EARLY BILINGUALISM AND
CHILD DEVELOPMENT

NEUROLINGUISTICS

An International Series Devoted to Speech Physiology
and Speech Pathology

13

Edited by

Richard Hoops, Ph. D. and *Yvan Lebrun*, Ph. D.

1984

SWETS & ZEITLINGER B.V. — LISSE

EARLY BILINGUALISM AND CHILD DEVELOPMENT

Edited by

MICHEL PARADIS and YVAN LEBRUN

1984

SWETS & ZEITLINGER B.V. — LISSE

CIP-GEGEVENS KONINKLIJKE BIBLIOTHEEK, DEN HAAG

Early

Early bilingualism and child development / ed. by Michel
Paradis and Yvan Lebrun. - Lisse : Swets & Zeitlinger. -
Ill. - (Neurolinguistics ; 13)
Met lit. opg.
ISBN 90-265-0463-2 geb.
SISO 803 UDC 616.8:159.946:800
Trefw.: tweetaligheid ; neurolinguistiek / ontwikkelings-
psychologie.

Typeset by Hoi studio B.V. Rotterdam
Printed in Holland by Offsetdrukkerij Kanters B.V. Alblasserdam

ISBN 90 265 0463 2

CONTENTS

CONTRIBUTORS

BRUCE BAIN, Department of Educational Psychology, University of Alberta, Edmonton, Alberta T6G 2G5 (Canada)

MARGARET BRUCK, McGill-Montreal Children's Hospital Learning Centre, 3640 Mountain Street, Montreal, Quebec H3G 2A8 (Canada)

JAMES CUMMINS, Ontario Institute for Studies in Education, 252 Bloor Street West, Toronto, Ontario M5S 1V6 (Canada)

YVAN LEBRUN, Neurolinguïstiek, Faculteit Geneeskunde, Gebouw F/R3, 103 Laarbeeklaan, 1090 Brussel (Belgium)

BARRY McLAUGHLIN, Department of Psychology, Stevenson College, University of California, Santa Cruz CA 95064 (U.S.A.)

MOLLY MACK, Department of Linguistics, Box E, Brown University, Providence, R.I. 02912 (U.S.A.)

MICHEL PARADIS, Department of Linguistics, McGill University, 1001 Ouest rue Sherbrooke, Montréal H3A 1G5 (Canada)

JEAN RONDAL, Institut de Psychologie et des Sciences de l'Education, Université de Liège, Sart-Tilman, 4000 Liège (Belgium)

RONALD TRITES, Neuropsychology Laboratory, Royal Ottawa Hospital, 1145 Carling Street, Ottawa, Ontario K1Z 7K4 (Canada)

JYOTSNA VAID, Laboratory for Language and Cognitive Studies, Salk Institute, P.O. Box 85800, San Diego, CA 92138-9216 (U.S.A.)

AGNES YU, Department of Educational Psychology, University of Alberta, Edmonton, Alberta T6G 2G5 (Canada)

TO BE OR NOT TO BE AN EARLY BILINGUAL?

Yvan Lebrun and Michel Paradis

It is not known when the controversy between proponents and opponents of early bilingual education began but, in all likelihood, theirs is an old debate. Statements about the effects of early bilingualism on the development of the child can be traced back to the early 19th century. In 1808, a German teacher named Jahn warned that bilingual education was likely to entail verbal and cognitive retardedness. Just as a child could have only one mother, so he could have only one mother-tongue, Jahn argued. If he were taught two or more languages, he would not be able to master any of them. In addition, he would have a confused mind, as each of his several languages offered a different world view. Ever since Jahn's time, the opponents of early bilingualism have emphasized these two major dangers over and over again. In 1899, Laurie stated that "if it were possible for a child or boy to live in two languages at once equally well, so much the worse for him. His intellectual and spiritual growth would not be doubled, but halved." This attitude was echoed by the French pediatrician Pichon (1936: 102-103) who claimed that having to learn more than one language required so much of the child's intellectual energy that the development of nonverbal cognitive skills was slowed down; moreover he believed that the child's young personality was torn between divergent *Weltanschauungen*, as each of his languages tended to interpret reality differently.

In Germany, especially under the Nazi regime, stress was laid on the shaping force of language and on the definite influence each language exerts on the thinking of those using it. This theory had its origins in the Romantic views of such writers as Johann Georg Hamann (1730-1788), Johann Gottfried Herder (1744-1803) and Wilhelm von Humboldt (1767-1835). It culminated in the teachings of Weisgerber (1929) and of Schmidt-Rohr (1933). Weisgerber contended that the way people thought could only be explained as a result of their using a particular language (p. 125), and Schmidt-Rohr, that two persons who spoke different languages could not have the same thoughts, feelings, or desires (p. xv). As a consequence, it was felt that

9

learning two or more languages in early childhood only led to intellectual chaos and personality disorders. The German psychologist Sander (1934) warned emphatically against these dangers, asserting that early bilingualism was bound to bring about a dissolution of the child's character and morals (p. 59).

In 1939 the North American neurosurgeon Penfield entered the controversy and took an opposing view. In an address given at Lower Canada College in Montreal, he stated that "before the age of nine to twelve, a child is a specialist in learning to speak. At that age he can learn two or three languages as easily as one." (Penfield & Roberts, 1959, p. 235). In subsequent publications Penfield expanded this view, arguing that "a child who hears three languages instead of one, early enough, learns the units of all three without added effort and without confusion." (Penfield & Roberts, 1959, p. 254). According to Penfield (1965) "the secret of the child's freedom from confusion lies in the action of a conditioned reflex that works in his brain automatically from the beginning... [This] remarkable switch mechanism enables him to turn from one language to another without confusion, without translation, without a mother-tongue accent." Penfield (1964) therefore recommended that children be given a bi- or multilingual education whenever possible, for "the bilingual child prepared for formal education by mother and nursemaid or mother and second-language kindergarten has undoubted advantage over other children, whatever the second language may have been and whatever the eventual work of the individual may prove to be." The bilingual child is better off not only because he masters two languages but also because, as an adult, he will find it easier to acquire foreign languages. The reason is that, because the child has been exposed to two languages in early childhood, he has had larger cortical areas committed to linguistic skills than monolinguals have (Penfield, 1965).

In this polemic, who is right? Jahn, Pichon, Sander, and the many others who have warned against the dangers of bilingual education? Or Penfield and those who, with him, advocate early bilingualism? What evidence is there to support the opposing assertions? What does the literature tell us about the effects of early bilingualism on the linguistic, cognitive, and psychological development of the child?

These all-important questions are addressed by McLaughlin in the contribution which opens the present volume. His careful review of published data leads him to conclude that the outcome of bilingual education depends to a nonnegligible extent on the parents' behavior. If the two languages are clearly differentiated in adult speech, the child will be more able to keep them apart and to avoid mixing their lexicon and syntax. Moreover, the quality of parental contributions to conversation and parents' attitude towards bilingualism have an influence on their child's linguistic achievements. Cummins, in his contribution to this volume, also acknowledges the importance of parent-child communication. Indeed, when there is a home-school language switch, a high level of bilingualism can usually be attained only if there is strong emphasis on the development of mother-tongue skills in the home. As a matter of fact, the role of the parents in bilingual education may be much more important than has usually been assumed. It may even be that bilingual education is more demanding of the parents than of the child (Lebrun, 1978a).

In his chapter, Cummins also tackles the difficult problem of the use of standardized test batteries to measure language-minority children's proficiency in the dominant language. Cummins stresses the discrepancy which may frequently be observed between a child's scores on verbal tests and his linguistic ability in actual communicative situations: often, language-minority students acquire peer-appropriate face-to-face communicative skills in the dominant language more rapidly than they achieve grade norms in dominant-language metalinguistic skills. A comparable observation can be made in connection with aphasics, i.e., adults who have lost part of their faculty of speech as a consequence of cerebral injury. Frequently, such patients prove to communicate more effectively in speech situations than might have been expected on the basis of their scores on formal verbal tests (Lebrun & Buyssens, 1982). It thus appears that traditional test batteries are ill-suited for the appraisal of the communicative abilities of linguistically disadvantaged individuals, whether their handicap be due to social or to pathological circumstances.

Since Jahn's gloomy predictions about the consequences of bilingual education, others have stated repeatedly that having to learn two languages may not only slow down, but also disturb, the child's verbal development. And various cases have been reported of children with language disorders deemed to be the consequence of early bilingualism. For instance, in their book on stuttering, which was published for the first time in 1937 and was reprinted in 1964, Pichon and Borel-Maisonny stated that in as many as 14% of their cases the child had had to use more than one language. In the authors' view, it was not all surprising that early bilingualism should be conducive to stuttering. In fact, they considered stuttering to result from what they called *insuffisance lingui-spéculative*. This is a lack of verbal immediacy: When a person with *insuffisance lingui-spéculative* wants to say something, the words he needs are not instantaneously available to him, it takes some time before he can form a phrase or a sentence to convey what he has in mind. In contrast with what happens in fluent speakers, thoughts are not automatically and speedily translated into words; they do not spontaneously engender their own verbal expression. Stutterers are dysfluent because they cannot smoothly and immediately convert their ideas into sentences. According to Pichon and Borel-Maisonny, having to learn two languages simultaneously can easily result in *insuffisance lingui-spéculative*, i.e., verbal tardiness: Because in the bilingual's brain each meaning is linked with two instead of just one word, there can be no automatic conversion of thoughts into utterances. Instead, each sentence must be laboriously constructed. Bilingualism then is conducive to the very situation that causes stuttering.

In support of this claim, Pichon and Borel-Maisonny presented reports of four clinical cases. (They described only three of them in some detail.) The reports fail to convince, however, because each of them can easily be matched, on the basis of symptomatology, with at least one case of stuttering in a monolingual reported elsewhere in Pichon and Borel-Maisonny's book. Now, if a monolingual and a bilingual stutterer each have the same kind of symptoms, the bilingual's speech impediment cannot be ascribed to his bilingual education without further justification. It must be demonstrated that it does not have the same origin as the monolingual's lack of fluency. It must be convincingly shown that bilingualism actually caused the speech disorder in the first case, while other factors were responsible for the occurrence of stuttering in the second. Such demonstration is wanting, however, in Pichon and Borel-Maisonny's work.

In an effort to avoid the pitfalls of subjective interpretation, Travis, Johnson, and Shover (1937) examined whether there was a correlation between bilingualism and stuttering. A total of nearly 5,000 school children ranging in age from 4 to 17 years were surveyed in the Chicago area with a view to assessing the incidence of stuttering in monolinguals as opposed to bi- or multilinguals. From the data obtained the three authors drew the conclusion that "it appears probable that there are significantly more stutterers among the bilinguals than among the children who speak only English; the respective percentages are 2.80 and 1.80, and the chances are about 98 in 100 that the difference is greater than zero." Travis et al. hastened to add, however, that "it is not to be overlooked that 97.20 per cent of the bilinguals do not stutter." The very high number of nonstutterers among bilinguals indeed falsifies the claim that bilingualism can easily result in stuttering. Moreover, when one looks at the incidence of stuttering in the subgroups comprising Travis et al.'s total population, one finds the following figures:

12

	N	% stutterers
White monolinguals (English)	1,734	1.03
Black monolinguals (English)	665	3.76
White or Oriental bilinguals (English + one foreign language)	2,322	2.80
White or Oriental multilinguals (English + two to four foreign languages)	89	2.38
Children who could not speak English	27	7.41
	4,837	2.61

This table shows that there was in fact a higher percentage of stutterers among black monolinguals (3.76) than among white or oriental bilinguals (2.80) and white or oriental multilinguals (2.38). Thus, although they favored an approach different from Pichon and Borel-Maisonny's, Travis and colleagues also failed to demonstrate that there exists a correlation between early bilingualism and stuttering.

However, this absence of correlation should not be taken to mean that there can never be any link between stuttering and childhood diglossia. As a matter of fact, there is a kind of bilingualism which may conceivably, if not engender stuttering, at least enhance an existing tendency to stutter. In some families, two or more languages are used concurrently and interchangeably. Indeed, they may even be used quasi-simultaneously, with a sentence begun in one language and finished in another. Most probably, this form of bilingualism requires the speakers to mobilize the whole of their linguistic knowledge (i.e., the various linguistic systems they are familiar with) when engaging in conversation with relatives. On the other hand, it has been shown (Lebrun, 1967) that monolingual stutterers not infrequently mix two synonymous words or phrases. Presumably the meaning the stutterer wants to convey calls forth two linguistic equivalents and he is unable to quickly select one of them and inhibit the other; as a result, he stammers in producing each of them confusedly. For instance, if the stutterer wants to say that something moved speedily, he may hesitate between *quickly* and *fast* and the word comes out as "qu... er say ... fick er quickly ... I mean fast." (Maybe Lewis Carroll's famous portmanteau words have their origin in the involuntary blends which the author of *Alice in Wonderland* made as a stutterer.) Interestingly, normal speakers who use spontaneous language under conditions of delayed auditory feedback may also combine synonymous phrases, e.g., "I am much interesting" instead of "I am much interested" or "I find it very interesting" (Meyer-Eppler & Luchsinger, 1955).

The phenomenon described above is just the opposite of what Pichon and Borel-Maisonny assumed to be the core of stuttering: while they posited that in stutterers the idea to be expressed often fails to call forth the word that corresponds to it, attentive examination of stutterers' verbal output indicates that sometimes the thought to be conveyed evokes more than one word and thus jams delivery. In fact, both symptoms — anomia and word blends — obtain in stuttering, but neither of them should be regarded as the central mechanism of the disorder.

In any one language, the number of synonyms or equivalent phrases is limited; moreover, each language user knows only some of them. In monolingual stutterers, word blends therefore occur only from time to time. But when two languages are used quasi-simultaneously, many meanings may call up two words at the same time, one in each language. If a child has a natural tendency to stutter and therefore finds it difficult to select only one of two equivalent linguistic items crossing his mind, this difficulty is likely to be increased if for many intentions two words are evoked. As a consequence, mixed bilingualism may be presumed to enhance stuttering. No such danger is to be feared, it would seem, when the two languages are never used quasi-simultaneously, for then the two linguistic systems can probably be activated one at a time and co-evocation is much less likely to occur.

Is stuttering the only language disorder which may under certain circumstances become more severe if the child is given a bilingual education? What about language-learning difficulties? Is delay in mother-tongue development likely to increase if the child is exposed to a second language? Does bilingualism aggravate retardation in the first language? Does it prevent the child from ever functioning at a normal level linguistically? Is the child not bound to become a semilingual, i.e., an underachiever in either language, while he might have been able, with appropriate help, to become a competent monolingual?

In her contribution to this volume, Bruck attempts to answer such questions by comparing the linguistic progress of four groups of young elementary school children: English-speaking pupils with and without a language problem in their mother-tongue and who are in French immersion programs, and English-speaking pupils with and without a language problem in their mother-tongue and who are in regular English classes. Statistical analysis of her data leads Bruck to conclude that French immersion programs appear beneficial to the language-impaired child, who manages to acquire proficiency in French without detriment to his English which, in fact, improves.

While Bruck's conclusions appear well-founded, it may be wondered

14

whether they can be generalized to other language learners. Can they be taken to mean that any language-impaired child will benefit from learning two languages instead of one? Is bilingual education to be recommended whatever the child's first-language problem? In the chapter he has written for the present volume, Rondal convincingly argues that while bilingual education may be adequate for children of normal intelligence with slight to moderate language-learning difficulties, it appears very risky with mentally retarded children: Exposure to a second language may easily endanger whatever little command these children have of their mother-tongue.

In his contribution to this volume, Trites contends that there is yet another group who should not be given an early bilingual education, at least not the one known as *immersion*. These children are those with a maturational lag of the temporal lobes. According to Trites, this lag prevents the children from making satisfactory progress when immersed in a second-language program beginning in kindergarten. However, since the delay in cerebral maturation is not permanent, they are likely to fare well if immersed after 10 years of age.

The pupils whom Trites identifies as having a maturational lag of the temporal lobes had normal intelligence and normal proficiency in their mother-tongue. The children in Bruck's experimental group also had normal intelligence but had mother-tongue learning difficulties. These difficulties cannot have been very severe, though, since their verbal IQ in kindergarten was dull normal. Moreover, their scores on various tests of proficiency in English improved between kindergarten and grade 2 more than those of the normal controls, although they received very little help for their language problem. Also, in grade 2 they were able to achieve normal scores on standard writing and reading tests. All this would hardly have been possible if Bruck's subjects had had a severe first-language problem. It may therefore be asked whether the conclusions of her inquiry are valid with respect to children who, despite normal intelligence, experience much difficulty in acquiring their mother-tongue.

A striking example of this sort of language-impaired child was Albert Einstein. Physically the boy developed well but his acquisition of language was so slow and so laborious that his parents thought for a while that he might be mentally retarded. At his primary school he was known as a silent, shy, and rather solitary child. He performed at a rather low level especially in language arts. Apparently, one of his teachers predicted that Albert would never achieve anything. When he was in the secondary school, his command of German was markedly below age level, and he found it very difficult to acquire some knowledge of classical Latin and Greek. On the

15

other hand, he was very good at mathematics and in this area surpassed all his classmates. He also liked science, art, and music, and he learned to play the violin. His family moved to Italy before he completed secondary school. A little later, he sat for the entrance examination at the Federal Polytechnic School of Zurich. His answers in mathematics were considered brilliant. Nonetheless he was not accepted because his knowledge of German, French, and English was deemed insufficient. A member of the examination board advised him to attend the school of Aarau for a year in order to improve his command of modern languages. Albert took the advice and a year later managed to pass the entrance examination at Zurich Polytechnic. He proved a very bright student. After he had taken his degree, he worked for some time at the Patent Bureau in Bern. Later he was appointed to a professorship first in Zurich, then in Prague. In 1922, he was awarded the Nobel Prize for physics. He taught in Berlin until he started being persecuted as a Jew. He went to the United States and became a member of the Institute for Advanced Study at Princeton. He retired in 1945 and died 10 years later.

Though he was considered a genius and achieved a world-wide reputation, Einstein was not very verbal: his linguistic skills were never commensurate with his other cognitive faculties. According to his biographer Reise (1931, p. 75) the great scholar did not like to address an audience and he used to compare his lectures to acrobatic feats. Vallentin (1954, p. 12) reports that Einstein was taciturn and that his delivery was often halting. Patten (1973) reveals that he was a poor speller and found it hard to set his thoughts down in writing. "Writing is difficult, and I communicate this way very badly" Einstein said. As a matter of fact, Einstein, although he did not stutter, appears to have suffered from what Pichon and Borel-Maisonny called *insuffisance lingui-spéculative* (see above): whenever he wanted to express himself "conventional words or other signs had to be sought for laboriously," as he himself confessed.

Should children with an endogenous first-language problem as severe as Einstein's be taught two languages when bilingualism is not necessary for academic education or socio-economic survival? Cummins' threshold hypothesis (1979) suggests that this question ought to be answered in the negative. The command which the child has of his mother-tongue is probably too limited for him ever to become a proficient bilingual. In such a case, bilingualism, it would seem, can only be subtractive. If, on the contrary, the child is given a monolingual education *and* adequate remedial teaching, his verbal agility is likely to improve markedly. It might of course be argued that if a child with a pronounced first-language delay is taught a second language, the competence he achieves in the second language — however limited — may reflect favorably on his command of his mother-tongue. While the possibility of such a transfer of ability is not to be denied, surely the influence which second-language learning may have on first-language acquisition cannot equal what can be achieved through special tutoring in the first language.

A comparison may make this argument more cogent. In the French-speaking part of Belgium those who want to retain Latin in secondary-school curricula often claim that knowledge of classical Latin will increase the pupils' command of modern French. While this may in part be true, due to the lexical kinship between the two languages, it is plain that Latin is in many respects — especially morphologically and syntactically — very different from French. Accordingly, greater progress would be made in the mastery of French if all the time spent on teaching specific features of Latin were directly devoted to improving the pupils' knowledge of their mother-tongue.

It follows that children with a marked first-language delay should probably be given a monolingual education whenever bilingualism is not made imperative by the socio-economic context. The same holds true, it would seem, with respect to children who, like Genie (Curtiss, 1977), have spent their early years in social isolation or who, like Nanga (Lebrun, 1978b, 1980), have received little verbal stimulation in early childhood. Once these children are placed in foster families it is probably wise not to teach them two languages. After a child is 6 or 7 years old, basic verbal skills develop so slowly that having to acquire two languages appears too arduous a task. Working from Penfield's hypothesis regarding the bilingual's cortical organization, it might be hypothesized that in the early childhood of such children, too restricted an area of cortical matter was committed to language for them ever to become proficient bilinguals. Indeed, adequate command of just one language may in their case prove an unachievable goal. In the chapter by Mack, the results of psycholinguistic experiments with adult monolinguals and adult early bilinguals are presented. Her data provide support for the notion that early bilingualism does not result in totally monolingual-like linguistic performance. This brings us to the issue of cerebral functioning in early bilinguals, late bilinguals, and monolinguals. This issue is addressed by Vaid in the present volume. Her experimental findings suggest that the three groups use different strategies in verbal problem solving and favor different modes of processing linguistic material.

Jahn, Pichon, and Sander (see above) were convinced that early bilin-

17

gualism not only slows down the child's verbal and cognitive development but in addition, by precociously confronting him with two different world views, jeopardizes his psychological balance: The child is torn between two cultures and this duality prevents him from developing an adequate self-image; in constant search of himself, the bilingual becomes "something of a problem child", to use Lowie's words (1945). In an effort to put this pessimistic view to the test and, at the same time, to avoid the drawbacks of local, parochial inquiries, Bain and Yu have undertaken a cross-class and cross-nation study of the development of body percept among unilinguals versus bilinguals. Their findings are reported in their contribution to the present volume. They show that the development of both body perception and object perception is influenced by the social-educational climate as well as by the school language program.

The chapters comprising this volume then address various contemporary issues pertaining to the relationships between early bilingualism and child development. It is hoped that the critical reviews offered and the experimental findings reported may help form a better judgment as to the advantages and dangers of bilingual education.

EARLY BILINGUALISM:
METHODOLOGICAL AND THEORETICAL ISSUES

Barry McLaughlin

INTRODUCTION

Parents in an increasing number of families face an interesting choice — that of raising their children in a bilingual or monolingual environment. In some cases parents who have learned a second language for educational purposes may wonder about the advantages or disadvantages of raising their children bilingually. In many cases husband and wife have different first languages and may wish to give their children access to both languages by using both in the home. In other cases the parents may have immigrated to a new country and may want to maintain the language of the old country while at the same time providing the conditions in the home for the children to learn the language of the new country.

How advisable is it to raise children bilingually? What consequences are there to bilingual upbringing? In his classic study, Jules Ronjat (1913) reported that his son Louis showed only positive consequences from having been raised in a bilingual, French-German home environment. Louis Ronjat learned to speak both languages as a native-speaking child would. He showed very few signs of interference between languages. Nor did his bilingualism have a deleterious effect on his cognitive development. His development was quite normal and it has been reported that by the age of 15 Louis Ronjat had equal fluency in both languages (Vildomec, 1963), preferring French for technology and German for literature. Many other researchers after Ronjat have come to the same conclusion — that early bilingualism has positive consequences for linguistic and cognitive development.

These positive consequences are not the inevitable results of a bilingual experience, however. Skutnabb-Kangas (1978), describing the experience of immigrant Finnish children in Sweden, reported that many of these children knew neither Finnish nor Swedish well. Often their Finnish pronunciation was heavily influenced by Swedish, so that they were unable to differentiate between long and short phonemes, a crucial distinction in Finnish. On the other hand, their Swedish was also limited, especially in vocabulary. Skutnabb-Kangas described these children as "semilingual", in the sense of not knowing either of their languages properly, at the same level as monolingual speakers of the same age.

What are the differences between the experience of Ronjat's child and the immigrant children that Skutnabb-Kangas described? Under what conditions is bilingualism an "additive" experience for the child and when is it "subtractive" (Lambert, 1977)? What conclusions can be drawn from research about the consequences of a bilingual experience on children?

These are the questions that I will address in this chapter. There are two major areas of concern: (1) the effects of early bilingualism on linguistic development, and (2) the effects of early bilingualism on cognitive development. In both of these areas there are important methodological issues, as well as theoretical implications that follow from what the research tells us. My focus throughout will be on these methodological and theoretical issues, since research can only provide answers to the practical concerns of parents and educators if it is well-grounded methodologically and theoretically.

LINGUISTIC CONSEQUENCES

What does the literature tell us about the effects of early bilingualism on the language development of the child? Does learning two languages simultaneously influence the development of either one? For example, if an American parent speaks both English and Spanish to her child, how will the child's English be affected? Is it better to speak only English than to use both languages? Research that bears on this question has concentrated mainly on lexical and syntactic development. I will discuss this research briefly and then turn to the methodological and theoretical issues that the research raises.

Lexical Development
In contrast to the monolingual child, the bilingual child has to learn two words for a single meaning. Some authors argue that this involves no particular problems. For example, Imedadze (1967) contended that bilingual children face no additional difficulties in the acquisition of meaning, since they merely extend to a corresponding word in the second language the word meaning they have isolated and come to associate with a particular real-world object in the first language. Her Georgian-Russian bilingual

20

subject used the Georgian word *ball* to denote a toy, a radish, and stone spheres at the park entrance, and then transferred the same set of denotations to the Russian word equivalent. In this early stage, Imedadze remarked, "differences in shades of meaning of corresponding words do not play an essential role" (1967, p. 3).

Later, however, the bilingual child has to learn that the meanings of some words have different extensions in the two languages that are being learned. For example, the English word *brush* can be used for a clothes brush, a shoe brush, and a paint brush, but the German word *Bürste* is not used for paint brush — instead *Pinsel* is used. Similarly the German word *Tuch* (cloth) can be used for the English *handkerchief, towel,* and *napkin.* In such cases the child must learn to utilize a somewhat different set of feature markings for corresponding lexical items in the two languages.

One might expect to find mis-extensions of various kinds based on ill-matched lexical areas across the child's two languages, and case studies of bilingual children indicate that such mis-extensions do occur. For example, Leopold, in his careful treatment of lexical extension (1949), mentioned a likely instance of such cross-linguistic interference, where the German *alle* is used (at 1;7-1;11) to mean *all gone* with reference to persons, as in *Mommy alle.* Standard German does not allow this since *alle* does not mean the same as the English *all gone* when applied to persons. Other instances of lexical mis-extensions have been reported by Vihman (Vihman & McLaughlin, 1982) and Ruke-Dravina (1967).

It sometimes happens that the bilingual child gives different extensions to words that have a single meaning for an adult. Volterra and Taeschner (1978) found that the German *da* and the Italian *la* (both of which mean *there*) had different meanings for one of the German-Italian bilingual children they studied. *La* was used for things that were not present and not visible, and *da* was used for things that were present and visible. Volterra and Taeschner argued that initially all words of the bilingual child's speech form a single lexical system; only gradually does the child differentiate the lexical items of the separate languages as those languages are experienced in different linguistic and nonlinguistic contexts.

In the process of differentiating the lexical systems of the two languages, the child may make lexical selections on phonological grounds. Leopold suggested that the bilingual child's choice of vocabulary from one language or the other "might be explained by a consciousness of articulatory difficulties" (1947, p. 267). Celce-Murcia (1978) emphasized this mechanism in her daughter's choice of French or English words, and Vihman noted it as well in her Estonian-English-speaking child's language (Vihman & McLaughlin,

1982). Another form of nondifferentiation is the use of blends, a phenomenon reported by Leopold (1939), Murrell (1966), Oksaar (1970), and
Vihman (Vihman & McLaughlin, 1982), whereby bilingual children settle
on a single phonological shape to express the same concept in either
language, the adult words bearing some phonological similarity in most
such cases.

In reviewing their own data based on two sisters acquiring Italian and
German and Leopold's (1939) data on his daughter Hildegard, Volterra and
Taeschner (1978) proposed a three-stage developmental sequence in child
bilingualism. In the first stage the child builds up a vocabulary repertoire
that involves a single lexical system with utterances containing mixtures of
words from both languages. This completely nondifferentiated stage is
followed by a second stage in which the child possesses two lexical systems
with mixed utterances continuing because corresponding words are learned
at different times and each word tends to be tied to the particular context in
which it is learned. Finally, in the third stage, two differentiated lexical
systems are acquired. A similar developmental sequence was proposed by
Nygren-Junken (1977) based on the speech samples of four French-English
children.

The question that many parents would like to have answered is how long
it takes the child to reach the third stage. Does bilingual exposure lead to
any retardation in normal lexical development? The answer to this question
seems to be that there may be some delay during the second stage, when the
child continues to strive to make a single unit out of the bilingual presentation. Leopold (1939) maintained that only when Hildegard became aware
that she was being presented two different languages did she begin to use the
appropriate word in both languages. When the child attains this metalinguistic insight, there is a spurt in vocabulary development in both languages
with no apparent negative consequences to either.

Authors differ with respect to the point at which they see the bilingual
child becoming aware of speaking two different languages. Ronjat (1913)
believed that his son had this awareness at 1 year and 6 months; Pavlovitch
(1920) also put the date of awareness relatively early — at 2 years. Other
authors (Elwert, 1960; Geissler, 1938; Imedadze, 1967) set the date some-
where in the 3rd or 4th year. The reason for this discrepancy is probably that
there are degrees of metalinguistic awareness: Leopold (1949) saw some
signs of awareness on the part of his daughter at 2 years, but it was only at
3 years and 6 months or so that the child had a good feeling for the
differences between the two languages.

Does this mean that mixing persists until the age of three and a half? The evidence suggests that it may, but that mixed utterances represent a small proportion of the child's total utterances. Swain (1974) observed the linguistic interaction of a French-English bilingual child over a 9-month period beginning at 3;1 and found lexical mixing to occur in only 4% of the child's utterances. Half as many lexically mixed utterances occurred at 3;8 as at 3;1, indicating that the child was progressing markedly during this period in differentiating the two languages. Swain (1972) claimed that bilingual presentation can have positive consequences, since she found that in both languages the total conceptual vocabulary of the bilingual child can exceed that of a monolingual child.

Syntactic Development

Is the acquisition of grammatical structures by bilingual children the same in its basic features and in its developmental sequence as for the monolingual child? There is evidence that structural features of the two languages of the bilingual child are not necessarily acquired simultaneously. As Slobin (1971) has noted, the syntactic realization of semantic relations (such as locative or possessive) can occur at different times within the two languages of the bilingual child, reflecting the perceptual salience of the features needed to mark the relationship in the two languages. Thus Serbo-Croatian-Hungarian bilingual children (Mikes, 1967) demonstrated locative relations in Hungarian (where the locative marker is expressed by noun inflection) earlier than in Serbo-Croatian (where noun inflection and preposition are needed to express the locative). This seems to reflect a processing strategy according to which simpler structures are learned prior to more complex ones.

Mikes (1967) pointed out, however, that the order in which various syntactic structures are acquired by bilingual children is the same as for monolingual children. The Serbo-Croatian locative construction is also acquired relatively late by monolingual speakers of that language. Furthermore, the syntactic development in languages of different structural types follows basically the same sequence. Mikes concluded that bilingual presentation has little effect on syntactic development.

The same conclusion was reached by Imedadze (1967), who found that the sequence with which grammatical categories appeared in the speech of a bilingual child depended on their difficulty — as is true of the monolingual child. Syntactic structures followed the same developmental order in both of the child's languages as they did for monolingual children. If both languages express a semantic relationship similarly, it tends to be acquired simultaneously in both languages; if it is more difficult in one language, it is acquired later in that language — as is true in the development of the monolingual speaker of that language.

This does not mean that there is no period of confusion in the syntactic development of the bilingual child's two languages. Volterra and Taeschner (1978) found that the two children they studied initially developed a single syntactic system that was applied to the lexicon of both languages. This syntactic system appeared to be different from that of either language. They argued that children initially fashion a unique system; then the system of the language with the more simple syntactic structures becomes dominant and mixing of syntactic structures from both languages occurs; finally, the two syntactic structures become differentiated.

The differentiation process is slower for syntactic than for lexical development. Swain (1974) reported that lexical consistency precedes structural consistency: At 3;9 her subject's lexicon was differentiated but the child's grammatical system remained essentially undifferentiated. Leopold argued that syntactic differentiation cannot occur prior to lexical differentiation because the child does not yet "use the two languages as separate instruments" (1949, p. 186).

The stage of syntactic mixing has been noted by a number of authors. For example, Oksaar (1970) reported that her child used Swedish morphemes with Estonian endings in the home, where Estonian was spoken; but with Swedish-speaking playmates the Swedish forms predominated. Burling (1959) found morphological and syntactic mixing, although his son seemed aware that he was mixing the two languages. Swain and Wesche (1975) found instances "in which the grammatical structure is French but the lexicon is English, and a few in which the structure is English but the lexicon is French" (1975, p. 20). For example, the French structure which apposes a noun or pronoun at the end of the sentence appeared in lexically English sentences, as did the French negative construction, with the negative element following the verb. To express possession, Swain and Wesche's subject used both French structure with English words and English structure with French words, suggesting that at this point both systems had been internalized, but their linguistic allocation was not yet under control.

In order to be precise about bilingual influence in the acquisition of syntax one needs data on the course of monolingual acquisition. Thus Bubenik (1978) pointed out that her child's use of an analytic construction for the expression of future tense with perfective as well as imperfective verbs in Czech could have been modelled on the English system. Similar errors, however, are common in monolingual learners of Slavic languages. Hence it is unclear whether the use of this construction (to at least age 5;7)

24

was attributable to the pressure of bilingualism.

In any event, the research suggests that the three-stage process of a unitary system, mixing, and differentiation characterizes syntactic development as it characterizes lexical development. The final stage of differentiation is seen to come later in the case of syntactic development, with mixing of syntactic structures continuing in the speech of some children throughout the preschool years.

Methodological Issues

There are a number of serious methodological problems with the research that has been discussed to this point. The data derive almost exclusively from case studies of a single or a few bilingual children. Many of the studies were carried out by linguists with their own children. One problem with such research is that of reliability. Especially when there is only one observer — and that observer is the child's parent — there is the problem of observational errors or selectivity. The child may be seen to have abilities he or she does not possess; ill-formed utterances may be transformed into well-formed sentences; mistakes may be overlooked or suppressed. The tendency is to see what supports one's hypotheses and to ignore the rest.

Even more serious, perhaps, is the issue of sampling bias. Most of the case studies were done with children from upper-middle or upper-class families. In almost all instances the parents were highly educated and intelligent. What are the linguistic consequences of bilingual exposure in lower socio-economic and less well-educated families?

There are two studies in the literature that speak to this issue. The first is by Carrow (1971) with lower- and middle-class Mexican-American children aged 3 to 10. Carrow found that there were specific areas where the children studied were, as a group, significantly delayed when compared to a control group of English-speaking children. In particular, the comprehension of pronouns, negatives, and some tense markers caused difficulty for children in the bilingual group.

Cornejo (1973) investigated the language development of 24 5-year-old Mexican-American children of lower-middle-class background and found a high degree of transfer, borrowing, and language mixture in the language samples. Interference from Spanish to English was most prominent at the phonological level, whereas interference from English to Spanish was most noticeable at the lexical level.

In addition to these studies there is Skutnabb-Kangas' contention that for many lower-class immigrant children bilingual exposure can lead to a state of "semilingualism":

> Many of the children do not know any language properly, at the same level as monolingual children. The language tests and estimates show that they often lag up to four years behind their monolingual peers in language tests in both languages (1978, p. 229).

It should be quickly pointed out, however, that Skutnabb-Kangas did not attribute this state of affairs to bilingualism per se, but to educational policies toward immigrant children.

That bilingual exposure can have different consequences for different children suggests that there are important intervening variables that have to be considered in research in this area. One such variable relates to the manner in which the child is exposed to two languages, which I refer to here as the conditions of presentation.

Conditions of presentation. Linguists have often noted that bilingual individuals occasionally make use of a separate code that includes mixing structures and vocabulary from two languages. This phenomenon has been found to be especially common in the speech of Mexican-Americans (Gumperz, 1970; Lance, 1969), and has been cited as an instance of interference between languages (Mackey, 1965). There is evidence, however, that bilinguals can eliminate such structures from their speech when talking to a monolingual individual, so that such mixing should be viewed as a sociolinguistic phenomenon, rather than as negative transfer due to bilingualism.

In their analysis of the mixing phenomenon in Mexican-American speakers, Gumperz and Hernandez-Chavez (1972) showed how the choice of speech forms is highly meaningful and serves definite communication needs. Speakers build on the coexistence of alternate forms in their language repertory to create meanings that may be highly idiosyncratic and understood only by members of the same bilingual speech community. Mexican-American speakers use mixed expressions when speaking to others of the same ethnic background in much the same way that American Jews use certain Yiddish expressions or Italians use certain Italian expressions to mark in-group identity. Often they are used by speakers who no longer have effective control of the first language.

The problem for the child learner is that, the more mixing of languages that occurs in adult speech, the more difficult it becomes to differentiate between the two languages. For example, Burling (1959) reported that his son's bilingual acquisition showed some mixing of Garo and English — Garo words being given English morphology and syntax. This was not too surprising, since all of the English-speaking adults around the child used Garo words in their English speech. Similarly, the Mexican-American child may find it difficult to differentiate Spanish and English if the adult input is mixed.

26

It seems that the mixing stage can be shortened if the domains of use are clearly defined and if the two languages are maintained somewhat in balance. This was true of the children of Ronjat (1913) and Pavlovitch (1920) and initially of Leopold's daughter (1949). These studies suggest that the optimal conditions for minimizing language mixing occurs when both languages are spoken in the home consistently by different persons. When the languages are mixed by adult speakers, or when one language becomes dominant, one finds more mixing in the child's speech (Burling, 1959; Engel, 1966; Leopold, 1949). If one language is spoken in the home and the second is acquired through acquaintances and playmates, balance seems to be upset and more mixing occurs (Murrell, 1966; Oksaar, 1970; Ruke-Dravina, 1967).

In short, conditions of language presentation have important consequences for language differentiation. Attaining bilingual competence is more difficult the more mixing the child is exposed to, although it seems likely that mixed exposure does not lead to permanent retardation in either language. In fact, researchers sometimes mistake mixing in the child's speech for confusion and language interference, when the child is actually using (or trying to use) mixed utterances rhetorically for sociolinguistic purposes, just as adult speakers in the child's linguistic environment do. More serious consequences for language differentiation follow from imbalanced presentation. This brings us to the next issue.

Active and passive bilingualism. For many children attaining bilingualism may be a more passive than active process. That is, the child may be exposed to a second language before being required to use it actively. The child's comprehensive abilities in the language may develop much faster than productive abilities. This is the case, for example, for many Spanish-speaking children in the United States for whom English is the dominant language of the larger social environment, but who have little opportunity to use English before entering school. For these children Spanish is the dominant language before school, but upon entering school emphasis is shifted to English. Throughout this process the input is imbalanced, first in favor of Spanish, then favoring English.

Children who acquire a second language passively by exposure and not by using it actively have a different bilingual experience than those children who grow up speaking two languages. Passive bilingualism is also a different process from learning a second language after a first language is established. On the one hand, the child is not learning two languages equally, since there is such a strong imbalance in favor of the language that is being used actively. On the other hand, the child is not a novice when it comes to learning the second language, since there has been considerable exposure to that language.

Often children from language-minority families acquire some knowledge of the language of the dominant culture in this more passive, imbalanced manner. Upon entering school, they may appear to be making fairly rapid progress in the majority language. This is likely to be an instance of the "linguistic facade" (Cummins, 1979; Skutnabb-Kangas, 1978), whereby children give the appearance of being rapid learners of a language because of their surface fluency, when in fact they have not mastered the language to the extent of being able to use it effectively in school-related tasks.

Failure to distinguish active and passive bilingualism creates a methodological issue for research on the effects of early bilingualism on language development because the consequences of the two forms of early bilingualism appear to be quite different. Although there has been no research specifically on this point, it appears that passive bilingualism — i.e., the situation where comprehension skills have developed somewhat without corresponding development of production skills — can lead to less successful acquisition of the two languages. Generally speaking, any situation in which one language predominates and the other is reduced to subordinate status leads to problems in differentiating the two languages (Burling, 1959; Leopold, 1949).

Defining differentiation. As we have seen, bilingual children pass through a stage in which they assume that the languages they hear belong to a single system, with a single lexicon and syntax. Arnberg (1981) has noted that it is difficult to say whether one language is interfering with another at this stage or whether the notion of "interference" should be restricted to a later stage, after the child is aware of possessing two separate languages. One of the problems in resolving this issue is how to define children's metalinguistic awareness that they possess two different languages.

We noted that authors differ with respect to the point at which they see the bilingual child becoming aware of speaking two different languages, and that the reason for this discrepancy is probably that there are degrees of metalinguistic awareness. The awareness that Imedadze (1967) saw to be necessary to enter the stage of discriminated language systems (at about 1;8) is obviously quite different from the awareness of language differentiation that Dimitrijevic (1965) described as occurring between the fifth and sixth year. Unless some greater clarity is achieved in defining degrees of metalinguistic awareness, this debate will never be resolved.

28

One attempt to be more precise in defining language differentiation was made by Swain and Wesche (1975), who distinguished between language mixing and spontaneous translation as evidence that the child was aware of the separation between the two languages. Lexically mixed data was taken to indicate that the child did not differentiate the two languages, whereas spontaneous translation was seen to show that the child was aware of speaking two different languages. As Arnberg (1981) pointed out, however, this approach is not without its critics:

> Other researchers disagree, however, stating that in lexically mixed material there is a high degree of "grammaticalness" (Cornejo, 1973) and that structural consistency of the utterance is maintained (Lindholm & Padilla, 1977, 1978). Word order is preserved, and the forms do not overlap in meaning (Padilla & Liebman, 1975). For example, the child would not say "*es un* a baby pony" because the use of the English article would be redundant. For this reason, these utterances cannot be taken as evidence of failure to distinguish between the languages (Bergman, 1976) (1981, p. 23).

The root of this disagreement is the contention on the part of some investigators (e.g., Bergman, 1976; Lindholm & Padilla, 1977, 1978; Padilla & Liebman, 1975) that the bilingual child, from an early age, is able to differentiate the two languages. These authors argue that, when the lines between the two languages are clearly drawn, the languages of bilingual children develop independently from each other and mirror their acquisition by monolingual children. How then is lexical mixing to be explained? These authors contend that lexical mixing is not due to failure to distinguish between the languages, but to the absence of the appropriate term in the child's vocabulary, memory lapses, salience factors (e.g., frequent use of a particular word on television), or language mixing by those who provide the child with input.

Even if the bilingual child eventually possesses two language systems, it seems unrealistic to suppose that the child differentiates the two languages from a very early age. The example given by Volterra and Taeschner (1978) of a child using the German *da* and the Italian *la* with different meanings suggests that the child is striving to develop a single system. Leopold's (1939) data also indicated that Hildegard initially used only a single word for a particular concept, adopting the strategy of giving things one name only. This was followed by a period of competition, with both words occurring and one being preferred. The competition ceased and Hildegard managed to use the appropriate words in both languages only when she achieved some realization that there were two languages in her environment.

What this realization involves needs to be more closely researched. The argument that the bilingual child separates the languages when he or she is aware that there are two systems in the environment is circular unless some criterion is provided for assessing what is meant by this awareness — other than that the child separates the languages. Most likely the awareness that the child achieves of the separateness of the two languages will differ with different conditions of presentation, but even in the clearest case — the one person, one language situation (Ronjat, 1913) — identifying words with the language spoken by one parent or the other does not necessarily indicate that the child has some awareness that the two languages are different, since young children are greatly influenced by the context in which words are first used.

What is needed is analysis of the *different levels* of metalinguistic awareness that the bilingual child passes through. The one attempt of this nature in the literature is that of Vihman (Vihman & McLaughlin, 1982). In her son's case, language differentiation was seen to begin at about age 2; awareness of the fact that words could be labelled by language and translated appeared to come slightly later, while consciousness of the bilingual situation as a whole seemed to dawn only at the end of the fourth year, with explicit awareness of the child's own bilingual capacities being acknowledged a few months later. Here again, however, clearly defined criteria are needed for each of the different levels of awareness.

Theoretical Implications
I would like to conclude this section on the effects of early bilingualism on linguistic development by discussing briefly two theoretical issues: (1) what early bilingualism tells us about the language learning process, and (2) what conclusions can be drawn about the manner in which the bilingual child stores and processes the two languages.

Early bilingualism and the language learning process. Using cognitive network theory (Rumelhart, Lindsay & Norman, 1972) Taylor (1974) argued that initial words are "labels" linked with concepts through a process of associative learning. Since the recurrent pattern of association between speech noises (words) and objects or events is less uniform for the bilingual than for the monolingual child, bilingualism was predicted to lead to a delay in the onset of the vocabulary spurt that marks the acquisition of the "label" metaconcept.

In a test of this notion, Doyle, Champagne, and Segalowitz (1978) found that French-English preschool bilingual children were not delayed in reported age of first word, but did score significantly lower than monolinguals

30

on vocabulary attainment in the dominant language on the Peabody Picture Vocabulary Test. Doyle et al. did not attribute these lower scores to the delayed acquisition of the "label" notion, but rather to the lack of variety of linguistic input in the dominant language.

A number of other investigators (e.g., Carrow, 1957; Skutnabb-Kangas, 1978; Smith, 1949, 1957) have also reported lower vocabulary scores for bilingual children, but as Carrow pointed out, the "bilingual handicap" may be due more to the family environment than to bilingualism per se:

> In homes where there is a language atmosphere that is favorable to wide experience in both languages and where good speech models are present, the bilingual child may not experience any problem in either language (1957, p. 378, cited in Arnberg, 1981).

It is to be expected that families that present a stimulating and diversified linguistic environment will promote language development in children — whether monolingual or bilingual. Wells (1981) reported that there are interaction patterns in the family that relate strongly to language development and success in school. One particular process is that of "negotiating meaning" (Wells, 1981) — that is, collaborating in conversation to express one's needs, ideas, and intentions. Wells' research indicated that there is a clear association between the quality of adults' contributions to conversation and their children's rate of oral language development in the preschool years.

Wells (1981) cautioned, however, that there is no necessary connection between social class and oral language development. A simple class-based distinction is not as enlightening as an approach that stresses the pattern of interaction between parents and children. In all likelihood there are differences between parents that are related to their own education and their perception of their role as the child's first teachers. These differences, in turn, affect the way in which parents interact with children and the extent to which they make meanings explicit.

In short, there is nothing unique about the language learning process in early bilingualism. Like research with monolingual children, research on early bilingualism suggests that language learning is a process that is greatly influenced by the conditions of language presentation to which the child is exposed. If the child experiences a rich and balanced language environment, the child will develop verbal proficiency in both languages. To the extent that the language environment is unstimulating and noncommunicative, language learning will be impeded.

Two systems or one? How does the bilingual child store and process the two languages? There are two positions on this issue. According to some authors (e.g., Swain, 1972) separate sets of rules for both languages would be inefficient in terms of memory storage. It is more efficient for the child to employ a common core of rules with those specific to a particular language tagged as such through a process of differentiation. Her data indicated that the rules acquired first in the acquisition of *yes/no* questions by French-English bilingual children aged 2;1 to 4;10 were those that were common to both languages. Rules that were language-specific or more complex were acquired later.

As we have seen, a different position was taken by Bergman (1976), who argued that each of the bilingual child's languages develops independently of the other. According to this position, the two lexicons of the bilingual child and the systems of rules that characterize the two grammars are kept separate from a very early age.

Research on adult bilingual subjects generally favors the view that there is a single storage for the semantic representation of words in memory and that the language tag is also stored in some way so that it can be correctly applied in output (Liepmann & Staegert, 1974; Lopez, Hicks, & Young, 1974). Furthermore, the hypothesis of separate language systems is unparsimonious. It is more economical to regard the bilingual child's two languages as separate linguistic codes, analogous to the separate codes of a monolingual speaker. There seems to be no reason to argue that the task of switching languages involves additional processes over and above those used to switch codes in a single language.

In some languages — Javanese is the example frequently given — there are a large number of different language codes associated with such variables as age, sex, kinship relation, occupation, wealth, religion, education, and family background. The complexity of code switching in these various communication situations is enormous, relative to what we are used to in European languages. Yet we do not postulate separate language systems for the various codes of a single language.

It seems consistent to hypothesize that the same is true of bilingualism. The ability of a speaker to move from code to code within or between languages does not seem to require separate systems. Each code can be thought of as part of a single system with some means of discriminating lexical entries and syntactic forms characteristic of a particular code (or language).

COGNITIVE CONSEQUENCES

How does early bilingualism affect a child's cognitive development? Research addressing this question has tended to center on two questions: (1) the effect of bilingualism on conceptual development, and (2) the effect of bilingualism on intellectual functioning. Again, this research needs to be read cautiously. We will see that there are serious methodological problems that limit the theoretical usefulness of much of this research.

Conceptual Development

Vygotsky (1962) believed that language brings about restructuring of cognitive processes both for social use and as a tool for thought. One might predict that two languages are better than one, that a second language gives the child a greater symbolic system and so enhances memory, perception, and creativity. Or does a second language interfere with competent cognitive functioning, confusing the child and producing a lack of clarity? Vygotsky maintained that bilingualism has positive benefits, enabling the child

> to see his language as one particular system among many, to view its phenomena under more general categories, and this leads to awareness of his linguistic operations (1962, p. 110).

Noting her child's precocious attention to speech at the end of her third year, Imedadze concluded that bilingualism

> can thus be looked upon as a factor which accelerates the appearance and development in the child of the ability to consciously recognize (objectify) words and speech (1967, p. 15).

A similar argument was made by Leopold (1949), who believed that one gain of bilingualism was that the normal childish habit of clinging to a single wording (e.g., in rhymes, songs, or bedtime stories) seemed to be missing in Hildegard. From an early age, she would render a story freely in both of her languages. When memorizing rhymes or songs, she would often destroy the rhyme with her own insertions of meaningfully related vocabulary. She readily accepted new names for objects already denoted in one language and asked to be given the name in the second language. Leopold attributed this looseness of the link between the phonetic word and its meaning to the fact that the bilingual child hears the same thing constantly designated in two different phonetic forms, so that form and conceptual meaning are not rigidly identified with each other.

Studies of conceptual flexibility. Ianco-Worrall (1972) tested Leopold's

33

hypothesis that bilingual children possess conceptual flexibility by comparing the responses of Afrikaans-English bilingual children and matched control groups of monolingual English- and monolingual Afrikaans-speaking children. In one experiment she gave children a semantic vs. phonetic preference test, a two-choice test on which similarity between words could be interpreted on the basis of shared meaning or shared acoustic properties. For example, the child was asked, "I have three words: *cap, can,* and *hat.* Which is more like *cap* — *can* or *hat*? A response of *can* was interpreted as indicating a phonetic preference, and the choice of *hat* was seen to indicate a semantic preference.

Ianco-Worrall found that in her bilingual groups, 4- to 6-year-old children responded predominantly on the basis of semantic meaning, whereas monolingual children of the same age tended to respond on the basis of phonetic meaning. For older children, aged 7 to 9, both monolingual and bilingual children responded mainly on the basis of semantic meaning.

In another experiment Ianco-Worrall asked children if names could be interchanged: "Suppose you could make up names for things, could you call a dog *cow* and a cow *dog*?" Less than 20% of the monolingual children, but more than 50% of the bilingual children consistently answered that the names of things could be interchanged. These findings led Ianco-Worrall to conclude that Leopold's observations were valid. Bilingual children seemed to be more aware of the arbitrariness of conceptual labels.

Cummins (1978a) also conducted a number of experiments to determine whether bilingual children have greater conceptual flexibility than do monolingual children. He studied third- and sixth-grade Irish children on three tasks: (a) meaning and reference, (b) arbitrariness of language, and (c) nonphysical nature of words. In the first task the children had to state whether words used to refer to animals, imaginary (*flimps*) and real (*giraffes*), cease to have meaning when the last of that type of animals dies. Bilingual children showed superior performance on this task, with differences for sixth-grade children reaching statistical significance. On the second task children were asked whether you could call the sun *the moon* and the moon *the sun.* Almost 70% of the bilingual children compared with 28% of the monolingual children answered that the names could be interchanged. On the third task children were asked questions such as "Is the word *book* made of paper?" On this task there were no significant differences between bilingual and monolingual children at either age group in the percent correctly answered. Cummins concluded that, in general, his research supported the hypothesis that bilingual children surpass monolingual children in conceptual flexibility.

There was one inconsistent finding in Cummins' research, however. About as many bilingual as monolingual children asserted that if a cat were called *dog* it would bark, in spite of the fact that pictures of a cat and a dog were in full view. This makes one a bit cautious in asserting that bilingual children have freed the phonetic word from its conceptual meaning.

Studies of symbol substitution and cognitive functioning. Ben Zeev (1977) reported that monolingual children aged 5 to 8 found a symbol substitution task more difficult than did Hebrew-English bilingual children. In this task the children were asked to substitute one meaningful word for another in a fixed sentence frame, including instances where the substitution resulted in a violation of the obligatory selection rules of the language. For example, the child was told that "In this game, the way we say *I* is to say *macaroni*." The children were then asked to tell how to say "I am warm", a correct response being, "Macaroni am warm."

The superiority of bilinguals in such a task was interpreted by Ben Zeev as indicating that bilinguals develop a more analytic orientation toward language than do monolinguals as a means of overcoming interference between languages. Ben Zeev's argument was that bilinguals, because they need to deal with two languages rather than one, habitually exert more processing effort in making sense out of verbal stimuli than do monolinguals. Bilinguals are more aware of the structural similarities and differences between their two languages and they develop a special sensitivity to linguistic feedback from the environment. This more developed analytic strategy towards linguistic structures is transferred, the argument runs, to other structures and patterns associated with different cognitive tasks. Hence bilinguals were thought to have cognitive advantages that monolinguals lack.

A similar argument has been made by a number of other authors. For example, Feldman and Shen (1971) found that bilingual 5-year-old children were better than their monolingual peers at relabelling objects and using labels in simple relational sentences. Landry (1974) found that sixth grade children in a foreign language program performed significantly better than monolingual children on a test of divergent thinking ability that measured such aspects of cognitive functioning as fluency, flexibility, and originality. Balkan (1970) found that bilingual 11- to 17-year-old children demonstrated greater cognitive flexibility than monolingual counterparts in a series of tests.

This research was interpreted to mean that bilingual children have greater cognitive flexibility than do monolingual children. Landry felt that bilingual

35

children have learned to overcome the negative transfer of their first language in learning their second, and this experience makes them less susceptible to negative transfer generally. As a result, bilinguals acquire a "flexibility set," that is beneficial in divergent thinking tasks requiring inventiveness and originality. The child is thought to have developed an adaptability in learning a second language that can be used profitably in other cognitive tasks.

How valid is this argument? There are sufficient methodological problems with this research, as we shall see shortly, to make one cautious in accepting the argument without scruple. In particular, it seems premature to assume that bilingualism leads to greater cognitive flexibility. Carefully controlled research (e.g., Bruck, Lambert, & Tucker, 1974) allows one to conclude only that no harmful effects to cognitive flexibility can be attributed to bilingualism.

Effects on Intelligence

Does being bilingual have any effect on a child's intellectual development? A number of contemporary authorities have argued that it has a positive effect, enhancing the child's intelligence. This contrasts with the findings of older studies that concluded that bilingualism has a permanent negative effect on intellectual development.

Some early investigators believed that when children think and speak in two languages they become mentally uncertain and confused. They saw bilingualism as a mental burden for children, causing them to suffer mental fatigue. Hence bilingual children are handicapped on intelligence tests, especially those demanding language facility. However, these generalizations were arrived at on the basis of studies that lacked adequate controls. There is no way of knowing whether the obtained results were found because of the children's bilingualism or because the children in the bilingual group were disadvantaged socially and economically relative to the children in the monolingual group. In fact, when appropriate controls were applied to studies showing negative effects on IQ from bilingualism (e.g., Morrison, 1958), the differences between monolingual and bilingual children disappeared.

In reviews of the early research, Darcy (1953, 1963) concluded that apparently contradictory findings arise largely from methodological differences between the various investigations and from the absence of an agreed definition of bilingualism. Investigators have often failed to separate the bilingual factor from environmental factors by not controlling for socioeconomic class. The general trend in the literature indicates that whereas

36

bilingual children suffer from a language handicap in verbal tests of intelligence, there is no evidence of similar inferiority relative to monolingual children when bilinguals' performance is measured on nonverbal tests of intelligence. Nor is there evidence that bilingualism negatively affects intelligence in the broader sense of basic, universal, cognitive structures.

Indeed, some research has been interpreted as indicating that bilingualism can have a positive effect on intelligence as measured by intelligence tests. Peal and Lambert (1962) compared French-English bilingual children with French monolingual children, matched for age, sex, and socioeconomic status. The children, 164 in all, were 10 years of age and were selected from a larger pool on the basis of measures of bilingualism. All children were given an intelligence test with verbal and nonverbal subsections. Bilingual children were found to score significantly higher than monolingual children in nonverbal intelligence and in total intelligence (verbal plus nonverbal).

These findings can be questioned, however, since Peal and Lambert chose their bilingual subjects on the basis of bilingual ability as measured by tests in French and English. Children were chosen for the bilingual groups whose English (the second language) matched their French. It seems likely that only more linguistically gifted and intelligent French-Canadian children are capable of acquiring, by the age of 10, a command of English equal to their command of French (Macnamara, 1966). Thus the method of selection may have led to a sample of children who were more intelligent to begin with than the monolingual comparison group. This brings us to the topic of methodological issues in research on the effect of bilingualism on cognitive functioning.

Methodological Issues
It has become apparent in recent years that there are serious methodological deficiencies in the research that has been carried out on the effects of bilingualism on cognitive functioning. I would like to discuss these problems briefly and then turn to some theoretical implications that can be drawn from our knowledge at present.

General methodological issues. Most research studying the consequences of bilingualism on cognitive functioning employs the following design:

Groups + *Independent Variable* –	*Dependent Variable(s)*
Group X Monolingual experience	Cognitive variable(s)
Group Y Bilingual experience	Cognitive variable(s)

In the best studies, Groups X and Y are matched on relevant variables, especially socioeconomic status and intelligence (if the dependent variable is some measure of cognitive functioning), although as we have seen, this was often not the case in early studies. But even when intelligence and socio-economic status are controlled, there remains the question of whether Groups X and Y are equivalent. There are possible differences in motivation, in parental attitudes toward bilingualism, school experience, ethnic identity, and so on.

Another methodological approach to investigating the effect of bilingualism on cognitive functioning is to study the longitudinal effects of bilingualism on cognitive variables. That is, rather than comparing monolingual and bilingual groups of children at one point in time (once-only design), it is possible to see what effect bilingualism has on a group of children over an extended period of time by measuring the cognitive variables in question repeatedly. This design, which can be called a matched groups, repeated measures design, can be illustrated as follows:

Matching +	Matching +	Independent —	Dependent
Groups	Variables	Variable	Variable(s)
Group X	Cognitive variable(s)	Monolingual experience	Cognitive variable(s)
Group Y	Cognitive variable(s)	Bilingual experience	Cognitive variable(s)

Here the groups are matched on all relevant variables and on the cognitive variable or variables in question. Subsequent measures of the cognitive variable(s) should indicate whether there is some effect of the bilingual experience on these measures of cognitive functioning.

Studies using this design have not shown positive consequences for intellectual or cognitive functioning. For example, in the St. Lambert project (Lambert & Tucker, 1972) yearly retesting of the students revealed no differences between bilingual and matched monolingual subjects on measures of intelligence or on measures of creative thinking. Other Canadian studies also reveal no differences between bilingual and monolingual subjects in intellectual functioning as a result of bilingual experience in full or partial immersion programs (Barik & Swain, 1974).

Another general methodological issue is that of the dependent variables themselves. A wide variety of measures of cognitive functioning and intelligence have been used, so that comparability between studies is usually impossible. Interpreting the meaning of some studies is difficult: Cummins (1978a) noted that children can give a "correct" response without understanding the principle behind their response. As we have seen, the bilingual children in his study were more willing to call a cat a *dog*, but as likely as monolingual children to assert that if cats were called *dogs*, they would bark. This suggests that results from such studies should be interpreted cautiously until the cognitive processes underlying performance on this sort of task are better understood.

Determining the direction of causality. We have seen that research on the effects of bilingualism on intelligence has raised the issue of the direction of causality. This is an issue for all research on bilingualism and cognitive functioning: Does bilingualism cause improvement in cognitive functioning or is the direction of causality from cognitive functioning to bilingualism? The second possibility has been posed by MacNab (1979), who reviewed research findings and concluded that there is no evidence in the literature that becoming bilingual leads to cognitive enhancement. Studies that show some positive consequences are, according to MacNab, questionable because of the criterion of "balance" demanded of bilinguals.

One issue is whether the measures used to determine balance are related to the dependent variables used to assess cognitive functioning. Is there some relationship between producing words in a word association test (a measure used in many studies to assess degree of proficiency in the bilingual's two languages) and the ability to list uses for common objects (often taken as a measure of divergent thinking)? If so, then there is a confounding between the independent and the dependent variable. In one such study, Cummins (1976) argued on correlational grounds that no such relationship existed in his data, but as MacNab pointed out, Cummins did not include nonbalanced children in his sample, so that the low correlation between association test scores and divergent thinking may have been spurious.

A second issue is that by choosing "balanced" bilinguals a selection factor might be introduced that affects the results. As MacNab put it, most research has been done on children who

> tend to come from homes where there is an open cognitive ambiance and where there is encouragement of learning in general and language learning in particular. In this environment the brighter, more able child picks up the second language and becomes bilingual, the less able child is less apt to become fully (or balanced) bilingual, in part because he has other options open and does not have to spend energies becoming fluently bilingual if that is difficult for him (1979, p. 251).

That is, the argument is that the nonbalanced child is likely to be slower to begin with and so will score lower on most measures of cognitive functioning.

If this is the case — that is, if research has tended to confound independent and dependent variables — then we are at an impasse with respect to the issue of the direction of causality. One way around this problem is to use stepwise regression procedures to test the alternative causal models. This was the strategy used by Hakuta and Diaz (in press), who studied a sample of 123 Spanish-dominant bilingual children in kindergarten and first-grade classes. The children were administered a test of nonverbal intelligence (Raven) and several tests of language ability in Spanish and English. More balanced children (those with higher scores in English) scored higher on the test of nonverbal intelligence, with age and Spanish ability partialled out. A stepwise multiple regression indicated that a model that claimed that degree of bilingualism affected nonverbal intelligence was more consistent with the data than a model that described the direction of causality as going from intelligence to bilingualism. It should be noted, however, that the relationship between degree of bilingualism and nonverbal intelligence obtained in this study, while significant, was relatively small ($r = .267$), so that there is a great deal of the variance in intelligence that was not accounted for by bilingualism (about 93%).

Theoretical Implications

What theoretical conclusions can be made on the basis of research on the cognitive consequences of bilingualism in early childhood? The first to be discussed here relates to the issue of the validity of Cummins' (1979) threshold hypothesis. The second relates to the question of how the consequences of early bilingualism on cognitive functioning — if there are such consequences — can be thought to come about.

The threshold hypothesis. To account for the possibility of negative as well as positive consequences from bilingualism, Cummins (1979) put forth the "threshold hypothesis," arguing that the positive or negative effects of a bilingual experience are a function of an intervening factor, the level of competence bilingual children achieve in their two languages:

> Specifically, there may be threshold levels of linguistic competence which bilingual children must attain both in order to avoid cognitive deficits and to allow the potentially beneficial aspects of becoming bilingual to influence their cognitive growth (1979, p. 229).

The threshold notion assumes that some limited knowledge of the second language must be attained before any of the positive benefits of bilingualism are achieved. Similarly, there must be a minimal proficiency in the first language, especially in linguistic minority children whose first language is threatened by the acquisition of a second language.

Cummins proposed that there are in fact two thresholds. The first is the

40

lower threshold which children must attain if they are not to suffer negative consequences from bilingualism ("subtractive bilingualism"). The higher threshold must be attained if the child is to experience positive benefits from bilingualism ("additive" bilingualism). Neither threshold can be defined in absolute terms, "rather [they are] likely to vary according to the children's stage of cognitive development and the academic demands of different stages of schooling" (1979, p. 230).

What support is there for the threshold notion? The strongest empirical evidence for the threshold notion, as it applies to language minority children in the United States, comes from research by Duncan and De Avila (1979). In this research language minority children who had developed high levels of first- and second-language proficiency, as measured by the Language Assessment Scales (LAS), performed significantly better than monolinguals and other subgroups of bilinguals (partial and limited bilinguals on the LAS) on a battery of cognitive tasks. This suggests that the proficient bilinguals had achieved high enough levels in both languages to experience positive cognitive effects.

What evidence is there for the lower threshold? In support of this notion Cummins (1979) cited the Swedish research of Skutnabb-Kangas and Tou-komaa (1976) that indicated that some groups of minority language and migrant children show less than native-skills in both languages, with detrimental cognitive and academic consequences. Presumably, these are children who did not reach the lowest threshold in linguistic ability and so experience subtractive bilingualism.

Again, however, there is the problem of the direction of causality. In the Duncan and De Avila study, it may simply have been the case that the less intelligent children were less successful at acquiring a second language (hence were less likely to belong to a "balanced" group) and scored lower on measures of cognitive functioning. This is a serious problem for much of the research investigating the effects of bilingualism on intelligence and cognitive flexibility.

Research with lower SES children is also open to alternate interpretations. Lower SES children are likely to be discriminated against socially, and these social and economic factors, rather than language per se, may have accounted for their poor showing on language tests in the Swedish research. MacNab argued that the minority language child is

> forced to learn the second language, no matter what the cost in other learning. This demand for second-language skills may be especially difficult for average and duller children because slowness in learning the language cuts into time needed for other learning and because they do not have the opportunity to specialize in other subject areas where they might find

41

learning easier. In addition, the subtractive environment is a stressful one because the child's cultural heritage is denigrated by the society (1979, p. 251).

In MacNab's view, positive and negative consequences of bilingualism can be explained by a model that stresses the child's opportunity for exposure to the second language, innate differences in learning ability, and differential rewards for learning the second language.

Although MacNab contrasts his model to Cummins' threshold hypothesis, there is no contradiction between the two approaches. Cummins was careful to include social and motivational variables in his framework, so that the factors that MacNab stressed are simply part of the larger "interaction" model that Cummins had proposed. Both Cummins and MacNab would agree that some children — those raised in "subtractive" environments — require special educational treatment if their bilingual experience is to be a successful one. This is an issue, however, that relates to later, rather than early bilingualism.

Language and cognition. There have been a number of proposals to explain claims of cognitive advantages for bilingual children. For example, Cummins (1976) and Ben Zeev (1977) have suggested that the cognitive advantages of bilinguals that they observed in their data could be explained by the bilingual's need to objectivize and manipulate linguistic structures. As we have seen, Ben Zeev argued that in order to avoid linguistic interference, bilingual children need to develop greater awareness and sensitivity to linguistic cues.

But is there a cognitive advantage for bilingual children? That is, has the bilingual child acquired an analytic frame of mind, a way of thinking about experience, that the monolingual child lacks? The findings of research on sound-meaning differentiation, in which the child is asked which of two words, *can* and *hat* is more like *cap*, are questionable, since the original findings (Ianco-Worrall, 1972) were not replicatable (Cummins, 1978b). Research on the interchangeability of words ("Can you call a dog *cat*?) is also questionable, since bilingual children do not show better understanding of the underlying principle than do monolingual children (Cummins, 1978a).

The superior performance of bilingual children on word substitution tasks, especially ones that require violation of syntactic selection rules (*macaroni* for *I*, as in Ben Zeev, 1977), can be explained on linguistic rather than cognitive grounds. As Aronsson (1981b) has noted, the bilingual child has more crucial experiences concerning syntactic form than a monolingual child has. Bilingual children not only know that something can be said in a

42

variety of ways (active vs. passive modes) — as all children do — but they come to understand that there are different formal means of realization in the two languages.

The underlying assumption of many investigators in this area is that bilingual children acquire some insight into the arbitrariness and complexity of language due to their bilingual experience, and that this sense of relativity generalizes to other cognitive tasks. Yet even monolingual children have to deal with lexical arbitrariness. As Aronsson put it:

> For instance, there is not really any reason to believe that the parallel existence of e.g. BOY:POJKE (English:Swedish) would assist the child's thinking more than the exposure to relative synonyms (e.g. BOY:GUY in American English) (1981b, p. 12).

Hence, the bilingual child's advantage may come more from a sensitivity to the formal aspects of language, than from any more general cognitive insights.

To investigate this hypothesis, Aronsson (1981a) tested 56 5- to 7-year-old Swedish-English children on phonological, semantic-syntactic, and syntactic tasks. The phonological task involved synthesizing words from phonological segments and breaking words down into phonological segments. The semantic-syntactic task involved guessing the meaning of novel compounds such as icecream-monkey/monkey-icecream. In the syntactic task the children were to transpose distorted sentences into grammatical ones. Bilingual children were found to be superior to monolingual children on the syntactic task only, supporting the notion that the advantage of bilinguals is primarily due to their superior linguistic awareness in the area of syntax.

What of other findings? Unfortunately, as we have seen, there are serious methodological problems with almost all research in this area, so that any statements about the positive (or negative) effects of early bilingualism on cognitive functioning should be viewed with scepticism. Until we have longitudinal studies with adequate controls (through random selection or via statistical procedures using multivariate techniques), no definitive statements are possible.

CONCLUSIONS

At the risk of some abuse to the English language, it is possible to distinguish two positions or stances on the issue of the consequences of early bilingualism: a "maximalist" and a "minimalist" position. Those who take a *maximalist* position hold that early bilingualism is essentially a positive experience for children. Not only do children acquire two languages, they do so with ease (whereas older children and adults need to exert considerable effort to learn a second language). In this view, there is no such thing as a "bilingual handicap." Studies such as Ronjat's or Leopold's are cited as evidence that children can learn two languages at once without one interfering with the other. Furthermore, the argument is made that early bilingualism leads to an analytic attitude toward language and toward cognitive tasks generally. Bilingual children are seen to be more cognitively flexible than their monolingual counterparts. Parents are urged to raise their children bilingually because of the linguistic and cognitive advantages that are thought to follow from such an experience.

The *minimalist* position holds that early bilingualism has little — or even a negative — effect on children. Although the older notion that early bilingualism leads to linguistic and cognitive confusion is usually rejected, advocates of the minimalist position point out that most case studies were done by linguists with their own children. Studies based on immigrant workers' children throughout the world do not show positive benefits from bilingualism. In fact, many of these children seem to have learned both of their languages poorly. The advice of some educators is that such children should attain mastery in one language before being taught a second.

There is an intermediate position possible between the extreme maximalist and the minimalist ones. According to this position what matters in determining the effects of early bilingualism on children is *how* the languages are presented to the child. If the two languages are clearly differentiated in adult speech, the child will be more able to keep them apart and to avoid mixing their lexicons and syntaxes. Children who have only passive exposure to one of their languages are less likely to deal successfully with that language. A critical predictor of success in mastering two languages is how active the child is in using both languages in conversation with adults and peers.

It seems clear that the child who has mastered two languages has a linguistic advantage over the monolingual child. Bilingual children become aware that there are two ways of saying the same thing. But does this sensitivity to the lexical and formal aspects of language generalize to cognitive functioning? There is no conclusive answer to this question — mainly because it has proven so difficult to apply the necessary controls in research. The ideal study would be one in which children, matched on relevant variables, were placed at random into groups receiving or not receiving the bilingual experience and were tested longitudinally on appropriate measures of cognitive functioning. Unfortunately, as we have seen, most studies have

44

not controlled for the relevant variables (especially for intelligence), have not been longitudinal, and have not used reliable dependent variables. Moreover, there have been no studies involving random assignment to bilingual and monolingual groups. This is a serious matter, as MacNab pointed out:

> Consider two families living side by side in similar houses with the fathers going off to very similar nine-to-five jobs. Both families have a five-year-old girl whose birthday is in August. The girls are matched for sex, age, and SES (measured by residence and father's occupation). One family sends their daughter to an immersion program. The other chooses the regular program. This choice probably means some basic difference between families or the children. For example, the family choosing immersion may be more open to people of different cultural background, more willing to try new experiences. Or the child in the other family may have been slower than 'average' in learning to talk (1979, p. 242).

Similarly, parents who decide to raise their children bilingually are likely to be different, in important ways, from other parents. The family environment is probably different from that where children are raised monolingually, and it becomes impossible to separate the linguistic and cognitive consequences due to family environment and those due to bilingualism per se.

If parents do decide to raise their children bilingually — either for educational and cultural purposes or because of immigration to a new country — it seems clear that the child must have the opportunity to "negotiate meaning" in both languages. The evidence from research on child language development indicates that the quality of parental contributions to conversation is a strong predictor of the child's language learning. Parents who habitually collaborate in conversations designed to encourage children to express their needs, ideas, and intentions will enrich their children linguistically, whether this be in an environment in which a single language is spoken or in a bilingual environment.

MINORITY STUDENTS AND LEARNING DIFFICULTIES:
ISSUES IN ASSESSMENT AND PLACEMENT

Jim Cummins

During the first half of this century, the inappropriate use of psychological tests with linguistic and cultural minority students has served both to reinforce educators' misconceptions about the detrimental consequences of bilingualism and to justify the active eradication of students' first language (L_1) in the school context (see Cummins, 1984; Mercer, 1973). In recent years there has been a greater awareness among educators in Western countries of the more obvious pitfalls associated with psychological testing of minority students. In the United States, for example, court litigation during the seventies highlighted the discriminatory use of IQ tests to label disproportionate numbers of minority students as "mentally retarded" and resulted in the adoption of assessment and placement procedures which attempt to take into account minority students' cultural and linguistic background. However, actual implementation of nondiscriminatory procedures has been slow as a result of both practical difficulties (e.g., lack of appropriate instruments and personnel) and conceptual confusion about many of the issues (e.g., what is a "learning disability"?).

Because research on nondiscriminatory assessment for minority language students is still in its infancy, researchers are very far from definitive answers to many of the questions faced with increasing frequency by practitioners. Teachers and school psychologists, who have had virtually no training in issues related to minority students, are increasingly faced with the necessity to make decisions regarding the assessment and placement of minority students. This derives both from the large numbers of minority students in many urban settings and the adoption in the United States and parts of Canada of mandatory procedures for identifying and treating exceptional students. An example of the rapid growth of the minority school population can be seen in the fact that in several Metropolitan Toronto school systems more than half of the students have learned English as a second language. Similarly, the ethnic minority student population in California is expected to become a "majority" (i.e., more than 50% of the total) by the mid-eighties.

The legal requirement to identify exceptional students' learning needs in the United States (as a result of Public Law 94-142, 1975) and in parts of Canada (e.g., as a result of Bill 82, 1979 in Ontario) means that an increasing number of minority students are being referred for educational and psychological assessment. Thus, clarification of the underlying issues concerned with the nature of academic learning processes among minority students has immediate practical significance.

In this paper two research studies which investigated some of these underlying issues are described and the findings are related to the assumptions of many educators regarding the assessment and placement of minority students. The first study involved a re-analysis of data from a large-scale survey conducted by the Toronto Board of Education in the late 1960s (Cummins, 1981a), while in the second study the teacher referral forms and psychological assessments of 428 students from English-as-a-second language (ESL) backgrounds in a Western Canadian city were analyzed (Cummins, 1983). The findings of the first study are relevant to the question of how long it takes ESL students to approach grade norms in English academic skills, while the second study analyzes the assumptions which educators bring to the teaching and assessment of ESL students.

Learning English as a Second Language: Proficiency and Time

There is evidence from several studies (e.g., Snow & Hoefnagel-Höhle, 1978) that within about one and a half to two years of arrival in the host country most immigrant students have acquired relatively fluent and peer-appropriate face-to-face communicative skills in the second language (L_2). Most teachers and psychologists would consider that immigrant students have sufficient English proficiency to be administered psychological and educational tests when they appear to have overcome obvious communicative difficulties in the L_2. However, it was found in the study of ESL students' psychological assessments (Cummins, 1984) that teachers and psychologists frequently commented on the fact that students' English communicative skills were considerably better developed than their academic language skills. The following examples illustrate the point:

PS (094): referred for reading and arithmetic difficulties in grade 2; Teacher commented that "since PS attended Grade 1 in Italy I think his main problem is language, although he understands and speaks English quite well." Verbal (V) IQ, 75, Performance (P) IQ 84.

GG (184): Although he had been in Canada for less than a year, in November of the grade

1 year, the teacher commented that "he speaks Italian fluently and English as well." However, she also referred him for psychological assessment because "he is having a great deal of difficulty with the grade 1 program" and she wondered if he had "special learning disabilities or if he is just a very long way behind children in his age group."

DM (105): Arrived from Portugal at age ten and was placed in a grade 2 class; three years later, in grade 5, her teacher commented that "her oral answering and comprehension is so much better than her written work that we feel a severe learning problem is involved, not just her non-English background." Her P IQ (grade 5) was 101 but V IQ was below 70.

These examples illustrate the influence of the environment in developing English communicative skills. In many instances in this study immigrant students were considered to have sufficient English proficiency to take a verbal IQ test within about one year of arrival in Canada.

How valid is the IQ score derived from such a test? The findings of the re-analysis of the Toronto Board of Education data provide a clear answer to this question. The original survey (Wright & Ramsey, 1970) involved 25% of the grades 5, 7, and 9 classrooms in the Toronto system. In this group of over 6,000 students there were 1,210 ESL students who had been born outside Canada. The re-analysis (Cummins, 1981a) was undertaken in order to investigate the effects of age on arrival (AOA) and length of residence (LOR) on students' academic performance. The results for one of the English language measures, an adaptation of the Ammons Picture

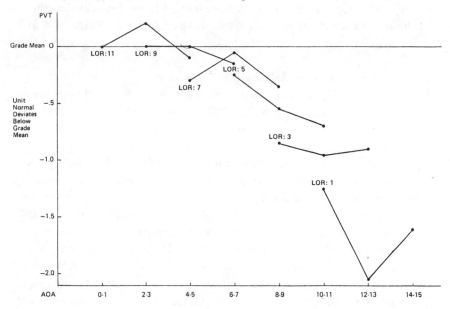

Figure 1: Age on Arrival, Length of Residence, and PVT Standard Scores

49

Vocabulary Test (PVT), are presented in Figure 1. Results for the other English language measures showed the same pattern.

It can be seen that it took immigrant children who arrived in Canada at age 6 or later between five and seven years (on the average) to approach grade norms in English vocabulary knowledge. The verbal skills measured on this test are very similar to those measured on verbal IQ tests such as the Wechsler Intelligence Scale for Children - Revised (WISC-R) - where the vocabulary subtest is typically the best predictor of overall IQ score. The developmental pattern shown in Figure 1 implies that IQ scores should not be regarded as valid indices of immigrant students' academic potential until students have been in the host country at least five years. It can be seen that students who had been in Canada for three years were still about one standard deviation (i.e., 15 IQ points) below grade norms, but continued to progress more closely to grade norms as their length of residence increased.

These findings carry an important theoretical implication in addition to their obvious practical implications. Specifically, they suggest that the language proficiency manifested in face-to-face interpersonal communicative situations differs in certain respects from the proficiency required in many academic or test contexts. Margaret Donaldson's (1978) distinction between embedded and disembedded thought and language provides a framework for understanding why ESL students appear to acquire peer-appropriate face-to-face communicative skills in L_2 more rapidly than they attain grade norms in L_2 academic skills (see Cummins, 1981b, 1984 for detailed discussion).

Embedded and Disembedded Language Skills

Donaldson (1978) points out that young children's early thought processes and use of language develop within a "flow of meaningful context" in which the logic of words is subjugated to perception of the speaker's intentions and salient features of the situation. Thus, children's (and adults') normal productive speech is embedded within a context of fairly immediate goals, intentions, and familiar patterns of events. However, thinking and language which move beyond the bounds of meaningful interpersonal context make entirely different demands on the individual, in that it is necessary to focus on the linguistic forms themselves for meaning rather than on intentions.

Donaldson offers a reinterpretation of Piaget's theory of cognitive development from this perspective and reviews a large body of research which supports the distinction between embedded and disembedded thought and language. Her description of pre-school children's comprehension and production of language in embedded contexts is especially relevant to

50

current practices in assessment of language proficiency in bilingual programs. She points out that

> 'the ease with which pre-school children often seem to understand what is said to them is misleading if we take it as an indication of skill with language *per se*. Certainly they commonly understand us, but surely it is not our words alone that they are understanding - for they may be shown to be relying heavily on cues of other kinds" (1978, p. 72).

She goes on to argue that children's facility in producing language that is meaningful and appropriate in interpersonal contexts can also give a misleading impression of overall language proficiency:

> "When you produce language, you are in control, you need only talk about what you choose to talk about... (The child) is never required, when he is himself producing language, to go counter to his own preferred reading of the situation - to the way in which he himself spontaneously sees it. But this is no longer necessarily true when he becomes the listener. And it is frequently not true when he is the listener in the formal situation of a psychological experiment or indeed when he becomes a learner at school" (1978, p. 73-74).

The relevance of this observation to the tendency of psychologists and teachers to overestimate the extent to which ESL students have overcome difficulties with English is obvious. In the following section the practical consequences of failure to differentiate between embedded and disembedded contexts of language use are illustrated.

Language Proficiency and IQ Test Performance among ESL Students

The WISC-R is perhaps the most frequently used diagnostic tool in psychological assessments. In the present sample a WISC-R Performance IQ was calculated in 264 cases and a Verbal IQ in 234. The median subtest scores on the WISC-R are represented graphically in Figure 2. Several things emerge clearly from the pattern of scores. First, students perform much more closely to the average range on Performance as compared to Verbal subtests. There is little variation among Performance subtests, although students tend to perform best on Coding where they come to within one scale point of the mean.

In contrast to the Performance subtests there is considerable variation among Verbal subtests. Arithmetic and Digit Span appear to be somewhat less culturally/linguistically biased against ESL students than the other Verbal subtests. The worst offender in this regard is Information where the median scale score is only 4.6. This is not surprising in view of the fact that the Information subtest is the one which most obviously reflects the prior learning experiences of middle-class anglophone children and consequently excludes the learning experiences of those who have grown up in a different cultural and linguistic milieu. This can be seen from the following items from

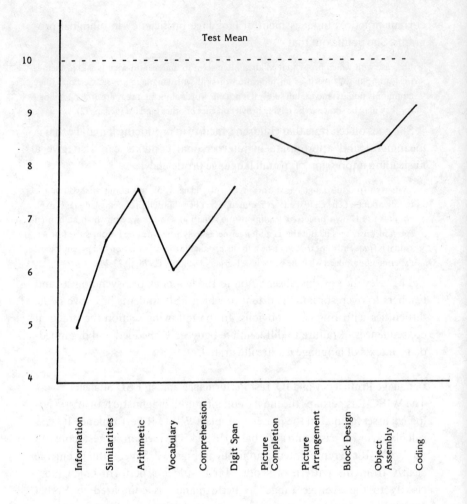

Figure 2. Median Scale Scores of ESL Children on the WISC-R

this subtest:
5. How many pennies make a nickel?
12. Who discovered America?
24. How tall is the average Canadian man?

It is ironic that the Information subtest is almost invariably administered in the assessment of ESL children, whereas Digit Span, the least biased of the Verbal tests, is often omitted. In the present sample, Digit Span was given only to 104 students while Information was given to 242. The extent of

52

the bias in the Information subtest can be seen from the fact that on this subtest, 70% of the ESL sample obtained a scale score of 6 or below and 34% obtained scores of 3 or below, compared to only 16% and 2.5% of the WISC-R norming sample. Yet in a large majority of cases, students' scores on the Information subtest were used in the calculation of verbal IQs.

It is worth noting that the pattern of ESL students' subtest scores shown in Figure 2 may have diagnostic significance. For example, when ESL children perform as poorly on Arithmetic and/or Digit Span as they do on the other Verbal subtests, this may indicate specific problems in these areas which are not attributable to ESL background. Similarly, lower scores on the Performance as compared to Verbal subtests departs from the typical pattern and is thus diagnostically significant.

In summary, it is clear that in this sample the WISC-R is assessing ESL students' present level of functioning in English academic tasks rather than their ability, aptitude or potential. The qualitative analysis of the psychological assessments illustrates the interpretation pitfalls faced by psychologists in attempting to make sense of students' test performance.

A. Qualitative Analysis of the Psychological Assessments: Inferential Paths and Pitfalls

The approaches that psychologists take to the assessment of minority children's academic potential are categorized in Figures 3 and 4. The major distinction is whether the psychologist makes allowance for the child's ESL background in administering and interpreting the test and in inferring academic potential on the basis of test scores. The majority of assessments did make some such allowance, but a substantial minority showed little understanding of the role of the child's cultural/linguistic background in test and academic performance. The different "inferential paths" that are involved within each of these categories will be illustrated by examples from the assessments.

(A1) ESL Background Ignored

Because minority children often manifest no obvious deficits in English fluency, teachers and psychologists often assume that the child's non-English background is not a relevant factor to take into account in interpreting test score performance. This is illustrated in the following two assessments.

PR (283): PR was referred for psychological assessment because he was experiencing difficulty in the regular grade 1 work despite the fact that he was repeating grade 1. The principal noted that "although PR was in

Figure 3. The Inferential Process in Assessment of Academic Potential in ESL Children

A. Psychologist takes no account of ESL background in inferring academic potential
(i.e. assumes that test score = potential)

(A2) Attributes deficiencies in academic *ability* to ESL background and/or bilingualism

ESL background essentially ignored in test score interpretation

Test Score Pattern

Aa. Low V¹
Low P¹

Ab. Low V
Average P

Inference

Low potential (retarded)

Low potential (learning disabled)

Placement Recommendation

Opportunity class

Resource room or learning centre

1. V = Verbal IQ
2. P = Performance IQ

Portugal for part (6 months) of the year there is a suspicion of real learning disability. WISC testing would be a great help in determining this". PR's scores on the WISC-R were VIQ, 64; PIQ, 101; FSIQ, 80. After noting that "English is his second language but the teacher feels that the problem is more than one of language", the psychologist continued:

> Psychometric rating, as determined by the WISC-R, places PR in the dull normal range of intellectual development. Assessment reveals performance abilities to be normal while verbal abilities fall in the mentally deficient range. It is recommended that PR be referred for resource room placement for next year and if no progress is evident by Christmas, a Learning Centre placement should be considered.

Comment. This assessment illustrates well the abuses to which psychological tests can be put. It does not seem at all unreasonable that a child from a non-English background who has spent six months of the previous year in Portugal should perform very poorly on an English Verbal IQ test. Yet, rather than admitting that no conclusions regarding the child's academic potential can be drawn, the psychologist validates the teacher's "suspicion" of learning disability by means of a "scientific" assessment and the use of inappropriate terminology ("dull normal", "mentally deficient"). An interesting aspect of this assessment is the fact that neither the teacher nor the psychologist makes any reference to difficulties in English as a second language and both considered that the child's English proficiency was adequate to perform the test. This again implies no obvious deficiencies in English communicative skills despite a severe lag in English academic proficiency.

AC (005): AC was born in Portugal and referred for psychological assessment in grade 1 because of reading difficulties. In referring the child, the principal noted that "AC learned English adequately while in the kindergarten but the teacher felt she would still have learning difficulties in grade 1". On the WISC-R, administered in May of the grade 1 year, the VIQ was 74, PIQ, 93; and Full Scale (FS) IQ 82. The psychologist commented:

> Psychometric rating as determined by the WISC-R places AC in the low average range of intellectual classification. There is a significant spread of 19 scale points between Verbal and Performance scores indicating higher aptitude for learning in the latter area of abilities... Overall, it is recommended that AC be considered for a resource room placement.

Comment. Logically, it is inadmissible to claim that the child's "aptitude for learning" is greater in the performance than verbal areas since the linguistic and cultural assumptions of the test are not met. This child was reassessed on the WISC-R five months later and her scores were several points higher on both Verbal and Performance scales (VIQ, 80; PIQ, 100; FSIQ, 88).

In summary, these assessments illustrate the fact that some psychologists have an extremely superficial understanding of the assumptions and consequent limitations of IQ tests. Because children's linguistic and cultural learning experiences were different from those assumed by the test, no inferences should have been drawn from the Verbal score. However, psychologists uncritically accepted the validity of WISC-R test scores, and consequently interpreted a low V, average-range P test pattern as indicative of low academic potential or learning disability. The usual recommendation was for resource room or learning centre placement. It is of course possible that this inference is correct, but it is equally possible that the low Verbal score is a temporary function of inadequate development of English language skills.

A variation of the first pattern is where the psychologist attributes the child's low academic potential (which has been inferred on the basis of test performance) to the negative influence of the child's ESL background.

(A2) Low Potential Attributed to ESL Background

When psychologists do take note of the child's ESL background, there is a tendency to assume that the test score is nonetheless a valid indicator of academic *competence* (as opposed to performance) and to attribute deficiencies in this competence to the child's ESL or bilingual background. The assumptions that some psychologists make about the role of bilingualism in ESL children's development and about the use of the L_1 at home emerge from many of these assessments. For example:

DR (110): "A discrepancy of 20 points between the verbal and performance IQ's would indicate inconsistent development, resulting in his present learning difficulties... It is quite likely that the two spoken languages have confused the development in this area" (VIQ 94, PIQ 114; grade 1).

BC (024): "BC, born in Italy, speaks Italian at home and this may be contributing to her problems at school... poor verbal abilities development is most certainly influenced by her Italian background" (VIQ 65, PIQ 78; grade 1).

CG (057): "The verbal IQ is 12 points lower than the performance IQ, although this is likely due to the effect of speaking both Italian and English... there is *very* poor development indicated in the area of general information fund" (VIQ 74, PIQ 86; grade 4).

PE (282): "It was noted that PE continues to have difficulty understanding and using the English language probably because the family speaks Italian at home. This seems to be a major handicap in PE's development of verbal skills" (PIQ 72, grade 2).

DA (125): "DA came to Canada from Italy at age 5 and learned English at

56

school. Italian is spoken in the home and this likely is contributing to overall below average verbal abilities development" (VIQ 80, PIQ 96; grade 7).

Comment. All of these assessments share the more or less explicit assumption that the child's experience with another language outside school exerts a detrimental effect on her verbal abilities development and on her school progress. What is wrong with this assumption? First, it assumes erroneously (see quantitative analysis) that the WISC verbal scale is a valid measure of verbal intellectual and academic *abilities* rather than indicative of present level of academic functioning in English. No attempt is made to ascertain what the child's verbal abilities might be in the mother tongue.

Second, there is no evidence that bilingualism or a home-school language switch, in themselves, have any negative effects on children's academic development (e.g., Bhatnagar, 1981; Cummins, 1981c). The research evidence, in fact, suggests that when continued development of minority children's L_1 is promoted (either in home or school), the resulting bilingualism is educationally enriching (see Cummins, 1981b).

Thus, the only conclusion that is logically possible in situations such as those considered above is that the child's poorer cognitive/academic functioning in both test and school situations in comparison to middle-class monolingual Anglo-Saxon peers, *may* (or may not) be due to the fact that her cultural experiences are different from those assumed by the test and school, and that her *English language* vocabulary, information, and concepts are *as yet* inadequately developed. No inference can logically be made about verbal abilities, aptitudes, or potential on the basis of test scores or present academic functioning.

Conclusion

The assessments considered above reveal a lack of appreciation of the assumptions underlying IQ tests such as the WISC-R and a lack of understanding of the ways in which a bilingual or ESL background influences academic development in an all-English school program. The psychologists and teachers, represented above, observe the fact that students from ESL backgrounds show low academic functioning in a school program oriented towards the linguistic and cultural experiences of middle-class Anglo-Saxon monolingual children, and perform poorly on IQ tests constructed specifically to reflect these same middle-class Anglo-Saxon experiences; they ignore the relativistic perspective within which tests and schools operate and make absolute statements about ESL children's academic abilities, aptitude, competence, or potential; and finally, many of them interpret the correlation between ESL background and low achievement as a causal relationship.

B. Allowance Made for ESL Background in Test Interpretation

The inferential paths that were evidenced when psychologists made allowance for children's ESL background in interpreting WISC-R scores are outlined in Figure 4. The first decision that the psychologist must make is whether to administer both Verbal and Performance batteries or only the Performance battery. If both batteries are administered, then a decision must be made as to the appropriate interpretation of the Verbal score. The assessments that fall into the present category are distinguished from those considered earlier in that caution was always exercised and recommended in the interpretation of Verbal scores. In some cases Verbal IQ's were not entered on the assessment report, in others they were entered but were clearly marked as minimal or invalid, while in the remainder, although the Verbal IQ was entered in the normal way on the referral form, inferences were made only in regard to the child's present level of academic functioning rather than in regard to academic potential or aptitude.

When only the Performance battery was administered, the interpretation of the test score was relatively straightforward, mainly because the screening it provided was relatively crude. There was no possibility, for example, of diagnostic interpretation of Verbal-Performance discrepancies.

Each of the inferential paths outlined in Figure 4 will be illustrated with examples from the assessment protocols.

B1. Both Verbal and Performance Scales Administered

(B1a) No Verbal-Performance Discrepancy
MT (245); MT was born in Yugoslavia and arrived in the school system in grade 3. Her grade 4 teacher noted on the referral that MT "is having difficulty with her school work, particularly written expression and comprehension. She tends to be inattentive and has poor work habits". The teacher wanted to know whether or not MT would benefit from repeating grade 4, and whether or not language was still a barrier, and if so, to what extent. MT's VIQ was 73 (4th percentile) and PIQ was 84 (17th percentile). The psychologist placed an asterix opposite the VIQ and FSIQ and indicated that "these scores are suspect due to foreign language origin of student". The report read as follows:

Figure 4. The Inferential Process in Assessment of Academic Potential in ESL Children

B. Psychologist takes account of ESL background in inferring academic potential

	B1. Both V and P administered		B2. Only P administered		B3. L1 Measures administered
	(B1a) No V-P Discrepancy	(B1b) V-P Discrepancy	(B2a)	(B2b)	
Test Score Pattern	Low V Low P → Average V Average P	Low V Average P	Low P	P average	
Inference	Low potential → Average-potential	Average potential	Low potential	Average potential	
Placement/ Remedial Recommendation	Opportunity class or resource room → Provide individualized help in regular classroom and review progress	Provide individualized ESL and academic help either in regular class or resource room and review progress	Opportunity class or resource room	Provide individualized help either in regular class or resource room and review progress	

V = Verbal Scale
P = Performance Scale

59

> MT appears to have low average ability - about 10-20 percentile. Verbal is of course suspect due to language but did not do much better on nonverbal tasks. Language mastery was considered more than adequate to grasp directions for nonverbal part of the test.

The psychologist suggested that language was still a barrier and made several recommendations for remedial assistance, among which was use of the resource room facility for areas such as reading and written and expressive language.

Comment. In the assessments that fall into this category the psychologists carefully consider the possible effects of cultural and linguistic background factors and interpret the Performance IQ as an indicator of the child's potential. When PIQ is low, special class placement is usually recommended; when PIQ is average or high, specific remedial suggestions are usually made for helping the child within the regular classroom. Because there is not a significant discrepancy between VIQ and PIQ, difficulties in interpreting test performance are reduced. However, as is illustrated in the next section, interpretation of low VIQ, average or high PIQ test patterns is essentially a matter of intuition.

(B1b) Significant Verbal-Performance Discrepancy

In response to a low V, average P subtest profile, those psychologists who take account of the child's ESL background in inferring potential usually regard the PIQ as an index of academic potential and attribute the low VIQ to cultural/linguistic factors. For example:

BI (044): BI arrived from Portugal in grade 3 and was referred by her grade 5 teacher because of reading difficulties. Her WISC scores were VIQ 73, PIQ 106. The assessment report read as follows:

> BI recently came from Portugal (1½ years ago). This, to a large extent, is reflected in a low overall Verbal score. I believe BI to be of at least average potential as can be inferred from the 106 IQ on the Performance subtests. BI requires enriched language arts experience. As with most new Canadians it is doubtful they can achieve at their grade placement. Resource room help is recommended.

RJ (312); RJ was a Chilean refugee who entered the school system in grade 3. The grade 3 teacher referred him in January noting that he is unable to work independently and finds it difficult to work for any length of time. She attempted to get him to do the Grade 3 Gates McGinitie reading test but reported that "he wasn't able to do it at all". RJ received a VIQ of 64 and a PIQ of 100. As with the majority of VIQ assessments, Arithmetic was highest (7) and Information lowest (1). The psychologist commented.

> It was quite evident that he has a great deal of difficulty with the English language... I would think that the Verbal IQ of 64 obtained is *not* a true indication of ability but resulted

primarily from language and cultural background. The nonverbal IQ of 100 is most probably more in line with this boy's verbal ability level.

The psychologist recommended that the itinerant ESL teacher be contacted for help.

Comment. Clearly, the conclusions drawn in these two assessments are reasonable and no other inferences can logically be drawn from the assessments. However, it is also quite possible that these children's academic difficulties derive from more than just their minority background. However, there is no way that potential long-term difficulties of this type can be detected from psychological testing administered only in English. The third example illustrates a case where it appears likely that serious learning problems were not identified by the psychological assessment.

UA (374): UA was born in South America and first referred by the grade 1 teacher who noted that she "needs individual help in all aspects of the program, since she's a new Canadian". Although UA was seen by a psychologist at that time there is no record of test scores. UA was again referred in October of the grade 2 year by the resource room teacher who noted that her teacher "says she cannot read. Has returned to grade 1 for reading period. UA also comes to me for help in Resource Room. She has extreme difficulty with word attack, particularly blending". The teacher wanted to know what her IQ and potential were.

UA was assessed on the WISC-R shortly after this referral. The psychologist noted that "UA was quite friendly during the test interview. She spoke freely..." Her WISC-R scores were: VIQ, 77; PIQ, 104. The psychologist commented that

While she is progressing in English, she is still behind, resulting in a low overall verbal score. Performance (score) was within the average range and this may well be a measure of the girl's potential. It is possible that family or other problems are impeding motivation toward intellectual work. No real disability is obvious other than auditory memory and a rather impulsive manner of attacking her work.

In April of the grade 2 year, UA was again referred for psychological and reading assessment. Her teacher noted that she had been in Canada for at least four years. "We have had her taking reading with the grade 1 class and her classroom teacher has given her individual help. Her progress is minimal and she does not appear overly concerned with her lack of progress... She was in the Resource Room and it was found that her phonic attack skills, after one year of special help, did not improve at all." The teacher wanted to know whether, in spite of the psychologist's first observation that "there was 'no real disability observed other than auditory memory'... UA has a sufficient degree of learning disability to warrant placement in a Learning Centre?"

Comment. The problem with attributing low VIQ performance to cultural/ linguistic patterns is that many children from monolingual backgrounds who experience reading difficulties also manifest a low V, average P pattern. Thus, what is usually perceived as one of the main diagnostic clues on the WISC-R is eliminated when the VIQ is discounted, and consequently, the possibility of early detection of learning problems is reduced.

However, the data presented earlier on WISC-R patterns suggest that administration of the V scale is not necessarily useless or inappropriate under all conditions. Provided the child has been in the school system for a reasonable length of time (probably two years minimum), an exploratory use of the WISC-R V scale may be informative. In the first place, the child may score relatively high (close to P score) on the V scale, thereby suggest- ing that s/he is making good progress in English cognitive/academic skills. Secondly, deviations from the typical pattern of V subtest scores among ESL children (see Figure 2) can be very informative. The peaks at Arithme- tic and Digit Span (when it is administered) are replicated in the vast majority of low V subtest profiles. Thus, a relatively low score on one of these subtests may provide a clue to a real learning problem.

The psychologists in the present sample who were sensitive to cultural/ linguistic barriers to test performance often administered only the Perform- ance scale. The inferential paths which follow from this decision are considered in the next section.

B2. Only Performance Scale Administered
When only the performance scale is administered, the PIQ is usually inter- preted as indicative of the child's potential.

GU (177): GU, whose parents were reported to speak mostly Polish, entered the system in grade 2 and was referred by her grade 3 teacher who noted that she was "having trouble with English vocabulary and its mean- ing. She is very competent in other areas such as arithmetic. But she is missing a great deal, not being able to understand what she hears and sees". The psychologist made no record of verbal scores (if administered). GU's PIQ was 73. The assessment read as follows:

> GU was rather quiet during the interview and had little to say. English is a second language for her and she has difficulty expressing herself. For this reason, the verbal scores on the test should be disregarded. On performance items, GU scored consistently below average. The scores may be somewhat lower that her actual ability level due to her lack of understanding oral instructions, however she probably would still score in the slow learner range.

Comment. Clearly, an average or high PIQ score provides useful information on students' nonverbal abilities, although a low PIQ needs to be treated somewhat more cautiously, depending upon the student's grasp of English. However, it is not necessarily valid to infer from an average or high PIQ that the student's overall academic potential is high, since reading and language arts achievement is generally more related to Verbal ability than to Performance. Possible visual perceptual difficulties may be noticed, but generally an assessment in which the P subtests alone are administered is usually capable of providing only limited answers to teachers' questions regarding academic potential or learning disability.

An obvious means of attempting to obtain more information on academic potential is to administer tests in the child's L_1. A handful of assessments in the present sample employed this strategy.

B3. Assessment of L_1 Abilities

Assessment of L_1 cognitive/academic abilities seems especially appropriate for the child who manifests a low VIQ, average PIQ WISC-R test profile and who has been in school in the host country for a relatively short time (less than two years). Testing L_1 after this period is likely to be of suspect validity because of possible regression of L_1 abilities due to lack of exposure to conceptually demanding input in L_1. The assumption underlying the assessment of L_1 abilities is that cognitive/academic abilities are cross-lingual or interdependent in L_1 and L_2 (see Cummins, 1981b, 1981c). In other words, an immigrant child's L_1 cognitive academic ability on entry to the school system will be an important factor determining the level of L_2 cognitive/academic achievement. Thus, if L_1 ability is well-developed it is likely that low VIQ and academic difficulties in English are a temporary function of ESL background. On the other hand, poorly developed L_1 and L_2 cognitive/academic abilities would suggest that academic difficulties are likely to be more long-term.

The greater confidence which can result from assessing the child's abilities in his/her stronger language is evident in the following assessment.

S (363): SS was referred by her kindergarten teacher who noted that she was immature and used baby talk. The speech and language assessment revealed that

> SS was operating at a 2.5 to 3.0 age level for comprehension of English as compared to her chronological age of 5.3.... Expressive language consisted mainly of one or two word utterances, or gestures.... In summary, SS exhibited a severe receptive and expressive language delay.

The psychological assessment showed SS's VIQ to be 51 and PIQ 70. The

63

psychologist noted that during testing SS was quite chatty, but difficult to understand. One of the psychologists in the system who spoke Italian (as an L_1) contacted the parents after these assessments and arranged to give SS an informal assessment in Italian in order to ascertain whether language development in Italian was normal; in other words, to ascertain whether the language delay was "real" or a temporary function of ESL background. This informal assessment revealed that although the mother felt SS's Italian was good, SS could not name many common objects in Italian, she tended to respond inappropriately to questions given in Italian and used segments or sentence fragments. Thus, the assessment team felt reasonably confident in their diagnosis because of the congruence of symptoms in the two languages.

Comment. One must presume in this instance that the psychologist who spoke Italian was sensitive to dialectal variations. Also, it is to be hoped that advice was given to the mother about how the family could help the child's speech and language development *in Italian* in order to complement the English speech therapy the child would receive within the school system.

In general, assessment of the child's L_1 proficiency can play an extremely important role in helping psychologists understand the nature of her academic difficulty. However, L_1 assessment is not a panacea. Problems may exist in regard to the cultural and linguistic appropriacy of the L_1 measure (e.g., dialectal variation) and no less caution in interpreting performance is called for than in an L_2 assessment.

SUMMARY AND CONCLUSIONS

The psychological assessments analysed in the present study illustrate the problems associated with applying assessment and placement procedures developed primarily to serve the needs of middle-class English-speaking students to students from linguistically and culturally diverse backgrounds. It is clear that there are many gaps in psychologists' and teachers' knowledge both about the limitations of psychological tests and about the development of academic skills in minority language children. Some of these gaps are due to the fact that the knowledge base has not existed; others are due to the fact that the data which are available have not been adequately communicated to teachers and psychologists, either in university or in-service courses. Some of the information which many psychologists, teachers, administrators, policy-makers, and academics concerned with special education and/or ESL students may not know about these issues is summarized below.

A. Test-Related Knowledge Gaps

1. *Psychological tests assess minority language students' present academic functioning, not potential.* Because IQ tests purport to assess academic potential, and because teachers explicitly request information about students' potential, many psychologists in the present study made inferences about minority students' potential, abilities, or aptitudes which are logically inadmissible given the assumptions of the test. These inferences about low abilities can result in overinclusion of minority students in special education classes, as documented by Mercer (1973). Contributing to psychologists' tendency to make logically invalid inferences is the apparent fluency of many minority students in English and the fact that psychologists and teachers have no information on how long it takes minority students to approach grade norms in English cognitive/academic skills. It is clearly not an easy task for a psychologist to admit that a psychological assessment has revealed little or nothing about a student's academic potential when the teacher has referred a student precisely in order to discover his or her academic potential so that realistic expectations can be established for the student.

2. *The WISC-R subtest pattern of minority students may provide diagnostic clues.* The quantitative analysis suggested that, in general, Performance subtests were more valid than Verbal subtests. Thus, provided the student clearly understands the task demands, it is reasonable to make cautious and tentative inferences regarding nonverbal intellectual abilities based on Performance scores. However, nonverbal abilities are usually less related to academic progress than are verbal abilities and thus are of limited usefulness as indicators of academic potential.

A large majority of low VIQ, higher PIQ, WISC-R profiles showed a characteristic pattern of peaks on Arithmetic and Digit Span and extremely low scores on Information. This implies that English language deficits interfere less with Arithmetic and Digit Span than with the other Verbal subtests. Thus, deviations from the typical pattern for ESL students may be diagnostically important. For example, relatively low Digit Span may indicate auditory sequential processing difficulties rather than English language deficits; no such inferences (however tentative) about abilities or verbal aptitude are warranted on the basis of relatively low Information, Similarities, Vocabulary or Comprehension scores.

65

Thus, it appears justifiable to administer the WISC-R Arithmetic and Digit Span subtests, as well as one of the other Verbal subtests (not Information) for comparison purposes, to minority students who have been in the country for a reasonable amount of time (i.e., who have developed fluency or have been here about two years). However, obviously no IQ should be calculated on the basis of these scores and inferences should be tentative.

The present data suggest that there is very little justification for administering the Information subtest to minority students; however, if it is administered and a student's score is lower than on the other Verbal subtests it should not be included in the calculation of an IQ score. For minority students Information rather than Digit Span should be the optional Verbal subtest.

B. Student-Related Knowledge Gaps

3. *ESL immigrant students take 5-7 years, on the average, to approach grade norms in English cognitive/academic skills.* There are many examples in the protocols where teachers refer for psychological assessment ESL students who have been in Canada for a relatively short amount of time (e.g., 1-2 years). Because the child's academic achievement is still poor, despite apparently good progress in English communicative skills, they wonder if some form of learning disability is involved or if the child has a low IQ. This is not surprising in view of the lack of any empirical data showing how long it takes immigrant students to approach grade norms in academic skills. The implicit assumption among teachers, psychologists, and policy-makers has been that English language deficits can no longer be invoked as a factor impeding school or test performance once the child has acquired relatively fluent English communicative skills. Normally immigrant children can speak and understand English very well within about two years of arrival.

The re-analysis of the Toronto Board of Education data (Figure 1) shows that these assumptions are fallacious. Despite the fact that ESL students may be fluent in English within about two years of arrival, it takes between 5-7 years, *on the average*, for students who arrive after the age of 6, to approach grade norms in English cognitive/academic skills, i.e., the skills required on a verbal IQ test or on a standardized reading test. The fact that students continue to approach grade norms with increasing length of residence suggests that inferences about students' academic potential based on a one-shot administration of the WISC-R within students' first five years in the host country are likely to underestimate potential.

66

4. *Interpersonal communicative skills are very different from cognitive/academic language proficiency*. The difference between these two types of language proficiency is clearly shown in the numerous referrals which noted that students spoke and understood English well but were experiencing considerable difficulties in reading and academic aspects of English. The data considered in the previous section show that it can take up to 7 years for immigrant students to approach grade norms in cognitive/academic skills despite the fact that their basic interpersonal communicative skills approach acceptable native-like levels much sooner.

The phenomenon is essentially the same as with preschool children learning their first language, where, as Donaldson (1978) points out, children's understanding and production can give a misleading impression of skill with language per se. Thus, ESL children's rapid acquisition of facility in understanding and producing appropriate language in meaningful interpersonal contexts is not surprising. Add to this facility a near-native accent and the use of stock peer-group expressions and the surface manifestations of the ESL background have disappeared.

However, functioning in a typical academic context (e.g., learning to read by phonically-based methods or performing verbal IQ tasks) often involves processing language which is stripped of its situational and interpersonal supports.[1] Just as in a monolingual context, children's facility in basic interpersonal communicative skills provides little or no information about their academic language skills, no inferences are warranted about ESL students' cognitive/academic language proficiency or the validity of verbal IQ scores based on their interpersonal communicative skills.

5. *ESL children's academic difficulties are not caused by the use of a non-English language in the home*. There were many instances in the protocols where children's low verbal IQ scores were interpreted as a valid reflection of verbal ability and attributed to the child's exposure to two languages. There were also several cases where the teacher or psychologist assumed that parents' lack of facility in English precluded them from helping their child academically at home and that the more exposure the child had to the mother tongue the greater the interference with the acquisition of English.

---

1. The academic difficulties of some minority students as well as students designated as "learning disabled" are greatly increased by the excessive "disembedding" of much instruction designed to teach literacy skills. The more "context-embedded" (Cummins, 1981b) or meaningful the instruction, the less such students (and all students) are handicapped by their language difficulties and the more rapidly will they overcome such difficulties.

There is considerable research data available to refute these assumptions (see Cummins, 1981c). A home-school language switch, in itself, does not cause academic problems. In fact, the research data suggest that the development of proficiency in two languages can be academically and cognitively enriching. However, in a minority language context a high level of bilingualism can usually be attained only when there is a strong emphasis, either in school or home, on the development of L_1 skills. One of the reasons why this emphasis has been lacking in many cases is because minority parents and educators have assumed that an emphasis on L_1 would be detrimental to English. Contrary to this assumption, the data suggest that a strong emphasis on developing L_1 skills in the home may make an important contribution to the development of English academic skills.

Several studies have shown that the ways in which adults communicate with children is important for children's future academic success. For example, in a longitudinal study recently conducted in England, Wells (1981) has shown that children's rate of linguistic development is significantly related to the quality of the conversation they experience with adults and also that children's knowledge about literacy on entry to school is strongly related to the level of reading skills they attain in school.

Given the importance of the *quality* of parent-child communication in the home and the fact that concepts developed in L_1 can easily be transferred to L_2, it is clear that teachers' or psychologists' advice to parents to use English in the home can have potentially disastrous results. In many cases, parents will use broken English or a mixture of L_1 and English and spend less time interacting with their children because they are not comfortable in using English. If minority language parents desire their children to become bilingual then they should expose them to as much L_1 as possible in the preschool years. Activities such as singing, playing, telling stories, and reading aloud to children are extremely important not only in developing a high level of L_1 proficiency but also in establishing a solid foundation for the acquisition of English skills and future academic success.

A clear policy implication of the present findings is that adequate interpretation of scores on a test like the WISC-R requires knowledge of more than just the characteristics of the test; it also depends upon familiarity with research findings on issues related to bilingualism and L_2 acquisition among minority students. Given the increasing numbers of such students in many North American school systems, and the fact that a disproportionate number appear to experience academic difficulties (see Cummins, 1981b), there is an urgent need for more than just token consideration of these issues in the training of school psychologists.

68

FEASIBILITY OF AN ADDITIVE
BILINGUAL PROGRAM
FOR THE LANGUAGE-IMPAIRED CHILD*

Margaret Bruck

As a direct consequence of English-speaking parents' dissatisfaction with pedagogical practices of teaching French as a second language, and as a result of their desire to provide their children with an opportunity to achieve mastery in Canada's two official languages, early French immersion programs have become increasingly popular across Canada. The main goal of such programs is to promote functional bilingualism in French and English among English-speaking children through a policy of home and school language switch (Lambert & Tucker, 1972). Specifically in these programs, English-speaking children receive all their instruction in the second language during kindergarten and grade 1. Thus the children are taught to read, write, and do mathematics in French (L_2) before they are taught these skills in English (L_1). In grade 2, English-language arts are introduced into the curriculum and with each successive year increasing amounts of L_1 are added resulting in a bilingual program by grade 5.

The results of numerous evaluations conducted across Canada consistently indicate that not only do the participating children develop normally in academic, cognitive, and social areas, but they also acquire high degrees of proficiency in French without any detriment to native language skills (e.g. Edwards et al. 1978; Genesee, 1978; Gray & Cameron, 1980; Lambert & Tucker, 1972; Swain & Barik, 1976). However, since these evaluations are based upon samples of "typical" French immersion students (i.e., children from middle-class backgrounds, with at least average intelligence, and normal development) little is known about the suitability of French immersion for children who deviate from these normal patterns (e.g., children of low intelligence, children from working class or minority backgrounds, children with deviant or slow patterns of development). The present study

* The research was supported by grants from the Quebec Ministry of Education and from the Department of Secretary of State and by the National Health and Welfare Research Development Program through a National Health Research Scholar award. This is manuscript No. 82-000, McGill-Montreal Children's Hospital Research Institute.

was designed to examine the feasibility of French immersion programs for one such subgroup, children with slow language development or language impairments.

The term language impairment refers to a heterogeneous group of children who, despite physical well-being, normal intelligence, and a healthy personality, acquire first language with painful slowness. Such children may display a number of different symptoms. For example, many children are relatively late in using words, in combining them, and in developing clear articulation and syntactic sophistication. These children may have problems in comprehending as well as producing speech. At school age, they often lack facility in oral language and miss the point of instructions, explanations, and informal conversations. Language impairment is usually sufficient cause for school difficulty (Jansky, 1978; Leonard, 1979). Recent estimates have indicated that 7% to 10% of the school age population exhibit some kind of language impairment.

In the present study language-impaired children, identified in French immersion kindergartens, were evaluated annually until the end of grade 3. Their development of first- and second-language oral skills as well as their academic achievement were compared to that of a similar group of language-impaired children identified in English kindergartens and to a control group of French immersion children with normal language development. This report details the progress of these children from kindergarten through grade 2 (for a complete description of the results through Grade 1, see Bruck, 1982; a preliminary analysis of the results based on only part of the total sample can be found in Bruck, 1978).

A study of the performance of language-impaired children educated in French immersion programs has practical as well as theoretical value. On a practical level, educators and parents require empirical data concerning the feasibility of immersion programs for the below-average child. Such data become more crucial as the program's enrollments grow, resulting in increasing numbers of children with various problems.

Presently, entry into French immersion programs is open to all children solely on the basis of the parents' desire to have their child learn a second language, and is not restricted on the basis of academic potential or achievement. Furthermore when children experience academic difficulty they are permitted, if their parents so desire, to continue in the program. Despite this current policy, the feasibility of French immersion education for such chldren and the optimal treatment for their problems are controversial issues which are best exemplified by the justifications for two opposing strategies currently employed to help poor-achieving French immersion

70

students. Some argue that the second-language situation causes or aggravates the observed problems and therefore the child who is experiencing difficulty should be switched to an English stream where all instruction is given in the child's first language; or if possible such children should be identified at the kindergarten level and placed in English classes. For example, Trites and Price (1976, 1977) argue that children with learning problems in French immersion programs exhibit unique neurological deficits which impede their ability to achieve in the French immersion program. They also report that when some of these children are transferred to an English program performance improves.

Others argue that many observed problems are a function of basic behavioral predispositions or specific underlying deficits inherent to the child who would display the same problems regardless of the language of instruction. Therefore it is suggested that children with problems continue in the immersion stream and receive help for their problems in the context of the program. For example, Genesee (1976) found that, when French immersion students with low IQ's were compared to similar students in English programs, both groups performed similarly on academic achievement and L_1 acquisition measures. When these low IQ children were compared to average or above average IQ French immersion students, while there were differences in academic achievement measures, the low IQ students were similar in terms of their acquisition of oral French communication skills. The grade 1 results of the present study (Bruck, 1982) are similar to those of Genesee. That is, the English-speaking children with language impairments attending French immersion programs demonstrated comparable cognitive, first-language, and academic skills to children educated only in their first language. While they were lower than the French immersion controls in academic, cognitive and linguistic areas, their comprehension of French was similar to that of the normal French immersion controls. These two sets of data indicate that while achievement in the French immersion program is related to cognitive and linguistic skills, this relationship is not specific to language of education in that the same patterns were found for similar children educated in their first language. Furthermore, these data indicate that despite poor L_1 or cognitive skills, such children can acquire proficiency in L_2 oral communication skills.

Theoretically the present study addresses the issue of which factors account for the success or failure of second-language programs, or of students within these programs. Two major theoretical models have been posited to account for the success of French immersion programs, which is especially notable when compared to the dismal failure of second-language "submersion" programs for the minority immigrant student (i.e., children from minority cultures who receive their total education in the majority culture language, e.g. Anderson & Boyer, 1978; Darcy, 1963; Skutnabb-Kangas & Toekomaa, 1976)). Proponents of the first model argue that the social, psychological, and sociolinguistic values of the social milieu primarily account for the success or failure of each bilingual program (Cohen & Swain, 1976; Lambert, 1975; Tucker, 1977). For example, the majority culture immersion child lives in a community whose members view L_1 as dominant and prestigious. There is also a concomitant value placed on learning L_2 which is viewed as socially relevant. As a result of these community conditions, the necessary cultural and educational supports are established to ensure that the children will add a second language to their linguistic repertoires at no cost to their first-language skills or to their cultural identity. These conditions are commonly referred to as additive bilingualism (Lambert, 1975). For example, teachers in immersion programs stress the necessity of using L_2 in the school setting even though they have positive attitudes towards the child's home language and culture. Furthermore, the voluntary nature of the program ensures that the participating children are from homes that endorse positive attitudes and motivations toward L_2 learning, and toward the maintenance of first-language skills and culture. Such conditions are thought to form the basis of positive attitudes and motivations in the learner which directly influence successful performance.

These conditions contrast with those found for the minority language child who is educated in a system designed to assimilate the student into the majority culture as quickly as possible and to replace the child's first language with the dominant language of the community. The school does not recognize or value the linguistic and cultural diversity of such children, who are often ridiculed by majority culture peers and teachers not only for their poor levels of L_2 proficiency but also for the use of their first language. As a result of both these conditions and of receiving no school instruction in the first language, minority children eventually lose proficiency in L_1, which is inadequately replaced by the more culturally dominant and prestigious language. These social psychological conditions, termed subtractive bilingualism (Lambert, 1975) or submersion programs (Cohen & Swain, 1976), are though to be the cause of the academic failure of many minority students.

The second theoretical model, while recognizing the importance of social psychological factors, emphasizes the individual learner's cognitive and linguistic abilities as primary predictors of success in the second-language classroom. The important role that these psycholinguistic skills play is reflected in Cummins' threshold hypothesis (Cummins, 1979). It is argued that there are minimal levels of L_1 competence that are necessary to avoid the negative consequences of L_2 instruction. Thus, because the French immersion children have acquired competence in L_1 upon program entry, they have the requisite cognitive-linguistic skills to learn L_2 and, therefore, can profit from the language interactions of the environment. Cummins (1979) has argued that minority children are exposed to home linguistic environments that do not promote vocabulary skills, metalinguistic insights, or decontextualized language which are necessary prerequisites for literacy skills. Therefore, because of inadequate exposure to L_1, minority children do not have the necessary linguistic competence in L_1; thus instruction in L_2 for children with poor L_1 skills will not only result in low levels of L_2 competence, but will also interfere with and severely retard the acquisition of L_1 skills. Such children have been called "semilingual" or "alingual" (Skutnabb-Kangas & Toukomaa, 1976).

The threshold hypothesis, however, is based mainly on empirical data from minority children educated in subtractive bilingual conditions (Cummins, 1979); thus it is not clear whether social psychological factors (i.e., subtractive bilingualism) or psycholinguistic factors are the primary causes of these children's poor achievements. In addition, the psycholinguistic position assumes that all French immersion children have intact or normal linguistic and cognitive abilities. This is not necessarily the case, in that entry into the program is based solely on parental willingness to have the child educated in two languages and is not restricted on the basis of academic potential. Consequently, there are some French immersion children with poor cognitive skills and psycholinguistic abilities.

The present study offers a more direct test of the relative contributions of the social psychological and psycholinguistic factors to achievement in home and school language-switch programs by examining the progress of children with low levels of L_1 competence who are educated in additive bilingual environments. Specifically, it examines the development of language-impaired majority culture children who attend French immersion programs. In the present context, the threshold hypothesis would predict that because of the language-impaired children's low levels of L_1 competence, they will do poorly and become semilingual if instructed in a second language. However, because the language-impaired children under investigation are from majority culture backgrounds and are taught in an additive bilingual environment, the social psychological model would predict that academic, cognitive, and linguistic development would not be adversely affected by instruction in the weaker language, but rather that development would be similar to that occurring in a situation in which language-impaired children were educated only in their first language.

While the sociolinguistic and threshold models were constructed to account for the relative success and failure of various programs (between program effects), with certain modifications they can also be used to account for individual variation within a program. That is, one would predict that students with more positive attitudes and motivations would perform better than those with less positive outlooks, and that students' performance would be a function of cognitive linguistic abilities.

While there is a significant literature detailing the contribution of attitudinal/motivational factors and cognitive variables to second-language achievement, there is a lack of specific data on individual difference in achievement of French immersion students. The available data suggest that the importance of motivational and cognitive variables change as a function of the criterion measure of achievement. For example, in a study of the relevance of cognitive and motivational factors to grade 1 French immersion children's L_2 achievement, Genesee and Hamayan (1981) found that both motivational and cognitive variables were associated with better listening comprehension and literacy skills but not with oral production skills. In Bruck's (1982) and Genesee's (1976) studies of language-impaired and low IQ students, cognitive linguistic ability was more associated with L_2 literacy tasks than with L_2 communication skill abilities.

In terms of the present study, although there were no measures of the individual children's attitudes and motivations toward the second language, there are measures of their cognitive linguistic abilities. These data will therefore allow one to examine more closely the association between cognitive-linguistic levels and various measures of L_2 achievement.

METHOD

Design
Children attending French immersion and English kindergarten classes were screened at the beginning of the school year to identify four groups of subjects:
1. French immersion children with language impairments
   (French problem - FP).
2. English stream children with language impairments
   (English problem - EP).
3. French immersion children with normal language abilities
   (French control - FC).

74

4. English stream children with normal language abilities
   (English control - EC).

Once the groups had been identified, the linguistic, cognitive, academic, and second-language skills of each subject were assessed annually in kindergarten, grade 1, and grade 2. To determine the feasibility of French immersion programs for language-impaired children, their performance and progress on the test battery was contrasted to that of the three comparison groups. Specifically, a comparison of the performance of the FP and EP groups in relation to the FC and EC groups would indicate whether language-impaired children in the French stream achieve at the same level as language-impaired children in the English stream, and whether any discrepancies are a consequence of general program factors affecting even the normal child. Comparisons of the discrepancies in performance between the two French immersion groups in relation to that of the two English groups would indicate whether French immersion schooling for the language-impaired child is more problematic than schooling in the first language. Simple comparisons between the two French immersion groups on French proficiency measures would indicate any specific problems the language-impaired (FP) children are encountering in acquiring a second language.

Subjects
In October, kindergarten children attending French immersion and English classes in one English school district were screened for language impairments. To correctly assess the linguistic capabilities of the students, a number of procedures were followed. First, all French immersion and English kindergarten teachers were asked to list any children from English-speaking backgrounds whom they felt had problems with language. (cf. Damico & Oller, 1980, for a discussion of teachers' good capabilities in making reliable judgments on children's linguistic problems). Next, the referred children were interviewed individually and then given a diagnostic screening test by a specialist in child language development. The test included an object manipulation test, a story retelling test, a sentence imitation test, and an echolalia test, for a total of 59 items. The items are similar to those used in other diagnostic tests of language skills, such as Boehm Test of Basic Concepts or Detroit Tests of Learning Aptitude. This test was specifically developed for the present project so that children with normal language development would have little difficulty, whereas children with language impairments would do poorly. The test took about 15 minutes to administer to each child.

Each problem child met the following criteria: On the screening test, the child scored lower than 35 (the scores within the problem group ranged from 11 to 35 with most being between 25 and 35); from the interview the experimenter felt the child had a language problem and that poor test performance was not due to shyness, dialect differences, etc.; and the child was of normal intelligence. All project children were given the Wechsler Preschool and Primary Scale of Intelligence. Any child not scoring above 85 on either the Verbal Scale of Performance Scale was eliminated from the project.

After the problem children were identified, each was matched with a control child on the basis of sex, age in months, classroom teacher, and father's occupation. In addition, each control subject satisfied the following criteria: The teacher indicated that the control child's language seemed normal; the child scored over 50 on the diagnostic screening test. On the basis of the interview the experimenter felt the child's language seemed normal; the child had normal intelligence as measured by the WPPSI.

Finally, in terms of the present analyses, in order to qualify as a subject, the children screened in kindergarten had to remain in their respective French immersion or English class through the end of grade 2. Because of the low incidence of language disabilities and because of subject attrition (children moving from the community or switching from French to English classes), it was not possible to identify a significant number of kindergarten subjects within 1 year. After 6 years of annual kindergarten identification, the following sample sizes were obtained for the grade 2 follow-up: 18 children in the FP (target) group, 31 in the FC group, 26 in the EP group, 26 in the EC group. The subjects in this study were predominantly middle class.

A comparison of the attrition rates across grades (Table 1) indicates that, while these were similar from kindergarten to grade 1 across groups, that by grade 2, the FP group had the highest rates. This differential loss was of concern because it might indicate that by grade 2 the children remaining in the FP group were those who were experiencing little difficulty while those with significantly more problems had transferred to an English stream. However, inspection of our records indicated that of the 9 children who had left the program between grade 1 and grade 2, five of these left because they had moved to a district which did not offer a French immersion program and only four, because of academic difficulty, were transferred to an English stream. Also the kindergarten and grade 1 test data of the 9 subjects who had left the project were similar to those of the 18 who were still in the sample. This suggests that, although the FP sample was greatly reduced over the project, the children who left were not necessarily the more disabled, and that qualitatively the characteristics of the group have remained constant since kindergarten.

76

Table 1

Number of children tested in kindergarten, Grade 1, and Grade 2

Group	Kindergarten	Grade 1	Grade 2
FP	36	27	18
EP	36	27	26
FC	40	34	31
EC	35	29	26

Tests

In the last school term of the kindergarten year, the children were administered a battery of tests to measure first language and cognitive skills. The children were then retested on the same measures one and 2 years later when they were in grades 1 and 2 respectively. Various measures were added to the grade 1 and 2 batteries to assess math skills, oral and written French skills, and English-language literacy skills.

Kindergarten battery. All kindergarten subjects were individually given four tests:
(1) Full Scale Wechsler Preschool and Primary Scale of Intelligence, (WPPSI):
(2) Peabody Picture Vocabulary Test, Form A, (PPVT);
(3) Receptive and Expressive subtests of the Northwestern Syntax Screening Test (NSST);
(4) Seven subtests of the Illinois Test of Psycholinguistic Abilities, (ITPA): Auditory Reception, Visual Reception, Auditory Association, Visual Association, Grammatic Closure, Auditory Sequential Memory, Visual Sequential Memory.

Grade 1 battery. All of the kindergarten tests were readministered at the end of grade 1 with the exception of the WPPSI. Form B of the PPVT was given rather than Form A. The following tests of first-language proficiency, cognitive abilities, and academic achievement were added: Vocabulary subtest of the Wechsler Intelligence Scale for Children (WISC); Similarities subtest of the WISC; Auditory Closure subtest of the ITPA; Sound Blending subtest of the ITPA: Sentence Imitation Test (Golick, 1977). The last measure assesses the child's comprehension of complex grammatical structures. The child was read a sentence and asked to repeat it. Repetitions that altered the semantic and/or syntactic structure of the original sentence were counted as errors. There were 21 sentences in the test.

77

To assess listening comprehension of spoken French, all children in the four groups were given the Ontario Institute for Studies in Education (O.I.S.E.) French Listening Comprehension Test (Barik, 1975)[1].

Grade 2 battery. All of the grade 1 tests were readministered at the end of grade 2. Form A of the PPVT was given. The following tests of English literacy and math skills were added: *Spache Diagnostic Reading Scales*, Reading, Math, and Spelling subtests of the *Wide Range Achievement Test* (WRAT), Math subtest of the *Metropolitan Achievement Test* (Primary Battery II).

Oral and written French-language skills were also evaluated. To examine French literacy skills, the FP and FC children were given the following tests: Decoding individual sounds; oral reading; reading comprehension; and dictation. These tests were developed during the course of the study by several psychologists and remedial therapists who had expertise in the field of assessment of learning disabilities. The development of such a battery was necessary given the lack of appropriate instruments to assess the reading and writing skills of young French immersion children. The O.I.S.E. Listening Comprehension test was readministered to all children in the four groups.

To obtain additional information on the children's skills and school achievement, the grade 2 class teachers were given questionnaires in which they were asked to rate the children's competence in reading, writing, math, expressive and receptive language skills. For the French immersion children, only French skills were rated and conversely only English skills were rated for the English stream children. These questionnaires were completed at the end of the school year.

RESULTS

Separate 2x2 ANOVA's were carried out on the kindergarten Verbal and Performance WPPSI IQ scores of the four groups to determine whether there were any differences between the verbal and nonverbal cognitive abilities of the two language problem groups and between the two normal control groups, which may have resulted as a consequence of not initially matching the children on verbal and nonverbal measures of intelligence.

1. Although the English stream children received no instruction in French reading and writing, they were given the oral test in that their kindergarten, grade 1, and grade 2 curriculum called for a daily period of French-as-a-second-language instruction (FSL) which was based on an audiolingual method.

The independent variables were language of instruction (French immersion vs. English) and linguistic ability (problem vs. control). The means for the Verbal and Performance IQ's are presented in Table 2.

On the Verbal Scale the control children performed significantly better than the problem children, $F(1,97) = 63.03, p < .001$. The French immersion children performed better than the English stream children, $F(1,97) = 4.09, p < .05$. There was no significant interaction effect. On the Performance Scale there was a significant linguistic ability effect, $F(1,97) = 19.59, p < .001$; a significant language-of-instruction effect, $F(1,97) = 8.71, p < .006$; and a significant interaction effect, $F(1,97) = 5.15, p < .03$. Teukey tests indicated that the EP group was significantly lower ($p < .05$), on the Performance Scale than the other three groups who were similar.

Table 2
Means of kindergarten IQ scores

Group	Verbal IQ	Performance IQ
FP	98.11	111.10
EP	93.65	98.65
FC	116.30	116.30
EC	111.50	115.00

The results of the IQ kindergarten scores deserve careful interpretation. Even though there was a difference between the French immersion and English stream groups on the verbal scale, this main effect was due to pooling the scores of the two French immersion and two English groups; when each immersion group was compared separately to its language-matched controls (i.e., FP vs. EP; FC vs. EC) the t tests were nonsignificant. Thus in terms of verbal ability as measured in kindergarten, the FP children were similar to the EP children. However, it does appear that the EP group had poorer nonverbal skills than the FP group. Therefore, to account for the possible influence of between-group differences in ability, Performance and Verbal IQ scores were used as covariates in all subsequent analyses.

Data from those tests administered in both kindergarten, grade 1, and grade 2 were analyzed by means of a multivariate analysis of covariance. Measures which were only given in grade 2 (e.g., English achievement tests) or in grade 1 and grade 2 (e.g., Sound Blending) were analyzed by separate univariate analyses of covariance. Performance and Verbal IQ's were the covariates. These analyses were then repeated without the covariance adjustment. A comparison of the results obtained from the covariance

79

technique and those obtained without covariance indicated that in most cases the levels of significance for the main effects and for the interaction effects were identical regardless of the statistical procedure. Discrepencies that occurred will be detailed in the discussion.

The data from the grade 2 teacher evaluations were analyzed qualitatively and were used to complement the quantitative findings.

Development of Cognitive and First-Language Oral Skills

A multivariate analysis of variance (MANOVA) and of covariance (MANACOVA) were run on the cognitive and L_1 linguistic measures administered in kindergarten, grade 1, and grade 2. The independent variables were: language of instruction (French immersion vs. English); linguistic ability (problem vs. control); and the repeated measure, grade at time of testing (kindergarten vs. grade 1 vs. grade 2). The dependent variables were: Vocabulary subtest (WPPSI-WISC); Similarities subtest (WPPSI-WISC); PPVT; NSST Receptive; NSST Expressive; Auditory Reception (ITPA); Visual Reception (ITPA); Visual Sequential Memory (ITPA); Auditory Association (ITPA); Visual Sequential Memory (ITPA); Auditory Association (ITPA); Auditory Sequential Memory (ITPA); Grammatic Closure (ITPA). A summary and comparison of the results for the MANOVA and MANACOVA analyses are presented in Table 3. The un-adjusted means for the dependent measures are presented in Table 4.

The overall MANOVA language of instruction effect was significant: the French immersion children performed better than the English stream children. However, this effect was nonsignificant for the MANACOVA. It should be noted that this is the only difference in results that was obtained from the MANOVA and MANACOVA analyses. It is unclear as to why there should be a significant language-of-instruction effect. However, in that this effect can be controlled by the covariance technique, and as will be shown below disappears over time, it is not felt that it interferes with the interpretation of the subsequent results.

There was an overall effect for linguistic level. In the MANOVA analyses, there were significant univariate F's for all 12 dependent variables. The number of significant dependent variables was slightly reduced in the MANACOVA analysis. All univariate analyses indicated that the control children performed significantly better than the problem children.

The overall main effect for time of testing was significant. The univariate F's for all dependent variables (except for Similarities and Vocabulary) were significant, indicating general improvement in performance as a function of grade level.

80

Table 3

Summary of MANOVA and MANACOVA Analyses

Significance Levels	MANOVA	MANACOVA
Language of Instruction - Immersion vs English		
Overall F	2.578* ($df = 12,86$)	1.16 ($df = 12,84$)
Significant dependent variables	Similarities[a.] NSST-Receptive NSST-Expressive PPVT Vocabulary	
Linguistic Ability - Problem vs Control		
Overall F	16.33** ($df = 12,86$)	6.94** ($df = 12,84$)
Significant dependent variables	All 12 dependent variables are significant	All dependent variables are significant except Similarities Visual Sequential Memory Visual Association
Language of Instruction x Linguistic Ability Interaction		
Overall F	1.56 ($df = 12,86$)	1.37 ($df = 12,84$)
Grade at Time of Testing		
Overall F	23.63** ($df = 24,366$)	23.63** ($df = 24,362$)
Significant dependent variables	All dependent variables are significant except: Similarities Vocabulary	All dependent variables are significant except: Similarities Vocabulary
Language of Instruction x Time of Testing Interaction		
Overall F	2.07** ($df = 24,366$)	1.99** ($df = 24,362$)
Significant dependent variables	NSST-Expressive Auditory Reception	NSST Expressive Auditory Reception
Linguistic Ability x Time of Testing Interaction		
Overall F	2.90** ($df = 24,366$)	2.93** ($df = 24,362$)
Significant dependent variables	NSST Receptive NSST Expressive Auditory Association Grammatic Closure	NSST Receptive NSST Expressive Auditory Association Grammatic Closure
Linguistic Ability x Language of Instruction x Time of Testing		
Overall F	1.16 ($df = 24,366$)	1.22 ($df = 24,362$)

a. All significant dependent variables are reported when $p < .05$ for the univariate F statistic

* $p < .05$

** $p < .01$

Table 4
Means for dependent variables of MANOVA

Measure	Year	French Problem	English Problem	French Control	English Control
Similarities	K	10.12	10.23	13.42	13.08
Scaled Score	1	11.06	9.69	14.26	12.85
	2	11.39	9.65	14.35	13.08
NSST Receptive	K	26.83	24.96	31.42	31.23
	1	30.44	31.12	33.97	33.50
	2	34.44	33.69	35.55	36.12
NSST Expressive	K	25.33	20.42	31.97	31.08
	1	30.50	29.46	34.48	35.85
	2	33.11	32.19	36.71	36.73
PPVT	K	101.2	94.69	113.8	107.7
IQ	1	98.22	88.65	109.8	107.2
	2	99.94	94.88	113.9	110.4
Vocabulary	K	9.5	8.85	12.71	11.31
Scaled Score	1	8.22	8.89	12.00	10.96
	2	8.5	8.85	12.00	11.50
Auditory	K	19.06	16.62	24.84	24.35
Reception	1	27.89	23.46	31.69	30.69
	2	27.67	31.31	34.65	35.73
Visual	K	15.89	15.04	18.87	20.08
Reception	1	23.33	22.77	25.06	23.85
	2	27.83	25.27	28.06	28.58
Visual	K	17.06	14.81	18.19	18.46
Sequential	1	20.94	19.96	21.71	19.27
Memory	2	22.72	20.27	23.26	22.27
Auditory	K	16.61	15.00	24.68	23.92
Association	1	21.94	21.69	28.29	27.54
	2	26.11	25.42	31.26	30.96
Auditory	K	14.83	14.00	25.48	26.58
Sequential	1	18.78	19.23	29.10	27.77
Memory	2	21.44	22.38	31.48	31.42
Visual	K	18.83	18.12	20.84	21.04
Association	1	21.78	22.04	26.71	24.65
	2	25.89	24.81	26.16	27.35
Grammatic	K	14.61	10.62	20.39	22.42
Closure	1	18.00	17.00	23.71	24.96
	2	22.72	22.31	27.32	28.38

N.B. Unless specifically noted all measures are expressed in raw scores.

82

There was an overall significant language of instruction x time of testing effect. The results of the Teukeys run on the two significant dependent variables (NSST Expressive and Auditory Reception) suggest that the overall effect is best interpreted as follows: even though the French immersion children's performance was superior to that of the English controls' in kindergarten, by grade 2, they were similar. It should be noted that since only two of the 12 variables adhered to this pattern the overall effect may be specific to only the two significant dependent measures of linguistic ability.

The overall linguistic ability x time-of-testing interaction was significant. Significant univariate F's were obtained for the following dependent variables: NSST-Receptive, NSST-Production, Auditory Association and Grammatic Closure. In all cases the variables were linguistic measures and results of the Teukey tests indicated that the problem children were more similar to the controls in grade 2 than in grade 1 or in kindergarten. It should be noted, however, that at grade 2 the two groups did not perform similarly: the normals still scored higher. These results are consistent with the notion that the problem children were maturationally slower in language skills (when screened in kindergarten) and that with time, will begin to approach normal levels of development.

Finally, the overall three-way interaction (linguistic level x language ability x time of testing) was not statistically significant, indicating that no specific groups made differential progress over the course of the three testing periods. Specifically, after 3 years of education in a second-language environment, the language-impaired children's linguistic and cognitive skills were similar to those of language-impaired children who had been totally schooled in their first language.

Separate 2x2x2 ANOVA'S with repeated measures were carried out on the Auditory Closure, Sound Blending, and Imitation test data. The independent variables were: language of instruction (French immersion vs. English), linguistic ability (problem vs. control), and the repeated measure grade at time of testing (grade 1 vs. grade 2). Analyses of covariance were also run on the data in which Verbal IQ and Performance IQ scores were used as covariates. A summary and comparison of the ANOVA and ANACOVA analyses are presented in Table 5. The unadjusted means for each of the three variables are presented in Table 6.

The ANOVA and ANACOVA results for the Imitation Test, a measure of the child's ability to comprehend syntactic structures, are identical. Control children performed better than the problem children. Performance was better in grade 2 than in grade 1. There was a significant linguistic ability x

Table 5

Summary of ANOVA and ANACOVA analyses for linguistic measures administered
in Grade 1 and 2

Test	ANOVA	ANACOVA
Imitation errors		
— Linguistic ability	$F = 98.45**, df = 1,72$	$F = 56.51**, df = 1,70$
— Language of instruction	N.S.	N.S.
— Time of testing	$F = 78.46**, df = 1,72$	$F = 72.63**, df = 1,71$
— Linguistic ability x time of testing	$F = 13.23**, df = 1,72$	$F = 11.38**, df = 1,71$
— Linguistic ability x language of instruction x time of testing	$F = 6.30**, df = 1,72$	$F = 5.11*, df = 1,71$
Sound Blending		
— Linguistic ability	$F = 41.83**, df = 1,97$	$F = 6.43**, df = 1,95$
— Language of instruction	$F = 32.18**, df = 1,97$	$F = 50.92**, df = 1,95$
— Linguistic ability x language of instruction	N.S.	$F = 3.92*, df = 1,95$
— Time of testing	$F = 76.66**, df = 1,97$	$F = 75.38**, df = 1,96$
— Linguistic ability x time of testing	$F = 6.42**, df = 1,97$	$F = 6.50**, df = 1,96$
Auditory Closure		
— Linguistic ability	$F = 49.73**, df = 1,97$	$F = 15.40**, df = 1,95$
— Time of testing	$F = 62.78**, df = 1,97$	$F = 61.90**, df = 1,95$

NB. Because the imitation test was developed during the course of the study it was not given to all subjects. For the reported analysis, the sample sizes are: French Problem = 12; English Problem = 23; French Control = 21 and English Control = 20.

* $p < .05$
** $p < .01$

Table 6

Means for linguistic measures administered in Grade 1 and Grade 2

Measure	Grade	FP	EP	FC	EC
Imitation	1	9.92	10.04	2.86	3.10
Errors	2	6.17	7.91	2.00	1.50
Auditory	1	13.39	14.23	19.00	17.92
Closure (raw score)	2	17.94	17.08	21.16	21.12
Sound Blending	1	10.83 (11.98)	18.38 (20.69)	20.03 (18.27)	24.50 (23.50)
(raw score)	2	20.50 (21.65)	25.88 (28.19)	25.65 (23.89)	28.35 (27.34)

Note. The adjusted mean scores are enclosed in parentheses.

time-of-testing interaction which indicated that the problem children showed greater increases over time than the control children. The signifi-

84

cant three-way interaction indicates that the FP group made more progress over time relative to the EP, and the control groups. While the FP and EP children performed similarly in grade 1, by grade 2 the FP children's performance was superior.

The ANOVA and ANACOVA results for the auditory closure test were identical: the controls performed better than problem children and performance improved for all children from grade 1 tot grade 2.

The ANOVA results for the Sound Blending test indicate that controls performed better than problem children and that the English stream children performed better than the French immersion children. A significant linguistic ability x time of testing interaction indicates that the problem children's performance increased more with time than did that of the controls. The overall effect for language of instruction is probably related to the fact that the test items required ability to synthesize English phonemes and that this task was similar to exercises given during English reading classes offered to the English control children for 2 years. Therefore the French immersion children who had had 1 year less of practice with English reading did not perform so well. The same results were obtained using the ANACOVA procedure with one addition: there was a significant linguistic ability x language of instruction interaction. Overall, the FP group performed more poorly than did any of the three groups.

The results of the cognitive linguistic tests suggest that children who were identified as language delayed in kindergarten continued to demonstrate deficits in cognitive-linguistic measures at the end of grade 2, even though they make gains in these areas. Most progress was made on linguistic measures requiring comprehension and production of syntactic structures (NSST Receptive, Imitation, NSST Expressive) morphological production (Grammatical Closure) and semantic-lexical relationships (Auditory Association). More importantly, except for 2 of 15 measures, language-impaired children in French immersion programs were similar to language-impaired children educated in English. That is, the progress of the target group was as predicted, given their language impairments and their language of education. The only measure on which they performed more poorly than all other groups was a test of auditory synthesis of phonemes (Sound Blending). However, the psychological significance of this finding is not clear. First, the result was obtained only with the covariance adjustments. Second, although the test performance may predict beginning reading skills, as will be shown below, the FP children did not perform particularly poorly on these tests. Last, although their performance on the Sound Blending test was significantly worse than that of the other children, in terms of age norms of the ITPA it is the only verbal subtest on which they performed at age level (i.e., like the EP children they perform 1 to 2 years below age level on linguistic tests). On the Imitation test, however, the opposite pattern is found. That is, the FP children performed similarly to the EP group in grade 1, but were superior by grade 2. Thus they make a great deal of progress in terms of understanding complex syntactic structures.

Academic Achievement - English Tests

Separate 2x2 ANOVA's were carried out on the WRAT Reading, WRAT Spelling, WRAT Math, the Spache, and the Metropolitan Achievement Math Subtests. The independent variables were language of instruction (English vs. French) and linguistic ability (problem vs. control). The dependent measures were grade 2 performance on each of the tests (expressed in raw score form except for the Spache scores which were grade levels). These analyses were repeated using Verbal and Performance IQ's as covariates. Summaries of these results are presented in Table 7, unadjusted means are presented in Table 8.

As can be seen from Table 7, the ANOVA and ANACOVA results are similar with one exception. For the ANOVA's, there was a significant linguistic ability effect. That is, on all measures except WRAT math the control children performed better than the problem children. In contrast there were no significant linguistic ability effects for the ANACOVA's; the controls were similar to the problem children. However, since this pattern does not change the interpretation of the present ANOVA results (i.e., the FP children were performing as expected, given their linguistic level and language of instruction) and since the ANACOVA artificially adjusts the problem group means (i.e., they appear to be functioning normally when in fact they are experiencing problems) only the ANOVA's will be discussed.

On the English reading and spelling tests, the control children performed better than the problem children and the English stream children performed better than the French immersion children. These data indicate that on tests of English reading and spelling the French immersion children who have had almost 1 year of English language literacy instruction did not perform as well as English stream children who had received almost 2 years of English language literacy instruction.[1]

[1] In certain ways, these data differ from those reported for other samples. For example, Lambert and Tucker (1972) reported that one class of grade 2 French immersion students performed similarly to controls on a spelling test but were poorer on a reading test; and that a second class of grade 2 immersion students were similar to controls on a reading test but inferior on a spelling test. In contrast, the French immersion children in the present study

Table 7
Summary and comparison of ANOVA and ANACOVA results for English Achievement Tests

Measure	ANOVA	ANACOVA
WRAT Reading		
— Language of instruction	$F = 11.62**, df = 1,97$	$F = 17.24**, df = 1,95$
— Linguistic ability	$F = 16.92**, df = 1,97$	not significant
Spache		
— Language of instruction	$F = 5.035*, df = 1,97$	$F = 8.62**, df = 1,95$
— Linguistic ability	$F = 15.78**, df = 1,97$	not significant
WRAT Spelling		
— Language of instruction	$F = 23.15**, df = 1,97$	$F = 27.76**, df = 1,95$
— Linguistic ability	$F = 11.90**, df = 1,97$	not significant
WRAT Math	no significant effects	no significant effects
Metropolitan Math		
— Language of instruction	$F = 5.93*, df = 1,97$	not significant
— Linguistic ability	$F = 20.84**, df = 1,97$	$F = 6.78**, df = 1,95$

$** p < .01$
$* \ p < .05$

In terms of math skills, the results of the WRAT math indicate to significant effects, while the Metropolitan math results indicate that the controls performed better than the problem children and the French immersion children performed better than the English stream children (N.B. This effect is eliminated in the ANACOVA).

The results of the English achievement test data indicate that, while the language-impaired children are having difficulty acquiring the basic skills of reading, spelling, and math, participation in a French immersion class does not differentially retard the acquisition of these skills. In fact the FP children's performance on these tests is better than expected when one considers the relative lack of remedial assistance for their problems. Accord-

footnote (continued)

were poorer than controls on both reading and spelling measures. The discrepancies may be due to time of testing: Lambert and Tucker tested the children during the month of May (the end of the year), while the children in the present study were tested in March. It may be that there is a steep increase in the learning curve during the last term of school. We will have to await the analysis of the grade 3 data to determine if the discrepent results are due to this difference in time of testing or whether the French immersion samples in the present study do not follow the well-documented trend of performing similarly to English stream children on English achievement tests after 1 *full* year of English language instruction.

Table 8
Summary of means for Grade 2 English Achievement Tests

Measure	FP	EP	FC	EC
WRAT Reading				
— Raw Score	39.40	46.81	48.68	57.73
— grade level	2.1	2.6	2.8	4.1
Spache				
— grade level	2.6	3.1	3.6	4.4
WRAT Spelling				
— Raw Score	27.78	31.23	29.71	35.23
— grade level	1.8	2.6	2.5	3.2
WRAT Math				
— Raw Score	25.72	25.69	25.61	26.85
— grade level	2.8	2.8	2.8	3.0
Metropolitan Math				
— Raw Score	52.06	43.31	57.16	55.5
— grade level	2.8	2.4	3.0	3.0

ing to the grade 2 teacher survey, 43% of the EP children were receiving specific educational interventions for school problems (e.g., a special remedial class or teacher); this was the case for only 25% of the FP children. The disparity in services cannot be attributed to the possibility that the FP children were not in need of extra attention, for the teachers indicated that of the FP children not receiving extra assistance 54% were in need of it. For the EP children not receiving help only 14% were felt to require it.

Second Language Skills
A 2x2x2 ANOVA with repeated measures was performed to analyze the number of correct responses on the O.I.S.E. Listening Comprehension Test which was given to all four groups of children in grades 1 and 2. The independent variables were linguistic ability (controls vs. problem), language of instruction (French immersion vs. English), and grade at testing (grade 1 vs. grade 2). There was a significant language-of-instruction effect $F(1,44) = 159.25, p < .01$, a significant time-of-testing effect $F(1,44 = 53.33, p < .01$, as well as a language-of-instruction x time-of-testing interaction, $F(1,44) = 40.08, p < .01$, and a language-of-instruction x linguistic ability x grade-of-testing effect, $F(1,44) = 4.02, p < .05$. Inspection of the means (Table 9) indicates that the French immersion children performed better

Table 9
French Test Results

Measure	Grade	FP	GC	EP	EC	Significance
OISE Listening	1	21.70	26.20	10.47	9.80	
Comprehension	2	31.90	34.70	9.20	12.40	
Decoding Individual Sounds	2	78.33	82.88	not given		not significant
Index of Oral Reading Quality — average or above	2	33%	52%			$\chi^2=3.23, p<.06$
Reading Comprehension	2	17.07	20.33			not significant
Dictation	2	4.00	6.10			$F=5.73, df=34, p<.02$

NB. Because these tests were developed during the course of the study, they were not administered to all project subjects. The following numbers received the OISE FP=10, FC=15, EP=10, EC=10. The remaining French tests were administered to 15 FP children and 21 FC children.

than the English stream children, and that the increase from grade 1 to grade 2 was shown only for the French immersion children. The three-way interaction clarifies this relationship even further by indicating that all groups except the EP children were better in grade 2 than in grade 1, and that the FP children made the most progress over the 1 year period.

The teachers' ratings complement and extend these findings. By the end of grade 2 they indicated that the oral comprehension skills of the FP children were at least average. However, the FP children were considered to be less proficient than their controls in terms of oral production (1/3 were considered below average). However, given the fact that they were slow to develop their first language and that at the end of grade 2 their skills were still not as developed as those of their controls, it is only plausible that they would demonstrate lags in L_2 communication skills. Their ability to acquire such skills, albeit more slowly than normal, is surprising, given reports in the literature of similar children's failure to learn a second language (e.g., Rudel, 1980) which is highlighted in the present study by the EP group's lack of progress after 3 years of daily 40 minute instruction in F.S.L.

The FP children's performance on the French reading and writing tests was compared to that of the FC group. The FP children were similar to the FC group in their knowledge of the basic French symbol-sound correspondences and their abilities to blend such sounds (Decoding). They also performed similarly on a reading comprehension test. However, their spelling and overall oral reading quality (as measured by speed and accuracy) was poorer. The French teacher ratings complement these findings: more problem children were considered to be having difficulty in reading and writing than were control children. It is interesting, however, that these discrepancies in ratings between the FP and FC children's achievement in French reading and spelling were almost identical to those between the EP and EC children's teacher ratings for English reading and spelling.

These data indicate that the FP children were learning their basic skills in French although not at the same rate as children without language impairments. By the end of grade 2 they seemed to have acquired the basic French sounds, and could understand short passages of prose which were read silently. They experienced more difficulty with spelling and reading orally for speed and accuracy.

DISCUSSION

English-speaking children with language impairments attending French immersion programs demonstrated comparable cognitive and first-language skills to similar children educated only in their first language. Adjusting for initial cognitive differences, overall there was no indication of specific interference or deleterious effects caused by 3 years of instruction in a second language.

While the FP children's L_1 literacy skills were poorer than those of the EP children, this discrepancy in achievement was similar to that of the EC and FC children. Thus lower performance on English reading and spelling test was not a function of a language impairment *per se*, but reflected some general effects of the French immersion program's sequencing of French and English instruction. It should be noted also that since FP children received so little assistance for their problems it was encouraging that they performed as well as they did and just as predicted given their language impairments and language of education.

In terms of L_2 skills, the French problem children's aural comprehension of French was similar to that of the normal immersion controls. Their good comprehension skill was evidenced not only by the teachers' ratings and the French test scores, but also by their performance on a math test. In that L_2

was used exclusively for math instruction, the children must have had sufficient understanding of French to have acquired the skills measured on the test. The FP children's L_2 oral production and L_2 literacy skills were poorer than those of the immersion controls. But in that they were also delayed in acquiring oral competence in their first language it would be unrealistic to expect them to acquire the same high levels of proficiency in oral and written aspects of the second language as nondisabled controls. Further work is needed to indicate whether, if given adequate exposure and time, the French problem children will eventually reach the same levels of proficiency or will remain consistently lower than the French immersion control children. For now one can conclude that the French problem children acquired some proficiency in French at no cost to first-language development, academic progress, or cognitive skills.

In terms of L_2 acquisition these data are consistent with those reported from other Canadian studies that have shown that the French immersion program is an efficient method for teaching second-language skills especially when compared to traditional second-language classes (e.g., Barik & Swain, 1975; Genesee, 1978; Lambert & Tucker, 1972). The present results indicate that this trend holds not only for the child with normal first-language skills but also for the child with impaired language abilities. In fact the French immersion program appears particularly beneficial to the language-impaired child who (as evidenced by the EP children's poor performance on the French oral test) fares particularly poorly in traditional second-language courses where the major teaching methods stress repetition of linguistic utterances in nonmeaningful contexts. The skills required to perform such tasks, such as memory for rote materials and good auditory skills, are often those that the language-impaired child has specific problems with in his first language. Therefore, it is not surprising that so many of the EP children did not benefit from traditional FSL approaches. However, as the present results indicate, given the appropriate conditions, children with poor first-language skills can acquire oral proficiency in a second language.

In general, the data reported in this paper are consistent with the hypothesis that cognitive linguistic skills in general predict achievement in a second-language program (Cummins, 1980). The language-impaired children attending French immersion programs did not perform as well as their controls in academic, cognitive, and first-language areas. However, this relationship was not specific to the language of education in that the same patterns were found for similar children (i.e., English problem group) educated in their first language. The relationship between cognitive linguistic skills and acquisition of L_2 oral skills is not so clear: production skills, but not comprehension abilities were related to L_1 and cognitive levels. These data are consistent with those reported in other studies (Genesee, 1976; Genesee & Hamayan, 1980).

Because both groups of problem children acquired skills to the same level of proficiency there is no evidence to support the threshold hypothesis or the psycholinguistic position that posits that second-language education for children with low levels of first-language competence (such as the language-impaired child) will result in poor levels of first- and second-language development as well as poor scholastic achievement (Cummins, 1979). The data suggest that the suitability of a home-school language switch is best determined by a constellation of social psychological conditions in the school and community. These conclusions are based not only on the results of the present study, but also upon indirect comparisons of these language-impaired children's performance with that of minority children (as described in the literature). While both the minority child and the language-impaired French immersion child enter an educational system where all instruction is given in a second language, and both types of children lack the cognitive linguistic skills necessary for literacy acquisition (see Cummins, 1979, for a discussion of the minority child's preliteracy skills), the prognosis for academic and linguistic development for the language-impaired immersion child is much more optimistic than that for the minority child. It is argued, therefore, that the major factors that differentiate the two groups and that predict achievement are not psycholinguistic abilities nor language of instruction, but rather are related to social psychological conditions. Two such conditions appear necessary (see Cohen & Swain, 1976; Tucker, 1977 for a detailed description of these and other conditions). First, the language-impaired immersion child is a member of a dominant prestigious culture which places primary emphasis on the development of first-language skills and therefore the child continues to develop linguistic competence in the native language. The minority child's environment does not place the same emphasis on L_1 acquisition, and thus exposure to and motivation to use L_1 is reduced, resulting in poor L_1 skills. It may be that the level of L_1 development, which is primarily influenced by social psychological conditions, influences the performance of children educated in L_2. Second, the language-impaired immersion children are positively reinforced for their L_2 skills, even though they may be less skilled in these areas than the normal classmates. As a result, the children are positively disposed to using and learning the language. This is not the case for minority children who are continually reminded by teachers, peers, and community members that they are not competent users of the language, and therefore their willingness and

92

motivation to learn the language are greatly reduced, resulting both in poorer L_2 skills and academic failure.

Based on the results of the present study, it is argued that the presence of the positive poles of the above social psychological conditions underlie the "relative" success of bilingually schooled language-impaired children, and that it is the presence of the negative poles of these same social psychological conditions rather than psycholinguistic deficits which primarily account for the often cited failure of minority language children.

In terms of the practical issue of whether French immersion programs are feasible for children who are slow to develop their first language, the answer is not completely straightforward. Depending upon one's sociolinguistic priorities, a case could be made for either side. If acquisition and competence in L_2 is not an important priority, the present data could be interpreted as showing that the FP children were below in reading and spelling in English and French (but so were the FC children lagging behind the EC in English reading and spelling; and the EP lag behind the EC on all tests) but of more importance they were receiving little help for these problems. Therefore, the argument could be made that they would be better served in an English stream where instruction would be suitably modified.

If, however, L_2 skills are an important priority then the argument could be made that overall the FP children's performance was as predicted given their slow language development and French immersion experience. Compared to the controls they were progressing normally. Moreover, their French language skills (specifically oral comprehension) were better than predicted and the French test data indicated slower but gradual acquisition of L_2 skills.

While the children may have lacked extra assistance for their problems in the present study, future generations of French immersion children need not function under such restrictive conditions. The lack of services in the present study was not due to philosophical or pedagogical outlooks but merely reflected a lack of trained specialists to teach the poor achieving French immersion child. It is hoped that in the future these conditions will change. That is, educational therapists in conjunction with classroom teachers will provide suitable remedial services and will restructure specific curriculum demands so that more children with mild to moderately severe problems can function and achieve academic success in the French immersion classroom. If this position is adopted, the focus of current concern, as reflected in the present study - "Are French immersion programs suitable for the language-impaired child?" - will change to "How can French immersion programs be made suitable for the language-impaired child?"

EARLY IMMERSION IN FRENCH AT SCHOOL FOR ANGLOPHONE CHILDREN: LEARNING DISABILITIES AND PREDICTION OF SUCCESS*

Ronald L.Trites

INTRODUCTION

In Canada, with its two official languages, there is an increasing interest in English-French bilingualism which has resulted in the development of several alternatives for the teaching of French to English-speaking school children. In the primary, or early, French immersion program, English-speaking children are exposed to French as the exclusive language of instruction in kindergarten and grade 1, with instruction in the English language being introduced and gradually increased in the later grades. The grade at which instruction in the English language is introduced may vary. Alternatively, exclusive instruction in the French language may be introduced at grade 6, 7, or 8, constituting a late French immersion program.

At present there is contradictory evidence regarding the success of early immersion programming as a means of acquiring proficiency in a second language without detrimental effects on native language skills. Studies describing a favourable outcome of immersion programming will be discussed below, followed by research outlining negative aspects.

Studies Reporting Success with Early Second-Language Immersion
One study supporting a favourable outcome of immersion programming was conducted in the St. Lambert area of Montreal, Canada. Lambert and Tucker (1972) described the linguistic, intellectual, and attitudinal development of English-speaking children in French immersion followed from kindergarten through grade 4, compared to English-speaking children in regular English classes as well as French-speaking children in regular French classes. In general, the results of this investigation indicated that French immersion programming results in satisfactory proficiency in the

* This work was supported by contractual research grants from the Ministry of Education for Ontario, Canada.

French language for English-speaking children, without detrimental effects either to English language skills or to progress in other academic areas. However, the experimental nature of this program, as well as the possible selectivity of the children (i.e., only the most capable children from an upper middle class area were in French immersion classes), along with tremendous parental involvement and commitment to this program, may have contributed to its substantial reported success.

Further investigations which followed the children in the St. Lambert French immersion program through grade 5 (Lambert, Tucker & D'Anglejan, 1973), grade 6 (Bruck, Lambert & Tucker, 1976), grade 7 (Bruck, Lambert & Tucker, 1974) and through grade 8 (Bruck et al., 1974) corroborated the success of French immersion programming in those schools.

Studies in other Canadian cities (Barik & Swain, 1974, 1975a, 1975b, 1976a, 1976b) compared samples of children in French immersion classes and regular English classes on measures of intelligence, achievement in reading and arithmetic, and French comprehension. Some attempts were made to follow the same children from kindergarten through grade 3, but the samples differed at each grade level. Results indicated that French immersion programming did not have negative effects upon cognitive development. English language skills lagged slightly in grade 1 for French immersion children, but this was overcome in grade 2 with the exception of spelling skills in some samples, after English Language Arts Skills had been introduced. The results were interpreted as attesting to the general success of French immersion programming. However, children with hearing, perceptual, or related problems were excluded from the testing and no information was provided regarding drop-outs from French immersion or children who did not do well. Children in French immersion had a significantly higher IQ in grades 2 and 3 (Barik & Swain, 1976a, 1976b), suggesting that the lower IQ and problem children had dropped out.

Although the above-mentioned studies are unanimous in reporting a favourable outcome of children enrolled in primary French immersion, several cautionary notes should be made. Of considerable importance, there is clearly some degree of attrition in the number of children who continued in the French immersion program. Very rarely did these studies include a clear statement either to the number or percentage of children who dropped out of the program, or to the reasons for dropping out. In the St. Lambert area of Montreal, 20 of the original 26 children in the pilot French immersion class were still in the program by grade 5 (Lambert et al., 1973) and only 15 by grade 7 (Bruck et al., 1976). Of the 38 children in the French

96

immersion follow-up class, 30 were still in the program by grade 4 (Lambert et al., 1973) and only 25 by grade 6 (Bruck et al., 1974). However, reasons for dropping out were not mentioned.

In addition, the follow-up French immersion studies did not consider the children who had difficulties in French immersion programs aside from the extremely small sample of 18 children with "language impairment" identified over a period of 6 years by Bruck and her colleagues (this volume, p. 77). There was also a tendency towards selectivity in the choice of subjects. Barik and Swain (1974) eliminated certain children from the analysis, such as "pupils who teachers indicated had special problems (for example, serious hearing or vision difficulties, emotional problems); pupils who teachers indicated had a very limited ability to understand and express themselves in English".

Thus, there are clearly important unresolved questions regarding the outcome of the French immersion program in Canada. The favourable results reported may be based in part on biased samples. Little is known about the failures or of the children who experience difficulty in the immersion programs. It is important that efforts be made to define the characteristics of the marginally successful and failing students as well as the successful ones.

Studies Reporting Failures with Early Second-Language Immersion

The above studies are unique in view of the fact that early immersion programming has not met with success in several countries. In Ireland, English-speaking children, for whom the language of instruction in school was Irish, did not achieve the same standard in written English as English monolinguals, or in written Irish as Irish monolinguals. The Irish immersion children also experienced retardation in problem-solving arithmetic but not in simple arithmetic computations (Macnamara, 1966).

Jones (1966) reported that English-speaking children taught in Welsh were below English monolinguals in English reading. A slight positive correlation was found between favourable attitudes toward learning Welsh and Welsh achievements. Conversely, if the parents' attitudes towards learning Welsh were negative, the children did poorly in this program.

In South Africa, it was observed that bilingual children taught in their mother tongue showed no adverse emotional reactions, but if children of lower intelligence were taught in the language with which they were less familiar, emotional disturbances could result (UNESCO Report, 1975).

Modiano (1968) found that children in Mexico whose native tongue was Tzeltat or Tzotzil, but who were given reading instruction in Spanish only, scored significantly lower on Spanish reading tests than children who were taught to read in their native tongue first and in Spanish later.

In the United States, there has been much attention directed towards the progress of Spanish-speaking children attending English-language schools. In general, children in this English immersion program have not achieved competence in the English language comparable to that of English monolinguals, and have had poor academic success (Macnamara, 1966; Gezi, 1974; Ortiz, 1982). In response to the failure of this immersion approach, bilingual education programs have been set up in which instruction begins in the vernacular moving gradually towards English. Improved academic success is observed among children in programs which offer instruction in their mother tongue (Gezi, 1974).

Engle (1975) reviewed 24 reports concerned with the use of the vernacular language in education. She raised two question: "1. Will a child learn to read more rapidly in his second language if he is first taught to read in his primary language? 2. Will the child achieve greater general knowledge of other subject matters if he is taught these subjects first in his native language?" Engle concluded that no definitive answers to these questions could be drawn since the reports varied in many ways and there are many confounding factors.

Variables Affecting Second-Language Learning
Irrespective of the manner in which a second language is introduced, considerable interest has been shown in individual differences in second-language acquisition. Two factors frequently cited as important determinants of success in second-language learning are: (1) linguistic aptitude, and (2) attitudinal variables (Barkman, 1969; Gardner & Lambert, 1959; Jones, 1966; Mackey, 1967; Pimsleur, Stockwell & Comrey, 1962; Stern, 1967). Little is known about differences in language aptitude among children below age 9 or 10; however, after these ages there is clear evidence that children vary in aptitude for foreign-language learning (Carroll, 1969).

Favourable attitudes towards the second language in the second-language community seem to facilitate second-language learning (Gardner & Smythe, 1973; Jones, 1966; Mackey, 1967). Sociological factors such as the relative prestige of the first and second language (Paulston, 1974) as well as perceptions and beliefs about the other ethnolinguistic group (Lambert, 1974) have been cited as possible factors affecting the success of early immersion programs. This factor may be important in explaining the seemingly contradictory results with early immersion programs in different countries.

98

Level of biological maturation has been stressed by some as an important determinant of success in second-language learning. Penfield (1953, 1965) was an influential figure in promoting the view that young children are the best language learners. He claimed that speaking, understanding speech, reading, and writing depend upon certain specialized areas of the cerebrum, and that there is an optimal age when these areas are plastic and receptive. In his view, functional localization of skills is established by ages 10 to 14, so that specific areas of the cortex become fixed as the speech cortex. Penfield (1965) held that second-language teaching, using the "mother's method" of direct language teaching, should begin before the age of 6 or 8 so that the child's brain will be conditioned early, thus becoming a better linguist. Much of this theory was based upon clinical evidence that following damage to the dominant hemisphere, children below age 10 or 12 recovered speech functions more completely, some by establishing a speech center in adjacent areas of the cortex or even in the previously nondominant hemisphere.

Lenneberg (1967) concurred with Penfield's view that there is a critical period for language acquisition which ends at puberty. However, the conclusions of Penfield and Lenneberg have been challenged. McLaughlin (1977) provides an excellent review of issues related to second-language learning in children. He points out that, contrary to popular belief, "older children do better on almost all aspects of language acquisition than do younger children in comparable circumstances" (p. 455). Krashen (1973, 1975) also challenged the conclusions of Penfield and Lenneberg and stated that establishment of cerebral dominance is not responsible for the critical period.

While there is no evidence then that the brain "fossilizes" at some prepubertal stage insofar as second-language acquisition is concerned, there clearly are fascinating aspects of brain function to be investigated in bilingual individuals (see for example Albert & Obler, 1978; Ojemann & Whitaker, 1978).

As mentioned, many disagree that adults lose an innate capacity for language learning or that they are less well equipped cognitively than children for second-language learning. Schumann (1975) suggested that affective variables are more important than biological maturation in problems associated with adult second-language learning. Social and psychological changes at puberty may interfere with second-language learning (for example, associate "different" with "bad", less able to internalize new norms). If affective variables such as attitude or motivation and empathy are positive, cognitive processes are allowed to work and second language is successful. Smythe, Stennet, and Gardner (1976) listed children's lack of self-consciousness, lack of fixed patterns, additional time in second-language learning, and motivation as factors thought to facilitate second-language learning and denied their superiority as foreign-language learners. Burstall, Jamieson, Cohen, and Hargreaves (1974) found that older children, (age 11) tended to learn French more efficiently that younger ones (age 8), when it was taught for a short daily period. They noted that some able students found learning French difficult because they found the emphasis on oral learning without support of visual cues intolerable. Catford (1971) cited different circumstances, rather than the loss of an innate capacity, as accounting for adults' less successful language learning (for example, occupational pressures, time constraints). Macnamara (1975) views first- and second-language acquisition as the same process and cites evidence from studies to show that adults are better than children in some aspects of second-language learning.

Thus, the debate continues. It does not seem to have been determined unequivocally that young children are indeed better language learners than older children or adults. Nor is it clear to what extent biological maturation, cognitive development, or affective and situational variables are implicated in success at second-language learning at different age levels.

Children with Learning Disabilities in French Immersion

Some children experience difficulties when they are immersed in the early grades in a second-language program. An early study in Montreal (Bruck, Rabinovitch, & Oates, 1975), focussed on the effects of French immersion programs on children with language disabilities. The investigators concluded that the children fare well, in that they learn to read in both English and French. They also concluded that first-language acquisition did not appear to have been retarded by placement in a French immersion program. However, there were several serious methodological difficulties with this study including the fact that the conclusions were based on an extremely small sample of subjects, basically a sample of three to six children depending upon the date of followup.

In a later study Bruck (1978 and this volume pp. 69-93) examined the suitability of primary French immersion for the language-disabled child. Achievement levels of children with language disabilities and normal controls enrolled in primary French immersion were compared to children with language disabilities and normal controls enrolled in the regular English program. The progress of the children was followed from kindergarten to grade 3. Bruck (1978) concluded that "children with language learning problems who attend French immersion programs can develop linguistic, cognitive and academic skills at a rate similar to that at which they would develop were they placed in an all-English classroom" (p.65). She concluded that children who encounter difficulty in French immersion should remain in the program and receive remedial assistance in the French language. However, the validity of these conclusions must be viewed with caution. The language-disabled children in the English program had significantly lower performance IQ scores in kindergarten and in grade 3 compared to the language-disabled children in the French immersion program. Nonverbal aspects of cognitive functioning may influence which children remain in French immersion and which children transfer out of the program. The problem group in French immersion had the highest attrition rates of all groups and the children who remained in the program to grade 3 likely represent a select, more able group compared to the problem group in the English program. Trites and Price (1977) found that the children who transferred out of the French immersion program had a lower Verbal IQ and were experiencing a greater degree of academic difficulty than children who remained in French immersion in spite of difficulties. Thus, one must consider that the groups compared by Bruck (1978) may not have been disabled to the same extent and that the more disabled children did not remain in the French immersion program to the end of the study. In addition, the progress of the problem groups in English reading tended to be at or above grade level. This suggests that the initial diagnoses of language disability are questionable. Further doubts about the exact criteria of language disability in this study is revealed in the present writeup (Bruck, this volume) in which it was found that it took 6 years to identify 18 of these children in a large metropolitan school board. It should also be noted that progress in the French language of problem children in French immersion was measured up to the grade 3 level by a test appropriate for grade 1 children. The scores at grade 2 and 3 may represent ceiling effects.

Second-Language Learning and Reading

Controversy exists over the advisability of introducing reading in a child's second language before he learns to read in his mother tongue. Downing (undated) has suggested that language mismatch between home and school language causes retardation in the development of reading skills. Studies cited earlier pointed to the retardation of reading skills in both the first and second language when the child was taught to read initially in the second language (Macnamara, 1966), to the retardation in native-language reading skills when initial reading was taught in a second language (Jones, 1966), and to improved reading ability in a second language when the child was taught to read initially in the vernacular (Modiano, 1968). Miller (1973) also pointed out the importance of the match of home and school environments for success in reading. Gezi (1874) reviewed studies of bilingual and bicultural education and stressed the importance of the mother tongue as a medium of instruction.

In contrast, studies of the reading skills of children in French immersion in Canada indicated that reading levels in French were below those of French monolinguals but that any retardation in English-language skills is overcome with the introduction of formal English reading instruction. Swain (1974) has suggested that it is easier to read in French than English because the former has a more systematic sound-symbol correspondence. The basics of reading are then easily transferred since the vocabulary and language structures are already established. However, contradictory findings regarding reading achievement in English arise when one compares children in partial French immersion programs who are taught to read in English initially to children in total French immersion programs who are taught to read in French initially. Swain (1974) reported that one group of children in a partial French immersion program were better readers in English in grades 1, 2, and 3 than children in a total French immersion program who had not had any English Language Arts instruction; however, grade 2 or 3 children in a total French immersion program who had received 1 year of English Language Arts instruction could read as well in English as children in the same grade in a partial French immersion program. Both immersion groups had lower English reading test scores than grade 2 and 3 children in the regular English program. Thus, in this sample learning to read in the vernacular did not appear to enhance reading skills. In contrast, another group of children in a partial French immersion program who were taught to read initially in English did appear to have enhanced reading skills in English. Children in a grade 3 partial immersion class were better readers in English than children in a total French immersion program regardless of the grade at which English Language Arts were introduced. With regard to reading skills in French, being taught to read initially in French appears to promote better reading skills in French, since children in total French immersion outperformed children in partial French immersion on French reading tests. However, when comparisons were made on the basis of amount of exposure to French, partial immersion programs appeared to produce levels of proficiency in reading French comparable to the reading levels achieved by children in total French immersion programs. Both immersion groups were poorer readers in French than French monolinguals.

102

Tucker (1975) reported that for pupils in grade 1 and grade 2 French immersion programs, reading achievement in French was a good predictor of reading achievement in English at each grade level. The apparently easy transfer of reading skills from French to English was stressed.

McDougall and Bruck (1976) investigated the effect on native-language skills when initial reading instruction was in the second language and when mother tongue instruction was introduced at different grade levels, i.e. grade 2 (early) or grade 3 (late). The French immersion students were in grades 3 and 4 when tested. The early and late English reading groups did not differ in English reading as measured by the *Spache Diagnostic Reading Scales,* nor did they differ from children in the regular English program. The authors concluded that a great amount of knowledge must be transferred from French to English and that this transfer is accelerated for the group receiving English reading beginning in grade 3. French reading levels were not compared. These results emphasize good progress in English reading following initial reading instruction in French. However, these results should be considered with caution. Only one measure of reading achievement was employed. The formal introduction of English reading in grade 3 does not necessarily reflect the actual amount of experience the children had in reading in English. They were from middle-class homes where parents probably encouraged and supported the development of mother tongue literacy (Tucker, 1975). The longer formal English instruction is delayed, the more likely it is that these parents would take an active role in promoting these skills.

Cziko (1976) examined reading achievement in both English and French among grade 4 children in different school programs. The groups were an early French immersion group (children in French immersion from kindergarten), a late French immersion group (children who were in regular English classes until grade 4 when they entered French immersion), a regular English program group, and a regular French program group. There were no significant differences among the first three groups in English reading. The late immersion group did as well as the early immersion group in French reading. French and English reading ability were positively correlated. The authors concluded that neither early nor late French immersion has detrimental effects on English reading and that there is a good transfer of reading skills across languages. However, there was no evidence of greater transfer from French to English than from English to French. The readingtest data did not indicate any advantages from an earlier start in learning French on French reading skills. Nor was there evidence that reading instruction in the vernacular initially enhanced reading in the vernacular or in the second language. The possible influence of parents upon French immersion children's mother tongue language skills may have influenced these results.

A 3- year study (McInnis & Donoghue, 1980) comparing the progress on English and French proficiency tests of two groups, namely primary French immersion and intensive French (90 minutes of French language instruction per day in an English language program) controlled for initial differences in the groups. Based on the outcome measures the authors concluded that "the immersion program results in an improvement in skills in French but does so at the expense of some loss of skills in English" (p.327).

In addition to the contradictory evidence from studies comparing children in total French immersion programs who are taught to read in French initially to children in partial French immersion programs who are taught to read in English initially, studies reporting difficulties in other settings are of interest. Cowan and Sarmed (1976) compared the performance of Persian-speaking children in English immersion or in a bilingual (50-50) English-Persian program with Persian-speaking and English-speaking children on measures of reading in English and Persian. The children in the immersion and bilingual schools were inferior to monolinguals in reading both Persian and English, especially Persian. The English immersion program did not produce higher reading levels in English compared to the bilingual (50-50) program which failed to enhance reading skills in either language despite the use of the vernacular. Reading in both languages was depressed in both the immersion and bilingual programs in contrast to the Canadian results (for example, Lambert & Tucker, 1972).

There is evidence that the simultaneous introduction of reading in two languages may cause confusion. Cohen, Fathman, and Merino (1976) compared Spanish-speaking children educated in an English school or in a Spanish-English bilingual program on measures of reading in English and Spanish. By grade 5, the English school children surpassed the bilingual program children on measures of English reading while the reverse was true on measures of Spanish reading. The poor performance by bilingual school children on English reading was attributed to the simultaneous introduction of reading in two languages by the same teacher.

However, in view of the contradictory evidence, further investigation of this problem is needed and, as yet, no definitive statement can be made regarding the optimal sequencing of initial reading instruction in bilingual education programs (Engel, 1975). Tucker (1975) discussed the conflicting results of studies on the sequencing of reading instruction in the vernacular and the second language. He claimed that initial teaching in the vernacular

104

failed to affect pupils' performance in some studies in contrast to others because several factors influence mother tongue development in children receiving initial reading instruction in their second language. The following factors may be important: the existence of a vernacular literacy transition, the encouragement of mother tongue literacy by parents and the community, similarity of orthographic representations, and the structural similarity of the two languages (Tucker, 1975).

Specific Neurological Substrates of Language Learning

Factors other than IQ, attitude, personality type, and age at which the second language is introduced must be considered in attempting to understand the progress or lack of it in an individual child in a second language learning program. One factor which obviously must be considered is adequacy of functioning of brain regions subserving language processes. The brain areas strongly implicated in language learning are the temporal lobes. Not only does this brain region contain the auditory cortex, but the temporal lobes have been implicated in verbal and nonverbal auditory processing and memory functions. Important studies dating back over 20 years (Kimura, 1961; Milner, 1954, 1958) have demonstrated the effect on psychological functions of damage or destruction of temporal lobe structures. The deficits in learning associated with disturbances in temporal lobe function are not restricted to gross alterations of behaviour, but may include difficulty in learning verbal associations and deficits in the delayed recall of verbal and nonverbal material (see for example Hécaen & Albert, 1978). The right and left temporal lobes subserve different psychological functions with impairment of the left temporal lobe often leading to deficits on verbal tests, while following right temporal lobe dysfunction, nonverbal visual symbolic and nonverbal memory deficits are more likely to result. The obvious psychological nature of the functions subserved by the temporal lobes, the verbal and auditory components in particular, give this brain region a high profile when considering a neurological model of language learning.

Summary

It is clear that immersing children in a second language at an early age has met with considerable success in some settings but with far less success in others. In addition to the age at which the language is introduced and the way it is introduced, research studies indicate that factors such as language aptitude, stage of cognitive development, affective variables and attitudes are also important factors to consider. We have also seen that an understanding of brain maturation, structure, and function may play a particularly important role in understanding more about second-language acquisition.

The French immersion program began in the Ottawa schools in 1969/70 with programs at the kindergarten level. It had become apparent by 1973 that increasing numbers of children from French immersion programs were experiencing learning difficulties and were being referred to the neuropsychology laboratory of the royal Ottawa Hospital for assessment. Children referred to the laboratory were given a 6 to 8 hour examination on tests standardized in Ottawa in French and English (Trites, 1977). The test battery was designed to determine the type of learning disability the child might have and to help in assessing the cause for the disability. The test battery, described more fully in the following section, included a variety of tests of psychometric ability, academic achievement, reasoning skills, language development, auditory perceptual functions, visual-motor functions, and motor and sensory tests as well as personality screening measures. It was soon discovered that most of the children with learning difficulties in the French immersion program had important deficiencies in their school progress in spite of at least normal intelligence, normal language functions, and no evidence of gross brain dysfunction. Nor did these children seem to have test profiles similar to that typically seen in children with dyslexia or primary reading disability, other types of perceptual or learning disabilities, or "minimal cerebral dysfunction". For this reason a 2-year investigation of learning disabilities amongst children in primary French immersion was undertaken with contractual research support from the Ministry of Education for Ontario.

Learning Disabilities in Primary French Immersion
In this first of 2-year investigations the goal was to see if the test profile of children who had either dropped out of the immersion program for academic difficulties or were still in the program but experiencing severe problems resembled in any significant way the test profile of children with more standard learning disabilities. The results of this investigation have been reported in detail elsewhere (Trites & Price, 1976, Trites, 1976; Trites & Price 1978/79). If the test profile of the French immersion learning difficulty group resembled one of the standard learning difficulty groups, such as a group of children with dyslexia or primary reading disability, this would tend to support the notion proposed by Bruck and her colleagues that the French immersion learning difficulty group does not have a unique learning difficulty and would have experienced difficulty in school in any event.

Sample

A sample of 32 children with learning disabilities in French immersion was selected from the files of the Neuropsychology Laboratory. A total of seven control groups were formed. There were 32 children in each group, all of whom, irrespective of group membership, were experiencing difficulty in school. In three comparison groups, language was a factor, namely:

1. Anglophone children in Francophone schools. For these children, as for the French immersion group, the home language was English and the classroom language was French. However, in this instance, the total school was French and the child was not in a specialized immersion program for anglophone children which is the case with the French immersion program.
2. Children from other ethnic backgrounds in anglophone schools. For this group the home language was something other than French or English and included children from German, Italian, Dutch, Polish, Chinese, and other language backgrounds.
3. Francophones in francophone schools. This was a group of 32 French-speaking children who were attending French schools and experiencing difficulty.

Four "traditional" problem groups were composed, each consisting of 32 children. In all cases, second language was not a factor since these were English-speaking children attending English-speaking programs. These groups included:

1. Primary reading disability. These were children who were having serious problems in reading and related language arts skills but who had met all the criteria of primary reading disability, including average intelligence or greater, no evidence of gross psychopathology, no gross neurological disturbance, adequate motivation and opportunity.
2. Children who were hyperactive. These were children who met the standard criteria of hyperactivity, including Connors' Parent and Teacher Rating Scale scores of over 1.5, physician's diagnosis of hyperactivity and a laboratory diagnosis of hyperactivity. To be included in this group the child also had to have a learning difficulty.
3. Behavioural and/or personality adjustment problems. These were children diagnosed by a psychiatrist as having adjustment problems which was then combined with laboratory test evidence of a learning disability.
4. "Minimal cerebral dysfunction" group. These children were diagnosed by a neurologist and/or pediatrician as having minimal cerebral dysfunction, usually based on history, physical neurological examinat-

ion, and mild or moderate EEG abnormality.

The above four comparison groups in which language was not a factor were carefully composed. Those with multiple diagnoses such as reading disability plus emotional disturbance or reading disability with minimal cerebral dysfunction were excluded. The eight groups of 32 children each represented a combined sample of 256 cases.

Procedure

Extensive history information was obtained on each of the 256 children in the study, including birth history, developmental milestones, medical and neurological history (including exact records where applicable, such as EEG recordings, details of drug use such as Ritalin, etc.), social and emotional development, family relations, socioeconomic level, and school performance. History information in each case was obtained from parents, school authorities, social agencies, and physicians. In addition, each child received an extensive 6 to 8 hour neuropsychological examination which has been described elsewhere (Trites, 1977). The following tests were administered: *Wechsler Intelligence Scale for Children* (Wechsler, 1949), *Raven Progressive Matrices Test* (Raven, 1960), *Peabody Picture Vocabulary Test* (Dunn, 1965), Halstead-Reitan tests adapted for children including *Halstead Category Test, Tactual Performance Test, Finger Tapping Rates, Fine Manipulative Skills, Steadiness, Maze Coordination, Foot Tapping Rates, Sensory Recognition,* all described in Trites, 1977), *Boston Speech Perception Test,* (Provonost & Dumbleton, 1953), *Frostig Visual Perceptual Battery,* (Frostig, Lefever & Whittlesey, 1966), *Illinois Test of Psycholinguistic Abilities,* (Kirk, McCarthy & Kirk, 1968), *Knox Cube Test* (Arthur revision, 1947), *Lateral Dominance Test* (Trites, 1977), *Developmental Drawings Test,* (Trites, 1977), *Wide Range Achievement Test (WRAT)* (Jastak & Jastak, 1965), *Early School Personality Questionnaire,* (Coan & Cattell, 1972), *Vineland Social Maturity Scale,* (Doll, 1965), *Myklebust Pupil Rating Scale,* (Myklebust, 1971), *Connors' Teacher's Questionnaire,* (Connors, 1969), *Connors' Parent's Questionnaire,* (Connors, 1970).

Results

The means and standard deviations for age, Full Scale IQ, and sex distribution of the groups are presented in Table 1. It can be seen from Table 1 that the French immersion group tended to be younger and had a higher Full Scale IQ than all but the reading disability group.

The large number of original dependent variables from the neuropsychological test battery was reduced through factor analysis to a small set of factor scores. The factor scores were used as new dependent variables in a stepwise discriminant function analysis in an attempt to see if the eight groups of subjects pooled into a sample of 256 subjects could be correctly assigned back to their proper group. This was an attempt to find test patterns which are characteristic of the French immersion group and which differentiate subjects in this group from all seven comparison groups. If the subjects could not be correctly classified back into their proper group (i.e., reading disability

TABLE 1

Age, WISC FSIQ, and Sex of the Eight Groups

GROUPS	AGE			WISC FSIQ			SEX	
	Mean	S D	t-prob.	Mean	S D	t-prob.	Males	Females
French Imm.	7.1	1.2		104.3	10.6		22	10
Anglophones in francophone sch.	8.2	1.7	.002**	97.7	12.5	.028*	26	6
Ethnic groups in anglophone sch.	8.0	1.5	.007*	95.3	13.7	.005**	24	8
Francophones in francophone sch.	8.4	1.1	.000**	94.0	10.7	.000**	27	5
Reading disabil.	8.3	1.0	.000**	104.8	8.5	.836	22	10
Hyperactive	7.2	1.7	.533	101.3	9.7	.244	30	2
Behaviour and personality prob.	7.8	1.1	.019*	101.8	11.5	.373	24	8
Minimal brain dysfunction	7.8	1.6	.058	96.9	10.2	.006**	21	11

1. The t tests referred to involve the comparisons of the French immersion group with each of the eight comparison groups.
* P <.05
** P <.01

subjects assigned to the reading disability group, hyperactive children assigned to the hyperactive group, etc.) it would either be an indication that the tests were not sufficiently sensitive to differentiate the various types of learning disabilities or alternatively, that there were no test scores or patterns of tests that could reliably characterize each of the groups. The eight group discriminant function analyses yielded highly significant results. It was quite striking that a statistically significant number of subjects were correctly classified in each of these groups as is seen in Table 2. The francophones in francophone schools were the easiest to classify while the hyperactive and anglophone in francophone school subjects were the most difficult to classify. The fact that the French immersion subjects were significantly differentiated from stringently defined control groups who also experienced difficulty in school gives strong support to the hypothesis that this is a unique group in terms of test profile. This provides support for the notion that unique factors are operating in their learning difficulty and that they cannot be considered, as a group, as having origins to their learning problems such as dyslexia, hyperactivity, minimal brain dysfunction, or behaviour and personality adjustment problems. It became very apparent from examining the test profiles of these children that they do not have language difficulties in English and are thus not similar to the type of subjects being described by Bruck in this volume. In view of the age and IQ differences revealed in Table 1, analysis based on restricted age and IQ groups were conducted. The same pattern emerged showing the results were not an effect of age or IQ.

TABLE 2

Percent of Cases Correctly Classified in the Discriminant function
Analysis of the Eight Groups

Group	Percent Correctly Classified
French immersion	34.4
Anglophones in francophone schools	18.8
Ethnic groups in anglophone schools	31.3
Francophones in francophone schools	62.5
Reading disability	43.8
Hyperactive	18.8
Behavior and personality problems	28.1
Minimal brain dysfunction	46.9

In order to further demonstrate the unique profile of the French immersion group, this group was compared with each of the other groups independently using discriminant function analysis. It can be seen from Table 3 that a highly significant number of cases were correctly identified in each two-group comparison. For example, in the French immersion versus reading disability comparison, 71.9% of the French immersion group was correctly classified and 75% of the reading disability group correctly classified.

Attempts were then made to identify which of the tests were most efficient in identifying children in each of the eight groups. Although it was hardly surprising, no single factor or test score could be identified which could reliably assign the subjects to their groups. However, a few measures were important in differentiating the French immersion group from the other seven groups. The important tests for differentiating them appeared to be:

TABLE 3

Percent of Cases Correctly Classified in the Discriminant Function
Analyses Involving Two Groups

Groups Compared	Percent Correctly Classified	Probability
French immersion vs.	71.9	.6047
Anglophones in francophone schools	68.8	.6028
TOTAL	70.3	
French immersion vs.	71.9	.6626
Ethnic groups in anglophone schools	81.3	.6806
TOTAL	76.6	
French immersion vs.	78.1	.7528
Francophones in francophone school	90.6	.7925
TOTAL	84.4	
French immersion vs.	71.9	.6132
Reading disability	75.0	.6312
TOTAL	73.4	
French immersion vs.	75.0	.6271
Hyperactive	71.9	.6276
TOTAL	73.4	
French immersion vs.	84.4	.6823
Behaviour and personality problems	81.3	.6802
TOTAL	82.8	
French immersion vs.	75.0	.6309
Minimal brain dysfunction	71.9	.6113
TOTAL	73.4	

WISC Performance IQ (except for behaviour and personality problems and reading disability groups), *Developmental Drawings Test* (except for reading disability group), *WRAT, Spelling* (except for ethnic groups in anglophone schools), *WRAT, Reading* (except hyperactive and minimal brain dysfunction groups), *Peabody Picture Vocabulary Test* (except reading disability, hyperactive and behaviour and personality problem groups) and most importantly the *Tactual Performance Test* (except anglophones in francophone schools, and minimal brain dysfunction groups).

Tactual Performance Test

A most important finding from the eight group analysis was that the French immersion group had significantly poorer performance levels on the *Tactual Performance Test* than all groups except anglophones in francophone schools and the minimal brain dysfunction group, both when all subjects were compared and also when age (between 6 and 9 years) and IQ (with Full Scale IQ between 85 and 109) were restricted. The fact that the French immersion group performed at poorer levels, similar to the brain dysfunction group, on this measure is of considerable interest. The *Tactual Performance Test* is a complex psychomotor problem-solving task in which the child, while blindfolded, is required to place six or eight blocks (depending on age) of varying shapes and sizes into a formboard, first with the dominant hand, then with the nondominant hand, and finally with both hands together. The time required for each of the three trials is recorded. Following completion of the task, the blindfold is removed and the child is required to draw the board and blocks from memory, attempting to keep them in the correct spatial position. Adequate performance on this test is dependent, among other things, upon integrity of the temporal lobes. As mentioned earlier, the temporal lobes are important brain structures in language, memory, and auditory-perceptual functions. The poor performance of the French immersion group cannot be considered as related to motor or sensory deficits since their performance was well within normal limits on motor and sensory tests.

In summary, the results of the eight group study indicated that children who experienced difficulty in primary French immersion were a unique group in the sense that they were not, as a group, hyperactive and did not, as a group, have characteristics of primary reading disability, minimal brain dysfunction, or personality problems. Rather, the French immersion group was composed of young, bright, and highly motivated children who gave no evidence of difficulty on basic motor and sensory tests. They stood out amongst the eight groups as having a well-developed vocabulary in English. However, they were also characterized by having the poorest performance of

112

all eight groups on a test highly sensitive to the functioning of the temporal lobe regions of the brain. The results were considered as indicative of a temporal lobe maturational lag in the French immersion learning difficulty group.

Cross Validation Study

The unique profile found in the French immersion learning difficulty group in the first study was possibly open to bias since all children had been referred to a clinic for investigation of their school failure. Thus a cross validation study was conducted (Trites & Price, 1977, 1978/1979) which avoided the possibility of that bias and importantly, was aimed at discovering the validity of the results of the first study and gathering further information bearing on a possible maturational lag hypothesis.

Sample

For cross validation purposes on a nonclinic sample, children who had dropped out of the primary French immersion program of one school in the Ottawa Board of Education were selected as follows: the names of 16 children who had dropped out of the program for academic reasons in the school years from 1971 to 1976 were obtained from the principal. The permission of the children's parents was then obtained to include the child in the study. A control group of 16 children who had remained in the French immersion program at the same school was formed. The Control children were matched with the Drop-outs on the basis of age, sex, and having been in the same French immersion kindergarten class. It was considered important that the Drop-out and Control French immersion students had shared the same teacher in order to minimize teacher variability. The descriptive information for the two groups is presented in Table 4.

TABLE 4

Descriptive Information for the Drop-out and Control Groups

		Drop-outs	Controls
N		16	16
Age	$\overline{X}$	8.6	8.7
	SD	1.3	1.1
Sex	Males	13	13
	Females	3	3

Method

Each child in the Drop-out and Control groups received an extensive battery of tests including the neuropsychological measures used in the previous study.

Results

Once again, as with the previous study, the large amount of data gathered was subjected to detailed statistical analysis, including factor analysis for data reduction and multivariate analysis. The Drop-outs and Controls could be classified into their appropriate groups at a highly significant level on the basis of the measures from the neuropsychological test battery. In addition to highly significant statistical differences between the two groups, the Dropouts and Controls could also be classified into their appropriate groups on the basis of different patterns of performance on the measures of the neuropsychological test battery. Data sheets summarizing the test scores on the test measures which included age, sex, and handedness as well as all of the cognitive, motor, sensory, language, and perceptual tests were prepared. Using a blind analysis of the test protocols, 14 of 16 Drop-outs and 16 Controls were correctly classified into their groups. These clinical results as well as the statistical analysis point clearly to the distinctiveness of the profiles of the two groups based on measures sensitive to the integrity of the central nervous system.

Tactual Performance Test

One of the tests revealed in the statistical analysis to be very important in differentiating the Drop-out and Control groups was the *Tactual Performance Test*. This finding was highly consistent with the results of the first study and again would be consistent with the interpretation of a maturational lag in the temporal lobe regions of the brain in the Drop-out group.

Follow-up Study

The 32 children from the original French immersion learning difficulty group were carefully followed for a number of reasons. For example, those children who had switched to a full English program were carefully assessed. If their original learning difficulty was particular to the second-language nature of their program they would be expected to accelerate quickly following enrollment in the English program, whereas if their original difficulties were simply manifestation of a generalized language difficulty (as predicted by Bruck et al., 1975) they would be expected to experience learning difficulties following the switch to the English program.

114

In addition, in order to test the maturational lag hypothesis, the progress was monitored carefully on the *Tactual Performance Test.*

A total of twenty-four of the thirty-two children were located for reassessment. Each child was assessed individually on a battery of tests including the *WISC, WRAT, Peabody Picture Vocabulary Test, ITPA, Boston Speech Perception Test, Conners' Parent's and Teacher's Questionnaires, Myklebust Pupil Rating Scale,* and *Tactual Performance Test.* The followup test results have been reported in extensive detail (Trites & Price, 1977). In terms of the children who switched to the English-language program, they showed significant acceleration in the development of reading and spelling skills in English as well as English vocabulary. None required learning-disability class placement in the English program and none were described by their teachers as presenting with learning disabilities in the English language program. These results suggest that these children do not have a primary language disorder or a generalized learning difficulty, but rather have a specific learning difficulty affecting their ability to be educated in a second language at an early age.

In terms of the *Tactual Performance Test* results, those children who were below age 9 or 10 at retest continued to have difficulty on this test while those children who were over age 10 at retest performed normally. These results were interpreted as consistent with the maturational lag hypothesis. Namely there was evidence of a psychomotor problem-solving deficit in the early ages which appeared to be resolved by ages 9 or 10. A detailed analysis of the *Tactual Performance Test* results is available (Trites & Price, 1977).

Discussion

The findings in the first study suggested that the student who fails in a primary French immersion program has a deficit in learning unique to that particular program and would not be classified as having a reading disability, minimal brain dysfunction, hyperactivity, or primary emotional-behaviour disturbance. The results of this study indicated that there are important neuropsychological test differences between groups of children who succeed when placed at a young age in an intensive second-language learning program as compared to those who fail. The findings in the cross validation study supported the first year's results in all important respects. In addition, clear evidence emerged which further defined the pattern of deficits in the group of children who drop out of primary French immersion. The maturational lag hypothesis received strong support from the results of the followup of the children assessed in the first year of study.

It is clearly of great importance to identify those particular children who would likely fail before they enter an early intensive second-language learning program such as the primary French immersion program. The finding of a unique pattern of deficits characteristic of children who experience difficulty led this investigator to an attempt to develop a battery of tests that could be administered to young children at age 4 and that would be predictive of their ability to function well in a second-language program. The following section presents the results of a 3 year project designed to identify a set of variables predictive of success or failure in primary French immersion programs.

Early Identification Project
Although a few attempts have been made to predict subsequent school success of kindergarten children already enrolled in a French immersion program (Edward & Smythe, 1976; Swain & Burnaby,1976), studies have not attempted to assess 4-year-old children prior to their entry in a French immersion program with a view to predicting their subsequent success in the program. Attempts have been made, however, to predict ability for second language acquisition in older children. Carroll (1975) reported an extensive evaluation of the teaching of French in eight countries to three age groups: 10-year-olds, 14-year-olds and end of high school. Analysis of variables predictive of success in reading French and in the comprehension of French indicated that the quality of instruction, the student's motivation and verbal IQ were important predictors. The amount of French instruction was found to be important, but the age or grade when French instruction was introduced was not a significant predictor. In English-speaking countries, sex was related to achievement in French, with girls favoured. This extensive study along with the studies just described in this chapter of a specific learning difficulty in the French immersion group points to the possibility that a set of predictors of achievement in early second-language immersion can be identified. This section presents the results of 3 years of investigation (Trites & Price, 1978, 1979, 1980; Trites, 1981) which began during the 1976-77 school year. The reader is encouraged to consult those reports for a detailed presentation of the neuropsychological test data, parent and teacher questionnaires, demographic data, and other findings pertaining to the studies. This section will only provide a brief overview of the results. The 3-year project was designed to identify a set of variables predictive of success or failure in primary French immersion programs. The predictive validity of measures obtained for children in the spring of their English 4-year-old kindergarten program was assessed in terms of criterion measures of academic achievement in English and French obtained in the spring of 5-

116

year-old French immersion kindergarten and again in the spring of grade 1 French immersion. The progress of the children is still being followed and a brief note will be made of the data just obtained when the children were assessed at the end of grade 4.

The Sample

Fifty-one of the principals of the 53 elementary schools in the Ottawa Board of Education offering an English 4-year-old kindergarten program agreed to participate in the early identification project. Teacher-rating forms and biographical and background information questionnaires were distributed to the teachers and parents of the 1,330 children in 77 4-year-old kindergarten classes in the 51 schools.

A random half of the 51 participating schools were selected for participation in the long-term follow-up study. The area served by the Ottawa Board of Education was divided into grids based on geographical boundaries, and a random half of the schools located in each grid were selected. Parents who had indicated their intention to enroll their children in a 5-year-old French immersion kindergarten in September 1977 were sent letters requesting permission to have their children participate in the early identification project. Parents of children for whom French would be a third language were not contacted. Two hundred eligible subjects were obtained.

Procedure

Questionnaire data (4-year-old kindergarten). The teachers of the 1,330 kindergarten children were asked to complete a brief rating scale for each child in their classes. The teachers' ratings provided information not only about characteristics of each of the 4-year-old kindergarten children, but also about those characteristics of the child held important by the teachers in advising whether or not the child should be enrolled in a French immersion class.

Teachers distributed a questionnaire to the parents of all children in their 4-year-old kindergarten classes. The purpose of this questionnaire was to gather biographical and background information that may have been related to selection of a particular school program, to identify characteristics of the child that parents considered important in program selection, and to provide a basis for assessing the representativeness or uniqueness of children enrolled in French immersion kindergarten. This questionnaire was concerned with the characteristics of the children, of their parents, and of their homes. The factors assessed included age, sex, hand dominance, preschool experience, socioeconomic status, number of books in the home, languages in the home, parental attitudes toward learning French, parents' reasons for choosing the regular English program or the French immersion program for their children in 5-year-old kindergarten, and characteristics parents considered to be important for success in French immersion.

Early Identification Assessment Battery. A variety of test measures and behaviour ratings were obtained for the sample of 200 children scheduled to enter 5-year-old French immersion kindergarten in September of 1977. The measures included five tests selected from *CIRCUS: An Assessment Program for Pre-primary Children* (1974). These tests assessed the children's knowledge of quantitative concepts such as counting, relational terms, and numerical concepts *(CIRCUS Number 2: How Much and How Many)*; letter and numerical recognition *(CIRCUS Number 5: Finding Letters and Numbers)*; auditory discrimination *(CIRCUS Number 7: How Word Sound)*; comprehension, interpretation, and recall of oral language *(CIRCUS Number 9: Listen to the Story)*; and problem solving *(CIRCUS Number 13: Think It Through)*.

Each child was administered an individual test battery by a member of the research team. This battery consisted of the following 10 psychometric tests, some of which were adapted specifically for this project: (WPPSI) (Wechsler, 1963); *Peabody Picture Vocabulary Test,* Form B (PPVT) (Dunn, 1965); *Raven's Coloured Matrices* (Raven, 1965); (WRAT) (Jastak & Jastak, 1965); Measures of Hand Dominance (Trites, 1977); *Tactual Performance Test* (three-block board) (Trites & Price, 1978); *Colour Naming* (Trites & Price, 1978); *Word Segmentation* (adapted from fox & Routh, 1975); *Renfrew Action Picture Test* (Renfrew, 1971); *Test Behaviour Observation Guide* (Atwell, Orpet, & Meyers, 1967); *Connors' Teacher's Questionnaire* (Connors, 1969); *Pupil Rating Scale* (Myklebust, 1979).

Results: 4-year-Old Kindergarten Study

Teacher ratings on 1,293 of the 1,330 children in 4-year-old kindergarten were obtained. This represented a very high response rate of 97%. A strong trend was apparent in the responses of teachers when they were asked whether or not they advised French immersion enrollment for a child. There was a highly significant trend to advise French immersion enrollment for children who were considered as above average in ability, social maturation, and motivation. For example, of the 107 children rated by their teachers as below average in ability, none were advised to enter primary French immersion in 5-year-old kindergarten. Of the 221 children considered below average in social maturation only 25 were advised to enter primary French

118

immersion while 196 were advised to enter the English program. Of the 130 children considered below average in motivation 3 were advised to enter French immersion and 127 the English program.

Based on the biographical and background information gained from the questionnaires returned by the parents, a number of differences were found between children who were to enter the French program and those who were to enter the English program. There were no age differences between the two groups, but there was a slight tendency for a greater number of females to be enrolled in French immersion. There were significant socioeconomic status differences. The socioeconomic level of the fathers, mothers, and families of the French immersion group was significantly higher than those of the English program group. The average socio-economic level for the French immersion group was in the lower-upper-class range compared with the upper-middle levels for the English program families. In addition, there was evidence that parents who enroll their children in French immersion are themselves more interested in speaking French than are parents who choose the English program. In fact many of these parents were taking or had taken a French language instruction course.

As mentioned earlier, all 200 children were assessed individually on a psychometric test battery. The average scores and standard deviations on a few selected measures of the assessment battery are presented in Table 5. As a group, the 200 children tended to perform well on all measures. Average scores on the *WPPSI* were in the bright-normal range and language skills as measured by the IQ, and *Peabody* were well developed. Readiness skills for reading were at the grade 1 level, while spelling and arithmetic readiness skills were at the mid to late 5-year-old kindergarten level. Thus, in general, this group was composed of very capable youngsters who were rated highly by their teachers, came from advantaged socioeconomic backgrounds, and performed very well on the psychometric tests.

In summary, the sample of children who were scheduled to be enrolled in 5-year-old French immersion performed very well on the measures of the early identification assessment battery. IQ scores were in the bright-normal to superior range. Ratings of behaviour by research staff and by 4-year-old kindergarten teachers did not indicate specific areas of difficulty for this group. The average English receptive vocabulary mental age score of 6 years and 2 months *(Peabody)* was well above the children's chronological 4-year-old level. Expressive language skills were within the $5\frac{1}{2}$ to 6-year range in terms of information, and within the 5 to $5\frac{1}{2}$-year range for grammar *(Renfrew)*. Tests of other skill areas also revealed competent performance levels.

Teachers tended to advise against French immersion for children whom they rated "below average" in terms of ability and social maturation. For children of "average" to "above average" ability, teachers were cautious about advising French immersion if the child's level of social maturation or motivation was rated "below average". These findings are consistent with the results reported earlier: Teachers give high priority to a child's general development, especially maturity, and emotional/social adjustment when advising against French immersion enrollment.

Parents and teachers were unanimous in recommending French immersion enrollment for a group of children that stood out in terms of high scores on PIQ measures and advanced receptive vocabulary; above average competency, as rated by teachers, in terms of auditory comprehension, spoken language, and motor coordination; superiority in performance rate and manual dexterity, as rated by research staff; and advanced readiness skills in the areas of identification of letters and numbers, auditory discrimination, and problem solving. Those children whose parents decided in favour of French immersion enrollment contrary to their teachers' advice performed more poorly than the previously mentioned group on the above measures as well as on the *Tactual Performance Test,* expressive language skills, *Colour Naming,* and readiness skills for reading, spelling, and

TABLE 5

Means and Standard Deviations Obtained by the Sample of 200 Children
to be Enrolled in French Immersion on Selected Measures of the
Early Identification Assessment Battery

Variables	$\bar{X}$	SD
Age	4.9	.3
WPPSI: VIQ	118.3	12.4
PIQ	115.8	12.0
FSIQ	118.9	11.9
Peabody: MA	6.2	1.3
IQ	114.0	14.3
Matrices Raw	17.3	4.6
Percentile	79.7	21.9
WRAT: Grade: Reading	1.05	.4
Spelling	.51	.4
Arithmetic	.80	.4

120

arithmetic. This group also had more behaviour problems and less competency as rated by teachers and research staff.

In conclusion, the first phase of the early identification project investigated various descriptive variables, with extensive test data collected for a sample of children whose progress in school would be followed for a number of years. The results indicated that there were describable patterns of differences at many levels for children entering different kindergarten programs (French immersion versus the regular English program) and within the group of children entering French immersion. The demographic data, parent ratings, teacher ratings, and early identification test information were all assessed at the end of 5-year-old kindergarten, grade 1, and grade 4 for their effectiveness as predictors of success in the French immersion program.

Five-year-Old Kindergarten Study

The follow-up assessments at the end of 5-year-old kindergarten, grade 1, and grade 4 indicated a moderate degree of attrition. An overview of the numbers of children remaining in the French immersion program and those who switched to the English program is presented in Table 6.

As can be seen from Table 6, 184 of the 200 children assessed in the spring of the 4-year-old kindergarten were reassessed in the spring of the 5-year-old kindergarten (1978). One hundred and fifty-nine of these children were enrolled in a 5-year-old French immersion program at the time of the kindergarten follow-up assessment. The parents of 11 children had opted for a regular 5-year-old kindergarten because they felt that their children were not ready for French immersion, or because it was not conveniently available. Six children had been transferred from the French immersion program to an English program during the 5-year-old kindergarten year. In most cases, parents did not make this decision on the basis of the particular learning difficulties encountered by the child, but rather on the basis of dissatisfaction with the situation of busing or with specific aspects of the school program (for example, in their opinion a lack of creativity, a lack of emphasis on basic skills, a lack of materials). Seven children were enrolled in a bilingual program. The parents had opted for this program because it offered additional support in the English language and/or it was located in a neighbourhood school.

Parents tended to express positive attitudes toward the French immersion program. The majority of parents ($N= 103$) had no concerns about the program. Although the parents of 26 children intended to enroll their children in an English grade 1 program and parents of three children opted for a bilingual grade 1 program, most of these parents considered the possibility of enrollment in French immersion in the future. This indicated a strong positive attitude towards the goal of having children learn French during the early grades.

The four kindergarten enrollment groups were compared in terms of the information obtained in the initial and follow-up assessments. Of considerable importance was the fact that the ratings of the 4-year-old kindergarten teachers did not discriminate significantly among the four kindergarten enrollment groups (transfers to English programs; transfers to bilingual programs; French immersion; and English kindergarten - no French immersion). However, the children who had transferred to the English program tended to have received a greater proportion of low ratings in ability.

Five-year-old kindergarten teachers did not recommend continued French immersion enrollment for 19 children (12%) who completed the 5-year-old French immersion kindergarten program. These children appeared to have encountered substantial learning difficulty in the program. The reasons cited by the teachers when advising for or against continued French immersion enrollment were examined. While teachers considered a child's ability level to be important when advising against French immersion enrollment, a child's level of maturity was considered to be highly important as well. The child's ability level was cited most frequently when French immersion was advised. These findings are similar to the results reported previously (Trites & Price, 1978). Teachers' reports of difficulty in kindergarten indicated that approximately half of the children in the English program, half of the transfers, and one third of the children in French immersion experienced difficulty. The main reason for difficulty was a

TABLE 6
Sample Size of Early Identification Study at Different
Stages of Follow-up

4-yr-old Kindergarten	5-yr-old Kindergarten	Grade 1	Grade 4
N = 200 - to be enrolled in F.I.	N = 159 in F.I. 17 in English kindergarten 16 moved. 9 miscellaneous.	N = 124 in F.I. 39 in English programs. 31 moved. 6 miscellaneous.	N = 94 in F.I. 37 in English programs. 62 moved. 7 miscellaneous

122

combination of immaturity and emotional-social adjustment problems. Thus, a child's level of emotional and social adjustment is an important factor associated with progress in the 5-year-old French immersion kindergarten program as judged by kindergarten teachers.

The four kindergarten enrollment groups were compared on the measures of the early identification assessment battery. On the whole, children enrolled in the bilingual program had higher IQ scores and performed well on all of the tests administered. The children who had enrolled in the regular English program and the children who transferred to the English program tended to have lower IQ scores than those of the other two groups, although they were within the average to high average range, and tended to have generally lower scores on the variables of the early identification assessment battery.

Few significant group differences were found on the measures of the kindergarten follow-up assessment battery. The transfers fared less well than the others, perhaps as a result of adjusting to two school programs during the school year.

The 159 children who were in the French immersion kindergarten in the spring of 1978 were considered in detail to determine the predictive validity of measures obtained in 4-year-old kindergarten. A statistical analysis was performed on 35 predictive variables of the early identification assessment battery and the 11 criteria and variables of the kindergarten follow-up assessment battery. Better prediction was accomplished for measures of the English language achievement than for measures of French language achievement. The best prediction was found for the *WRAT* reading percentile score. Prediction of achievement in French and English was related to similar measures, including colour and picture naming in English, readiness measures of quantitative concepts and knowledge of letters and numbers, arithmetic scores, expressive language skills in English, and behaviour ratings by research staff and teachers. It is interesting to note that academic achievement in reading, spelling, and arithmetic measured in English was best predicted by IQ. IQ was of greater importance when predicting achievement measures in the English language than when predicting achievement in French. Of great interest, *Tactual Performance Test* scores entered into the multiple regression equations for French language measures but not for English language measures.

Although much of the variance was left unaccounted for in the evaluations of the predictive validity of 4-year-old kindergarten measures, the relationships established at the 5-year-old kindergarten level were encouraging. Much more variation in academic progress was expected to be evident in the grade 1 program, where structured learning situations are more demanding

123

Thus, it was expected that the measures obtained at the end of 4-year-old and 5-year-old kindergarten would have greater predictive validity when they were assessed against criterion measures obtained in the spring of grade one.

Further encouraging results with regard to the prediction of achievement in French immersion were found in the comparisons of groups of high and low achievers formed on the basis of percentile scores on the French comprehension test. As can be seen from Table 7, important differences were found between these groups on measures of the early identification assessment battery and of the kindergarten follow-up assessment battery. Low achievers were younger, had lower IQ scores (but still in the bright-normal range), had lower scores on the *Tactual Performance Test* and generally performed less well on tests of oral fluency, word segmenting, and related tasks.

In summary, the early identification assessment battery seems to have considerable promise. Significant differences were found among groups of children enrolled in the various kindergarten programs, among high achievers and low achievers on the French comprehension test, and among various achievement groups formed on the basis of teacher ratings at the end of 5-year-old French immersion kindergarten. This tended to strongly suggest that measures obtained in 4-year-old kindergarten were related to subsequent achievement in the second-language immersion program. It was predicted that these trends would likely become much stronger during the grade 1 year.

Grade 1 Study

At the end of grade 1, 169 of the initial 200 children were located and assessed. A total of 124 children were still in French immersion, while most of the remainder were in an English program. Twenty-five of the children in the English program were clearly established as drop-outs from the French immersion program on the basis of academic factors. It must be stressed that the recommendation that the child transfer from the French to the English program was usually made by the teacher or other school personnel, and that at no time were the results of the testing from this project made available to either the parents or the school authorities.

The 124 children who attended the French immersion program to the end of grade 1 and the 25 children who dropped out of French immersion for academic reasons were similar in terms of family socioeconomic status, sex, and preschool experience. Both groups were from advantaged home backgrounds. Parents of both groups expressed a positive attitude toward the French language.

124

TABLE 7

Means, Standard Deviations, and t scores for Significant
t test Comparisons of High and Low Achievers on the Early
Identification Assessment Battery

	High Achievers		Low Achievers			
	X̄	SD	X̄	SD	t SCORE	df
Age	5.0	.3	4.8	.3	2.52*	65.4
WPPSI VIQ	124.4	12.4	116.2	11.1	2.89**	66.0
FSIQ	123.8	11.4	117.9	10.7	2.20**	65.8
Matrices Raw Score	18.6	5.9	15.9	4.0	2.20*	62.3
WRAT Arithmetic Grade Score	1.0	.4	.8	.4	2.19*	64.3
Formboard: †						
Total time	97.5	1.2	96.7	1.7	2.31*	65
Nondominant time	99.2	.6	98.8	1.0	2.27*	65
Time per block (Nondom)	33.1	.2	32.9	.3	2.21**	65
Colour-naming	9.7	.6	8.8	1.5	3.29**	66
Word Segmenting:						
Total segmented	14.6	3.1	12.0	5.4	2.41*	66
Total (syllables)	10.3	3.2	7.7	3.7	3.08**	62.4
Observer's Checklist:						
E: Attention	5.4	1.5	4.6	1.9	2.07*	60.2
Renfrew: Information	26.5	2.6	23.7	3.6	3.68**	66
Grammar	28.6	5.3	26.4	3.4	2.06*	66
Conners Teacher Rating:+						
Inattentive-passive	13.3	17.2	23.6	19.2	−2.33*	62.6
Myklebust Pupil Rating Scale:						
Auditory Comprehension	14.2	3.2	12.4	2.3	2.77**	63
Spoken Language	17.4	3.2	15.5	2.8	2.54*	66
CIRCUS						
2 : How Much & How Many	32.8	4.4	29.1	5.7	2.98**	57.5
5 : Finding Letters and Numbers	18.2	1.6	16.6	3.7	2.25*	66
7 : How Words Sound	40.4	3.1	38.6	3.3	2.36*	63.9
9 : Listen to the Story	18.3	2.7	15.8	3.3	3.36**	59.8
13: Think it Through	22.6	3.9	18.9	4.1	3.72**	64.2

†   Higher scores represent better performance.

+   Higher scores indicate a greater incidence of problems.

* $p < .05$.

** $p < .01$.

The reliability of the recommendations of 4- and 5-year-old kindergarten teachers with regard to French immersion enrollment as predictors of which children would drop out of the program was examined. The results indicated that the advice of the 4- and 5-year-old kindergarten teachers did not reliably predict which children would drop out of the French immersion program. Four-year-old kindergarten teachers rated the children in terms of ability, social maturation, and motivation prior to their enrollment in French immersion 5-year-old kindergarten. The grade 1 French immersion and drop-out groups did not differ significantly on these scales. Thus one cannot predict which children are likely to drop out of a primary French immersion program on the basis of these ratings by 4-year-old kindergarten teachers.

The comparisons of the French immersion group and the drop-outs on the early identification assessment battery are presented in Table 8 and indicate that the French immersion group had higher IQ scores. However, the drop-outs were within the bright-normal range of intelligence and capable of good progress in most school programs. Although the French immersion group had higher scores on the *WRAT* reading and arithmetic measures, both groups scored at least 6 months in advance of the 4-year-old kindergarten level when tested at the end of 4-year-old kindergarten. With regard to *CIRCUS* readiness measures, the French immersion group outperformed the drop-outs and were better prepared for the 5-year-old kindergarten program. When IQ differences were statistically controlled in analysis of covariance, the drop-outs continued to differ significantly from the French immersion group on *CIRCUS* readiness measures. However, the drop-outs were not deficient in terms of readiness skills and were well able to cope with the demands of a regular kindergarten program. It is clear from the test profile characteristic of this drop-out group that this group does not have a language disability in English and as such is vastly different from the type of child investigated by Bruck (this volume).

The significantly better performance of the French immersion group on the *Tactual Performance Test* (dominant hand time per block) even when Full Scale IQ was controlled statistically, was consistent with the findings of previous investigations of children encountering difficulty in French immersion and of drop-outs from the French immersion program (Trites & Price, 1976, 1977). Again, the drop-outs performed more poorly on this measure in comparison with the children in the French immersion program. The finding was consistent with the maturational lag hypothesis proposed in the earlier studies. Of considerable interest, and suggesting that the drop-out group's difficulties were in the French language skills only, at the grade

126

TABLE 8

Means, Standard Deviations, and Significant t-test Comparisons
of the French Immersion Group and Drop-out on the
Early Identification Assessment Battery

| | French Immersion | | Dorp-outs | | |
	X̄	SD	X̄	SD	t-prob
	n = 124		n = 25		
WPPSI:					
VIQ	120.6	11.7	114.5	12.8	.035
PIQ	116.9	12.0	111.6	12.0	.050
FSIQ	120.7	11.5	114.6	11.8	.022
Vocabulary	13.6	2.5	12.2	2.5	.020
Arithmetic	13.3	2.5	11.8	1.0	.002
Sentences	10.7	2.7	8.9	3.3	.016
Picture completion	13.2	2.5	11.9	2.7	.035
WRAT					
Reading grade	1.1	.4	.9	.3	.004
Arithmetic grade	.9	.4	.6	.4	.000
Colour-naming	9.4	1.0	8.9	2.2	.050
Word Segmenting:					
Total	13.8	4.0	10.7	6.3	.002
Syllables	9.6	3.7	7.1	4.6	.018
Observer's Checklist:					
C: Manual dexterity	5.4	1.4	4.7	1.2	.024
Renfrew: Information	25.7	3.4	23.6	3.5	.011
Myklebust:					
Auditory comprehension	13.5	2.8	12.3	2.1	.019
Verbal	29.9	5.4	27.7	4.9	.044
Total	77.7	12.4	73.0	9.1	.032
CIRCUS					
2: How Much &How Many	32.1	4.2	28.3	4.7	.001
5: Finding Letters and Numbers	17.7	2.4	16.0	3.7	.004
7: How Words Sound	40.4	2.8	37.7	3.6	.001
9: Listen to the Story	18.0	3.1	15.7	3.7	.005
13: Think it Through	21.5	4.4	18.9	4.5	.013
Tactual Performance Test:					
Dominant time per block	32.8	0.8	33.6	3.0	.020

one level the drop-outs outperformed children who continued in French immersion on measures of reading and spelling in English. Thus, the drop-outs responded well to instruction in the English language and made normal progress.

Once it was established that, based on the 4-year-old kindergarten assessment, it was possible to differentiate, at highly accurate levels, between those children who would still be in French immersion by the end of grade 1 and those who would have dropped out, it was decided to further subdivide the 124 children who were still in French immersion into high achievers and low achievers, on the basis of both teacher assessments and a variety of French-language tests. A detailed discussion of the socioeconomic level, preschool experience, teacher assessment, parent questionnaire information, and related factors for the drop-outs, low achievers, and high achievers is available (Trites & Price, 1980). This section will primarily summarize the test results.

The extent to which the drop-outs could be discriminated from the high achievers and low achievers in French immersion on the basis of predictive data gathered in 4- and 5-year-old kindergarten was assessed in stepwise multiple discriminant function analyses. The drop-outs and high achievers were easily predicted. As can be seen in Table 9, the children in these groups were classified correctly into their groups with 100% accuracy on the basis of the early identification assessment battery. Univariate analysis of the 4-year-old test battery yielded significant differences between the high achievers and the drop-outs on measures of IQ; readiness skills including quantitative concepts, and knowledge of letters and numbers, auditory discrimination, and problem solving; *WRAT* spelling test scores; ability to segment words into syllables; levels of manual dexterity, self-confidence, cooperation, and interest; level of inattentive-passive behaviour as rated by teachers; and teacher ratings of auditory comprehension, spoken language, and personal-social behaviour. The high achievers obtained better scores than the drop-outs on all of these measures. Of the above measures, the highest weights in the discriminate function were given to inattentive-passive behaviour, knowledge of letters and numbers, interest, spoken language, auditory comprehension, problem solving, auditory discrimination, and quantitative concepts. Thus, using a combination of 14 tests on the early identification assessment battery administered at the end of 4-year-old kindergarten one could predict with extreme accuracy those children who were likely to encounter difficulty in a primary French immersion program, or drop out of the program, versus those who were likely to progress very satisfactorily in a French immersion program. The 14 test measures would

128

TABLE 9

Discriminate Function Comparison of the Drop-outs and High Achievers
on the Four-Year- Old Kindergarten Variables

Actual Group	N	Predicted Group a			
		Drop-Outs		High Achievers	
		N	%	N	%
Drop- Outs	17	17	100	0	0
High Achievers	22	0	0	22	100

a overall correct classification: 100%

include IQ, *CIRCUS* readiness tests, the *Tactual Performance Test,* Picture and colour naming, the *WRAT* spelling test, word segmentation, and the *Renfrew Action Picture Test.*

As can be seen from Table 10, high levels of correct classification were also obtained in the discriminant function analyses of the drop-outs versus low achievers by the end of grade one. Based on the early identification assessment battery, 88% of the children were correctly classified according to group. Many of the same tests that differentiated the high achievers from drop-outs were equally effective in differentiating the low achievers from drop-outs.

Among those children remaining in French immersion at the end of grade 1 it was also possible to differentiate the low achievers from the high achievers based on the 4-year-old kindergarten early identification assessment battery. As can be seen from Table 11, 87% of these children could be identified correctly.

TABLE 10

Discriminate Function Comparison of the Drop-outs and Low Achievers
on the 4-Year-Old Kindergarten Variables

Actual Group	N	Predicted Group a			
		Drop-Outs		Low Achievers	
		N	%	N	%
Drop-Outs	17	17	100	0	0
Low Achievers	17	4	23.5	13	76.5

a overall correct classification: 88.24%

TABLE 11

Discriminate Function Comparison of the High Achievers
and Low Achievers in French Immersion
on 4-Year-Old Kindergarten Variables

Actual Group	N	Predicted Group a			
		High Achievers		Low Achievers	
		N	%	N	%
High Achievers	22	22	100	0	0
Low Achievers	17	5	29.4	12	70.6

a overall correct classification: 87.18%

An important finding of the above mentioned discriminant function analyses was the role of the *Tactual Performance Test* in separating dropouts, low achievers, and high achievers. In the studies reported earlier in this chapter (Trites & Price, 1976, 1977) it was found that children who encountered difficulty in French immersion had a unique pattern of skills and deficits characterized by a high IQ, excellent motor and sensory function along with normal perceptual and language functions, and yet performed poorly on the *Tactual Performance Test,* (a complex psychomotor problem solving test). The findings were interpreted as evidence of a maturational lag in the temporal lobe regions of the brain. The results reported here are again consistent with that hypothesis. The *Tactual Performance Test* constructed for young children was selected by the stepwise procedure.

On the basis of the information gathered in 4-year-old kindergarten, including the biographical and background information questionnaire, teachers' ratings and the early identification assessment battery, the following picture of the future drop-out from the French immersion program emerges. The drop-out has bright-normal intelligence. Four-year-old kindergarten teachers rate the drop-out as average or above average in ability and as average in social maturation and motivation. There are no important sex differences and he or she is likely to have attended preschool. The child is likely to have come from an advantaged socioeconomic background and the parents generally have positive attitudes towards French immersion, and the French language and its speakers. His or her 4-year-old kindergarten may have advised French immersion enrollment; however, if the 5-year-old kindergarten teacher advises against French immersion enrollment, it is likely that the child will encounter difficulty in

130

the French immersion program. The drop-out tends to have poor auditory discrimination skills and receive low ratings on auditory comprehension and spoken language when compared with a successful student; however, when compared with the average child, he or she generally performs well. The drop-out lags behind the successful French immersion peer in terms of knowledge of basic concepts of numbers and letters, quantitative concepts, and colour naming. The drop-out is less flexible in terms of problem solving, both manually *(Tactual Performance Test)* and verbally (word segmenting *CIRCUS Number 13)*. The drop-out is less adept in manipulative skills as indicated by poorer performance on the *WRAT* spelling subtest, which involves copying marks, poorer performance on the *Tactual Performance Test,* and lower ratings of manual dexterity. Despite these lower performance levels, drop-outs make good progress in acquiring reading, spelling, and arithmetic skills in English, and have well developed receptive and expressive language skills in English, indicating that their learning difficulties are specific to the second language only.

As can be seen from Table 6, 138 of the original 200 children were reassessed at the end of grade 4. Ninety-four were still in French immersion while 37 were in English language programs in the Ottawa area. The test data have not been analysed as yet. However, it should be stressed that 36 of the 37 in English programs are in regular classes none of whom require special education programs for learning disabilities. The 37th child is in a special class, but this child was one of those whom the parents decided not to put in the French immersion program before school started in the 5-year-old kindergarten year. The normal school progress of the 36 children in English language programs is what would be expected based on the findings of our earlier years of investigation, which indicated the learning disability was in the second language program only.

Summary and Conclusions
The five studies summarized in this chapter were aimed at furthering our understanding in a second-language program at school at a young age, and at the development of a battery of tests that can be administered to young children to predict their ability to succeed in a second-language immersion program. The results of the first year of study demonstrated clearly that the neuropsychological test profile of children who are unable to make satisfactory progress when immersed in a second-language program beginning in 5-year-old kindergarten is substantially different from that of children who have the more "traditional" type of learning disabilities such as primary reading disability, emotional disturbance with learning disabil-

ity, hyperactivity with learning disability, difficulty or "minimal cerebral dysfunction" with learning disability. In addition, it was most interesting to see that the learning disability profile of the immersion group was distinguishable from those of francophone children failing in a francophone program, anglophone children failing in a francophone school, and children from other ethnic backgrounds failing in an English language program. It was possible, based on the first year of study, to tentatively propose that children who fail when placed in a primary French immersion program appear to have a maturational lag in the temporal lobe regions of the brain. The temporal lobes are important brain structures for auditory perceptual abilities as well as for verbal and nonverbal perceptual and memory functions.

The second study, conducted a year later, was designed to see if the results of the first year could be validated. The second study not only completely replicated the results first noted, but also further clarified the maturational lag hypothesis by demonstrating that the neuropsychological deficits were apparent in children below 9 years of age but were no longer found in those over that age. Presumably children who have evidence of the specific maturational lag and are not able to progress satisfactorily when immersed in a second-language program in 5-year-old kindergarten would be able to make completely satisfactory progress if immersed at grade 3 or 4, or later. Follow-up studies of children who had been transferred to an English language program from French immersion due to academic difficulties indicated that the children progressed rapidly in the development of the English language arts skills.

The first 2 years of study suggested that it may be possible to develop an early identification battery that could be administered to 4-year-old children that would be predictive of their ability to progress satisfactorily in a French immersion program beginning in 5-year-old kindergarten. A large representative sample of 4-year-old children was assessed at the end of their 4-year-old kindergarten school year. They were tested individually on selected measures, and extensive teacher observation information and questionnaire data from parents were obtained. Follow-up assessments were obtained at the end of 5-year-old kindergarten, at the end of grade 1 for both those children who remained in the French immersion program and the children who were transferred out of the program for a variety of academic, behavioural, and other reasons, and lastly at the end of grade 4 for all groups. Results from the longitudinal investigation indicate that it was possible to identify with 100% accuracy, based on the 4-year-old assessment, those children who would subsequently drop out of French

132

immersion for academic reasons as opposed to those children who were able to remain in the program and do very well. It was even possible to identify with 80 to 90% accuracy the drop-outs as opposed to those children who would remain in the French immersion program in spite of experiencing academic difficulties. The best predictors were the individual neuropsychological measures, several of which were specifically designed for the early identification assessment. The test findings supported the interpretation given to the first 2 years of investigation, namely, that there are certain children who, in spite of being bright, highly motivated, coming from an advantaged socioeconomic background, and being free from personality or neurological impairment, have a mild maturational lag, which is easily identified as early as 4 years of age. These particular children progress normally when they are educated in the vernacular, but are unable to progress satisfactorily in a second-language immersion program.

BILINGUALISM AND MENTAL HANDICAP: SOME PROGRAMMATIC VIEWS

Jean A. Rondal

STATEMENT OF THE PROBLEM

Most investigations of the relationship between bilingualism and cognition, on the one hand, and between bilingualism and verbal abilities, on the other hand, conducted prior to or around 1960 have generally concluded that bilingual individuals perform at a lower level than unilinguals (e.g., Macnamara, 1966). It has also been reported that bilingualism may adversely affect scholastic achievement. Many of the early studies, however, suffered from serious methodological defects. Among other weaknesses, they failed to control for confounding variables such as socio-economic status, sex, onset of exposure to the two languages, and degree of practical knowledge in the two languages.

More recent studies offering a better control on these independent variables tend to indicate that bilingualism can accelerate the development on nonverbal as well as verbal abilities, facilitate aspects of cognitive flexibility, and enhance divergent thinking skills (see Cummins, 1976, and McLaughlin, 1977, for detailed reviews of the literature). Whether these more recent findings are firmly established or can be questioned on methodological grounds (see McLaughlin, this volume) still remains a matter for further investigation and discussion.

Cummins (1976) has analyzed and tried to resolve the inconsistencies between the results of the older studies and of the more recent studies on early bilingualism and child development. As a first step, he suggests abandoning the optimistic expectation that research into the psychological and educational consequences of bilingualism should produce completely consistent results. Cummins states that there is an enormous variety of bilingual learning situations which are likely to affect cognition in different ways depending on the age at which the languages are learned, the opportunities for using both languages in the home, school, and social environment, etc., and whether they are learned separately or simultaneously.

The major methodological difference between early and more recent studies on early bilingualism and cognitive as well as verbal development seems to concern the level of competence reached by the subjects in the two languages (Cummins, 1976). Earlier studies did not select only bilingual subjects who had developed balanced linguistic skills in the two languages. The majority of more recent studies, starting with Peal and Lambert's (1962) research, have, however, tried to ensure that the bilingual subjects had developed a similar or at least a closely related level of competence in both languages. On the basis of the inconsistencies between the results of the earlier and the more recent studies of early bilingualism, and on the basis of the correlated differences in the methodology used in the two sets of studies, Cummins (1976) has hypothesized that the level of linguistic competence[1] attained by the bilingual child may "mediate" the effects of his bilingual learning experience on cognitive and verbal development. This is the so-called "threshold hypothesis" of linguistic competence. In other words, a bilingual child, it is supposed, should attain a definite level of linguistic competence in order to avoid the deficits reported by the earlier studies and to allow the full cognitive and linguistic benefits of becoming bilingual as reported in more recent work.

Cummins adds that the threshold level of bilingual competence should be considered an intervening rather than a "basic causal" variable in accounting (potentially) for the cognitive growth of bilinguals. The attainment of the threshold is indeed itself determined by a number of other factors: social, educational, cultural, cognitive, and language-learning aptitude.

While Cummins' hypothesis is of interest to the question of the relationship between early bilingualism and development in the language-impaired child as well as in the mentally handicapped individual (I will develop this latter point below), it is clear that its use would require at least a minimal operational definition of the "threshold bilingual competence".

1. As is often the case in the current developmental and applied psycholinguistic literature, and as will also be the case throughout the present chapter, Cummins (1976) is using the term "competence" as a synonym for knowledge or capacity (herein linguistic knowledge and capacity). No claim is made that this knowledge must have reached any conscious level in the individual and no specific hypothesis is made regarding the origin (or origins) of this knowledge (i.e., whether it is experiential, innate, or an interaction between innate ideas and predispositions and linguistic experience and practice). This concept of competence is broader than the one used by Chomsky in his classical writings (e.g., Chomsky, 1965). Chomsky's concept of (intrinsic) linguistic competence centers around the notion of a system of generative processes, i.e., a generative grammar, supposed to be stored in an ideal speaker-listener and put to use in concrete verbal exchanges.

Only a few hints are offered by Cummins (1976). The threshold cannot be defined in absolute terms. It may vary with the type of cognitive operations expressed through the second language (for example, concrete and formal operations in the Piagetian sense) because language is likely to increase in importance as a cognitive instrument between the time the child can only reason concretely and the time he can function at the formal propositional stage. It may also vary according to the type of bilingual learning situation (full immersion program, partial immersion program, home situation, etc.) because a greater proportion of the child's meanings and cognitive operations (particularly in school) must be expressed through the medium of the second language.

In fact, there might be two thresholds. The attainment of the first threshold would permit the child to avoid cognitive retardation, but a second and higher level of linguistic competence in the second language might be necessary to lead to accelerated cognitive growth.

However, beside these general indications, no other insight is given as to what the threshold of bilingual competence could be. In particular, nothing is said regarding the several components of the language system, i.e., the sound system, lexicon, morpho-syntax, structural semantics, pragmatic rules and constraints, discourse integration. It is obvious that any threshold should have to be defined multiply, according to the various components of the language system. Indeed there is no reason to believe that, say, lexical competence can be regarded as an index that could subsume development in the other components of the system. The large body of data available today on language development in the child indicates quite clearly that linguistic growth proceeds unequally over time for the lexicon, syntax, articulation, productive and receptive capabilities, use and awareness of rules, etc.

Variables other than threshold bilingual competence have been found to affect second-language learning. One is *general linguistic aptitude*. Carroll (1969) and others have gathered data showing that children vary in aptitude for foreign-language learning. The evidence is particularly clear for those children older than 8 or 9 years. For first-language learning, it is well known that there are important individual differences in linguistic aptitude even and perhaps especially in younger children (McCarthy, 1930; Maccoby & Jacklin, 1974). *Stage of cognitive development* must also be considered. Whether one wants to consider cognitive development within the general framework of Piaget's theory or not, it has been argued recently (Macnamara, 1975; McLaughlin, 1977) that older children and adults regularly outperform younger children on most aspects of second-language acquisition when they are placed in comparable circumstances. This opinion, based on recent data, is in contrast with previous views such as Penfield's (1965) and Lenneberg's (1967), which imply that second-language learning yields better results because the brain of the child can be "conditioned" linguistically before he reaches 7 or 8 years of age.

Affective, attitudinal, and sociological factors are also of importance in second-language acquisition. It is easy to understand that second-language acquisition is facilitated and can come more "naturally" if the first-language community is favourably inclined to the learning of a foreign language (e.g., Mackey, 1967). Personal motivation to learn a foreign language and positive empathy for a culture other than the native one of course can and do facilitate second-language learning. Finally, factors such as the relative economical, cultural, historical, and/or political prestige of the two languages have been cited as possibly potent variables in explaining the results obtained with early immersion programs in different countries or regions. Lambert (1974, 1977) has developed the notions of "additive" and "subtractive" bilingual experiences to capture the general effects of such sociocultural realities on second-language acquisition.

In a situation of additive bilingualism, the ethnolinguistic group sees the learning of the language of the other linguistic group as positive and not threatening to its own cultural and political well-being or survival. This seems to have been the case, for example, for the English-speaking residents of Montreal, Quebec, whose children have learned French. In such a situation, the second language is learned more easily and at no cost to the first language of the individual, for it is felt to be a valuable addition to the developmental background of the child. For many minority ethnic groups, however, the learning of a second language (usually the majority language) is likely to (or can be believed to) lead to a gradual replacement or weakening and hybridization of the native language. In this type of bilingualism, the bilingual individual's competence is likely to reflect some sort of subtraction from the first language and an addition to the second language.

In summary, early bilingualism is affected by the child's capacity to deal with structural aspects of language, by his level of maturational and cognitive development, as well as by affective, attitudinal, and sociocultural factors. It is possible that most of the deficits sometimes associated with early bilingualism can be avoided and some cognitive and linguistic benefits gained only when a given threshold of linguistic competence is achieved in second-language learning.

So far, I have only considered the case of children of average or above average intellectual ability who have acquired their first language quite normally, i.e., without delay and without any particular difficulty. But what about second-language learning and bilingual education in language-delayed or language-impaired children and in developmentally delayed children — particularly mentally handicapped children?

One easy answer could be that it may not be necessary to raise such children bilingually as they appear to have enough problems learning their first language. In some cases this attitude is appropriate. However, the question of the possible benefits of early bilingual education on the cognitive and linguistic development of these children should be taken into serious consideration, perhaps even more so than for normal children. If such benefits are real and can be found to apply to language-delayed and language-impaired children, one is morally obliged to use bilingual education as a remedial tool for these children in conjunction with other instruments and techniques for intervention because they already have language problems. In a number of other cases, the decision to renounce bilingual education is not an easy one and sometimes it is simply not feasible. For example, the child's family may be bilingual, with the father and mother being native speakers of different languages. Or in the social milieu, a language that is different from the one spoken in the family of the child may be used. This is typically the case with first-generation immigrants. Or in the immediate external milieu, one language that differs from the official language of the larger social group or from the national language may be used. This is often the case with minority groups or with local people in linguistically autonomous provinces or regions that are part of larger political entities (Siguan & Serra, 1981).

BILINGUAL PROGRAMS FOR THE LANGUAGE-IMPAIRED CHILD

Very little is known about the suitability of early bilingual education for children of normal intelligence with deviant or slow patterns of language development such as marked delays in using and combining words, in developing clear articulation, and in showing mastery over the usual syntactic structures of their language. These children may represent between 5 and 10% of the school-aged population according to recent estimates (cf. Rondal & Seron, 1982). Moreover, the existing data are contradictory (Bruck, 1978; Bruck, this volume; Bruck, Rabinovitch, & Oates, 1975; Trites, 1976; Trites, this volume; Trites & Price, 1976, 1977, 1978/1979).

Bruck and her collaborators have followed and evaluated the development of first- and second-language oral skills as well as school achievement in about 20 English-speaking children. All were from middle-class backgrounds and were diagnosed as having language impairment. The children were living in Montreal and attended French immersion classes. They were assessed annually in kindergarten, grade 1, and grade 2. Their performance and progress were compared with those of three other groups of children matched with the target children on a number of categories: English-speaking children with language impairments placed in regular monolingual English-speaking classes; English-speaking children with normal language development placed in French immersion classes; and English-speaking children with normal language development placed in regular monolingual English-speaking classes.

The language-impaired children were screened in immersion and regular classes through the use of a set of language tasks including story retelling and sentence imitation. They were also given the Wechsler Pre-school Primary Scale of Intelligence to make sure that they had normal intellectual aptitudes. Any child scoring below 85 on the WPPSI was eliminated from the study. The children were given a battery of tests to measure first-language and cognitive skills at the end of the kindergarten year, first grade, and second grade. The battery included tests like the WPPSI, the Peabody Picture Vocabulary Test, the Northwestern Syntax Screening Test, several subtests of the Illinois Test of Psycholinguistic Abilities, a Sentence Imitation Test, and a French Listening Comprehension Test to assess comprehension of spoken French.

On the whole, the data obtained indicated that the English-speaking children with language impairments demonstrated cognitive and first-language skills after 1, 2, or 3 years of instruction in a second language essentially comparable to skills of other language-impaired children educated only in their native language. Expectedly the competence levels reached by the language-impaired children after 1, 2, or 3 years of schooling were markedly lower than the ones attained by the normally developing children with no interaction between language aptitude and modality of instruction.

Regarding second-language skills, the language-impaired children placed in immersion classes acquired some receptive and productive proficiency in French. Their productive skills, however, proved markedly poorer than those of the immersion control children. This result was expected given these children's delays and difficulties in acquiring oral competence in their native language.

Bruck concludes from her data that immersion programs in additive bilingual situations are an efficient method for developing second-language skills in children at no cost to first-language acquisition, and that this

140

conclusion holds true for language-delayed or language-impaired as well as for normally developing children.

If one tries to relate this conclusion to Cummins' threshold hypothesis, the implication may be interpreted in one of two ways. Either there is no evidence to support a strong threshold hypothesis that posits that children with low levels of first-language competence will inevitably do poorly in second-language development and exhibit general cognitive and linguistic deficits, or Bruck's language-impaired subjects had already attained the necessary threshold level in first-language competence permitting them, according to Cummins' hypothesis, to proceed harmoniously and beneficially in second-language learning. The latter implication immediately suggests another hypothesis that can be formulated in the following way: the general threshold level of competence in first language that is necessary for efficient second-language learning is lower than the proficiency level reached by Bruck's language-impaired subjects around 5 or 6 years of age. It is regrettable in this respect that the exact description of the linguistic levels of Bruck's subjects when entering the immersion program in kindergarten and in grade 1 was not given.

Trites and collaborators have concentrated their research efforts on a number of young English-speaking children of average or higher intellect from middle- or upper-class socio-cultural background who failed when immersed in a second-language program in the early school grades. Dropouts from the immersion classes have generally not received much individual attention in the classical immersion studies by Lambert and associates in Montreal or by other researchers in other towns (e.g., Barik & Swain, 1976). There has been a tendency to eliminate from the immersion programs children with emotional problems or children who were delayed in their ability to understand and to express themselves orally in their native language. This was the case, for example, in Barik and Swain's Toronto study (see Barik & Swain, 1974).

Trites (this volume) expresses serious doubts regarding the validity of Bruck's conclusions as to the so-called demonstrated suitability of the early immersion programs for language-delayed or language-impaired children. Basically, he questions the diagnosis of language disability put by Bruck and collaborators on their sample of target children as well as the validity of certain tests to assess the children's knowledge in the immersion language.

Trites reports on the results of a 3-year study conducted in Ottawa. The objective was to discover more about the learning difficulties of 32 young English-speaking children who had dropped out of the French immersion programs for academic difficulties or who were having serious problems

141

with the program. This sample of children was compared with seven control groups on a number of cognitive, perceptual, and linguistic tasks as well as on several personality and motivation questionnaires. The control groups included anglophone children placed in regular francophone schools, children from German, Italian, and other ethnocultural backgrounds placed in regular anglophone schools, francophone children in regular francophone schools, hyperactive children, children with "minimal cerebral dysfunction," among others.

The results suggest that the students who fail in the early immersion programs have a learning deficit distinct from that of hyperactive, emotionally disturbed, or reading-disabled children or children with minimal brain dysfunction. There seem to exist important differences in various neuropsychological tests between the children who succeed and those who fail when placed at a young age in an intensive second-language learning program. These differences seem to point to the validity of the hypothesis that those children who drop out of the immersion programs exhibit a marked maturational delay. If there are characteristics specific to the children who are likely to fail in an immersion program, it should be possible (and would be of great importance) to identify these children before their entrance in the program. Trites (this volume) presents the results of a long-term project designed to identify a set of predictive variables for success or failure in early immersion programs. Among other characteristics, the drop-outs tend to have rather poor auditory discrimination skills and to receive low ratings in auditory comprehension and spoken language when compared with successful immersion students. They also lag markedly behind successful immersion students in basic concepts of number, letter, quantities, color naming, problem solving, and manipulative skills.

Trites' description of his subjects who dropped out of immersion programs in Ottawa seems to match Bruck's indications regarding her language-impaired children in Montreal as far as language capacities and basic intellectual aptitudes. It is probably the case that Trites' drop-out subjects were less behind in terms of language skills than Bruck's subjects judging from the reports presented by these authors. The results of the two sets of investigations therefore are clearly contradictory. For Bruck, the language-impaired child is perfectly able to participate in and to benefit from an early immersion program providing that the general socio-political context makes up for an additive bilingual experience. Judging from Trites' data, however, the only possible implication is that comparable children are very likely to fail in an early immersion program although they may progress well in regular monolingual stream classes.

142

The question of the suitability of early additive immersion programs for language-impaired and/or learning-disabled but emotionally well-adjusted children of normal intelligence cannot be resolved on the basis of the existing contradictory data.

BILINGUAL EDUCATION AND THE MENTALLY HANDICAPPED CHILD

To the best of my knowledge, there are no immersion programs operating for the mentally handicapped children at the present time. Neither do I know of any systematic attempt to teach second-language skills to mentally handicapped individuals. The rest of this chapter therefore is programmatic and speculative. Many questions may be asked: when bilingualism is not imposed by the living conditions of the family, is it advisable to engage mentally handicapped children in second-language learning? Could they benefit cognitively from a prolonged bilingual exposure? In those situations where bilingualism is a fact of life, how should one proceed with the retarded child? When is it preferable to start second-language exposure and learning? How much of the second language is the handicapped child capable of learning? How much can he take in at a time? What about possible negative interferences between first- and second-language learning, etc?

In trying to give a hypothetical answer to some of the preceding questions in the absence of direct empirical data, it is necessary to take into account the different psychometric levels of mental retardation. There are indeed as many important differences in psychological functioning between mildly retarded individuals (with IQ's between roughly 50 and 75) and moderately and severely retarded subjects (with IQ's between 25 and 50) as there are between the former and subjects of average intelligence. There is no reason therefore to justify making general statements for mental retardation in toto disregarding differences in the retarded individuals at different levels of the psychometric scale.

Genesee (1976) has tried to evaluate the suitability of early French immersion programs for English-speaking children with low IQ's (who were within the normal range, however). He compared the academic and linguistic performance of a number of these children with similar students placed in regular English programs. Both groups of children performed similarly on academic achievement and first language acquisition measures. The low IQ children placed in immersion programs were reported to be similar to average or above average IQ French immersion students in terms of their acquisition of oral French skills.

Genesee's data and conclusions may be overly optimistic. They seem to suggest, however, that low-IQ children can benefit at least minimally from regular immersion programs at no cost to their academic progress and first-language development. The same suggestion could be made tentatively for mildly mentally retarded individuals in life situations calling obligatorily for bilingual education. At what age should one advise possible placement in immersion classes for such children or, in the absence of regular immersion programs, at what age should one start systematic second-language learning?

Most immersion programs in Canada (doubtless the leading country in this respect) start at the kindergarten level, i.e. around 5 years of age (see the Montreal, Toronto, and Ottawa programs referred to in this volume and other publications). The rationale behind this decision is that it is around 5 years that most normally developing children reach the level in first-language development where they are able to make rapid progress in second-language learning at minimal cost to their native language. At this time, they can also benefit cognitively and academically from the immersion program. Let me assume on this basis that the threshold competence level (in Cummins' sense) in first-language acquisition for starting potentially successful systematic second-language learning is reached around a mental age of 5 years. Quite obviously, this does not mean that the children cannot learn elements of foreign languages before the age of 5. They can and sometimes do.

With mildly mentally retarded children the same figure in terms of mental age is usually not attained before 7 or 8 years (chronological age) at the minimum.[2]

It could be suggested tentatively that systematic second-language learning could be started around 8 years of age with mildly retarded subjects provided that the necessary motivations have been established and that the general situation allows for an additive bilingual experience. It would probably be useful or perhaps necessary to arrange the second-language setting or the immersion conditions in such a way that additional or remedial teachers would be able to assist the regular classroom teachers in individually helping the retarded pupils to accommodate to the particular difficulties and problems of second-language learning. Specific curricula would have to be constructed taking into consideration the special needs and learning characteristics of the retarded pupils.

2. This indication is obtained through the following computation:

$$\frac{60 \text{ months}}{80 \text{ months}} = .75 \times 100 = IQ, \text{ where}$$

60 months represents mental age (5 years), 75 the approximate upper IQ limit for child mental retardation, and 80 months chronological age.

The above considerations are based on the implicit hypothesis that mildly mentally retarded subjects develop speech and language in much the same way as nonretarded children do, except for rate of development and final stage reached. In other words, language development in these subjects is a similar but delayed and incomplete process by comparison with normally developing children. This hypothesis is accepted by most experts in the field of mental retardation (Yoder & Miller, 1972; Rondal & Lambert, 1983).

In summary, for mildly retarded subjects, it could well be the case that systematic second-language learning or adapted versions of the regular immersion programs starting later than with normal children could meet with success provided that the general context is favourable to second-language experience. At this time, I do not see any particular scientific reason that would preclude such attempts in situations where bilingualism is an inescapable fact of life.

The picture may look completely different, however, when moderately and severely mentally retarded individuals are taken in consideration. These subjects have IQ's between approximatively 25 to 50 points. Their retardation is most often the phenotypical expression of genetical aberrations or the consequence of maternal infections, traumas, or biochemical imbalances during pregnancy. The speech and language development of moderately and severely retarded children has been systematically studied in the last 20 years or so yielding a considerable amount of data. It may be necessary to take a detailed look at these data in order to provide a basis for giving a meaningful answer to the question of the suitability of second-language learning in these children.[3]

FIRST-LANGUAGE ACQUISITION IN MODERATELY AND SEVERELY RETARDED INDIVIDUALS

A search through the literature has yielded the information summarized in Table 1. This table is organized in such a way as to allow systematic comparisons between retarded individuals' linguistic performance and knowledge and that of normally developing children of comparable chronological age, mental age, or level of language development.[4]

3. For more details, the interested reader is referred to Spradlin, 1963; Zisk & Bialer 1967; Rondal, 1975; Rondal & Lambert, 1983; Rondal, Lambert & Chipman, 1981.
4. Data concerning Down's syndrome children and retarded children of other etiologies are presented separately in view of the fact that Down's syndrome children are often reported to be inferior to other types of retarded children in all aspects of linguistic functioning (cf. Rondal & Lambert, 1983).

TABLE 1

The data were obtained using a mental age (MA) matching procedure, or a matching on level of linguistic development (with mean length of utterance, MLU, as the criterion variable) with normal and moderately and severely mentally retarded children - either Down's syndrome (DS) children or retarded children with other etiologies (O). V means retarded children of various etiologies including Down's syndrome; P means production, and C, comprehension; + indicates that no difference was found between normal and retarded children; and - means that one difference was found between normal and retarded children (with the normal children performing better).

Number	Linguistic aspect	Matching procedure	Mentally retarded children's CA in years	Normal children's CA	Children's MA in years*	Production/comprehension	Etiology of retardation	Result
1	Frequency of phonological errors made spontaneously and in imitation (Dodd, 1975)	MA	9-15		4-8	P	DS&O	D.S.-O+
2	Understanding the lexical items on the Carrow Test of Linguistic Comprehension (Bartel, Bryan, & Keehn, 1973)	MA	9-13 (and beyond)		2-6	C	V	+
3	Basic vocabulary of use (Lozar, Wepman & Hass, 1972)	MA	5-15		3-9	P	V	+
4	Responses on word association tasks (Sersen, Astrup, Floidstad, & Wortis, 1970; O'Connor & Hermelin, 1963)	MA / MA	6-14 / 10-20		3-9 / 5-7	P / P	V / V	+ / +
5	Type-token ratio (an index of lexical diversity of speech (Rondal, 1978a)	MLU	3-12	20-32 months		P	DS	+

146

TABLE 1 (continued)

Num-ber	Linguistic aspect	Match-ing proce-dure	Mentally retarded children's CA in years	Normal children's CA	Chil-dren's MA in years*	Produc-tion/ compre-hension	Etiology of retar-dation	Re-sult
6	Frequency and type of basic semantic relations expressed in speech (Rondal, 1978a; Layton & Sharifi, 1979)	MLU	3-12	20-32 months		P	DS	+
			7-12	34-64 months		P	DS	+
7	Comprehension of basic semantic relations (Duchan & Erick-son, 1976)	MLU	4-8	20-32 months		C	DS&O	+
8	Use of familiar English inflec-tions as assessed by the subtest Auditory-Vocal Automatic or Grammatical Closure of the Illinois Test of Psycholinguistic Abilities (Mueller & Wea-ver, 1964; Bate-man, Bilovsky & Share, 1965; Glovsky, 1970)	MA	16 (mean) 14 (mean) 14 (mean)		5 (mean) 4 (mean) 4 (mean)	P	V	—
9	Progressive use of imperative, active affir-mative, negative and interrogative sentences with increasing MA (Lackner, 1968; Gordon & Panagos, 1976	MA	6-16 7-12		2-9 3-5	P	V DS	+ +

TABLE 1 (continued)

Num- ber	Linguistic aspect	Match- ing proce- dure	Mentally retarded children's CA in years	Normal children's CA	Chil- dren's MA in years*	Produc- tion/ compre- hension	Etiology of retar- dation	Re- sult
10	Comprehension of grammatical words, gender and number agreement, subject-verb number agreement and double object construction (Bartel, Bryen & Keehn, 1973; Lambert, 1978)	MA MA	9-13 6-12		2-6 3-6	C	V	—
11	Comprehension of active nega- tive, affirmative passive, and negative passive sentences (Dewart, 1979; Chipman, 1979)	MA MA	7-18 8-15		3-9 4-8	C	V	+
12	Comprehension of temporal pro- positions and temporal rela- tionship between propositions (Barblan & Chipman, 1978)	MA	6-10		3-7	C	V	+
13	Upperbound (i.e. length of the longest utterance in a corpus of speech) (Rondal, 1978a)	MLU	3-12	20-32 months		P	DS	+
14	Number of modifiers per utterance (Rondal, 1978a)	MLU	3-12	20-32 months		P	DS	+

148

TABLE 1 (continued)

Number	Linguistic aspect	Matching procedure	Mentally retarded children's CA in years	Normal children's CA	Children,s MA in years*	Production/comprehension	Etiology of retardation	Result
15	Incidence of utterance without verb. (Rondal 1978a)	MLU	3-12	20-32 months		P	DS	+
16	Proportions of imperative, declarative, wh-interrogative, and yes-no interrogative utterances (Rondal, 1978c)	MLU	3-12	20-32 months		P	DS	+
17	Word order (Ryan, 1975)	MLU	5-9	2-4 ys.		P	DS&O	+
18	Word order in early combinatorial speech (Dale, 1977)	MLU	4-6	20-42 months		P	DS	+
19	Strategies used to identify agents and objects in the basic strings received (change performance first, semantic-lexical strategies second, and responses based on word order third) (Dale, 1977)	MLU	4-6	20-42 months		C	DS	+

TABLE 1 (continued)

Num-ber	Linguistic aspect	Match-ing proce-dure	Mentally retarded children's CA in years	Normal children's CA	Chil-dren's MA in years*	Produc-tion/ compre-hension	Etiology of retar-dation	Re-sult
20	Reversal of order of subject and copula or auxili-ary verb *be* in interrogative sen-tences (Develop-mental Sentence Scoring Procedure) (Rondal, 1978b)	MLU	5-12	24-27 months		P	DS	—
21	Frequency and type of indefinite pronouns (Developmental Sentence Scoring Procedure) (Rondal, 1978b)	MLU	5-12	24-27 months		P	DS	—
22	Developmental level of pronouns used (Developmental Sentence Scoring Procedure) (Dale, 1977	MLU	4-6	20-42 months		P	DS	—

* When this indication is available. By definition, normal children have identical CA's and MA's.

A few additional comments may make it easier to understand the preceding table. They are organized according to the components of the language system.

BABBLING AND PHONOLOGICAL DEVELOPMENT

A large proportion of moderately and severely retarded children have articulatory and voicing difficulties as well as stuttering problems (Spradlin,

1963). There is some agreement that the incidence of speech disorders including stuttering is higher among Down's syndrome children than in the rest of the retarded population (Keane, 1972; Zisk & Bialer, 1967).

As to phonetical development or babbling, Smith and Oller's (1981) and Dodd's (1972) studies clearly indicate that babbling proceeds in the same way in Down's syndrome as in normal infants.

Smith and Oller (1981) have extended their search into the phonological development of their Down's syndrome subjects. They have concentrated on the development of three phonemes /k/, /f/, and /ð/. They report a marked delay in the onset of meaningful speech but the articulatory approximations and substitutions made by Down's syndrome children are of the same type as those made by younger normal subjects (i.e., the order of development was /k/, /f/, and /ð/, and the easier phonemes /k/ and /f/ tended to be substituted for the more difficult phoneme /ð/). Dodd (1979) has compared the phonological errors made by normal, Down's syndrome, and other severely subnormal children matched for MA. She reports that the number and type of errors (for example, consonant cluster reduction) made by the non-Down's syndrome children are the same as those of their MA-matched normal pairs. But the Down's syndrome children made far more errors and were more inconsistent. A lower intelligibility of speech than expected on an MLU basis was also reported by Ryan (1975) and by Rondal (1978a) for Down's syndrome children between 3 and 12 years of age.

Dodd (1975) has suggested that the articulatory deficit of the Down's syndrome children is due to a basic difficulty in programming the motor movements of speech. Such a hypothesis is consistent with the findings of Frith and Frith (1974) that the motor disability in Down's syndrome subjects is due to an inability to use long-term motor programmes for sequences of movements. The articulatory problem in Down's syndrome subjects, therefore, may be more a symptom of a type of general motor disability than the expression of a different type of phonological development.

LEXICAL DEVELOPMENT

The retarded children are comparable to younger normals in the way they acquire lexical knowledge. They understand, use, and associate as many words and similar types of words as their MA-matched normal pairs. When matched for MLU with normal children, the retarded appear to use a more diversified set of vocabulary terms. Recent theories (e.g., Clark, 1973) have proposed that lexical development proceeds through the addition of discrete features of meaning and the subsequent reorganization of the lexical field. Cook (1977) has found that Down's syndrome children acquire the meaning of words like *big, long, in, on,* and *under* in the same order as the normal children (i.e., *big* before *long*, and *in* before *on*, and then *under*).

SEMANTIC STRUCTURAL DEVELOPMENT

The semantic structure basic to multiword expression and understanding (i.e., the notions of agent, object, possessor, benefactor, instrument, presence, absence, attribution, location, etc.) seems to be organized along the same lines in the normal and retarded subjects. The explanation for this is probably that the sensory-motor cognitive knowledge on which the basic semantic structure of language appears to rest (Fillmore, 1967; Chafe, 1970; Piaget, 1954; Brown, 1973; Edwards, 1973) is a prerequisite for the onset of combinatorial speech.

It is possible, however, as some data collected by Willis (1978) on mildly retarded children indicate, that retardates are limited in their ability to combine several semantic relations in order to set the semantic framework for a more complex utterance.

This ability should be distinguished from the morphosyntactic organization of surface structure strings. Retarded children have a great deal of difficulty understanding and applying complex morphological and syntactical rules. It is also possible that they are deficient in the ability to embed two-term relations in order to realize complex semantic structures.

GRAMMATICAL MORPHOLOGICAL DEVELOPMENT

The data on this aspect come mainly from the Grammatical Closure subtest of the Illinois Test of Psycholinguistic Abilities (see Ryan, 1975, however). In this subtest, the child is presented with a set of pictures and has to complete statements like *Here is a bed, here are two – (beds).* The test looks for the productive knowledge of the rules of plural, progressive, past tense, past participle, third person present tense, and comparative form inflections applied to real words located in final position in the sentence. The retarded lag far behind the normal children in the use of grammatical morphemes. They may fail to acquire the complete morphological system and/or settle for some peculiar morphological organization yet to be defined.

SYNTACTICAL DEVELOPMENT

Superficially, it looks like the retarded children develop syntactical knowledge in the same way as normal children. They advance through the early stages of language development with increasing mental age. When matched with normal children for MLU, the Down's syndrome children have identical upper-bounds, number of modifiers per utterance, and incidence of utterance without verb. They produce the various syntactic types of utterances in proportions similar to normal children. As to word order, the evidence collected by Dale (1977) suggests that the early combinatorial speech of Down's syndrome and normal children follows similar patterns. Identical strategies are used by the two groups of children in interpreting the relational structure of elementary sentences (i.e., identifying agent, action, and object).

However, as *more sophisticated aspects of syntactic knowledge* are examined, MLU-matched normal and Down's syndrome children are no longer comparable. Lee's Developmental Sentence Scoring Procedure has been instrumental in revealing some finer differences between the two groups of subjects. The retarded often fail to invert the order of subject and copula or auxiliary verb in interrogative sentences, except in stereotyped questions like *what's that, who's that*, or the like. They seem to have difficulties with the personal, as well as with the indefinite pronouns (for example, *some, all, a few, both, several, somebody, anybody*, etc.), again except in simple constructions like *all done* which may function as single lexical units (Dale, 1977). A difficulty with the indefinite pronouns has also been observed by Willis (1978) in his study of mildly retarded children.

The Down's syndrome children studied by Rondal (1978b) had higher proportions of grammatically correct sentences than their MLU-matched normal pairs. The Down's syndrome children also used more elementary main verbs whereas the normal children constructed more sentences with secondary verbs according to the Developmental Sentence Procedure. Dale (1977) reports that at comparable MLU levels the normal children use more grammatically progressive but erroneous forms. They seem to be taking more risks, henceforth committing more errors, in trying to construct more sophisticated syntactic structures. Willis (1978) has reported a markedly greater use of conjunctions than embeddings in mildly retarded subjects compared to younger normals.

Whether these indications are suggestive of a freezing process taking place in the language development of the Down's syndrome and other retarded subjects or whether they signal a different organization of the advanced syntactic aspects of language is a matter requiring further investigation.

On this basis, it is possible to speculate as to whether the moderately and severely mentally retarded individuals can ever be expected to attain a competence level in first language that could be considered sufficient for engaging in systematic second-language learning.

THE QUESTION OF MINIMAL LINGUISTIC COMPETENCE IN MODERATE AND SEVERE MENTAL RETARDATION

Let me first continue to assume that 5 years mental age is a valid chronological indication of the attainment by the child of a minimal threshold competence level in first language necessary for efficient and relatively rapid second-language learning. Let me assume also that we find ourselves in an ideal situation when the affective, attitudinal, motivational, and sociological factors that contribute significantly to efficient second-language learning in normal children are present and play the same positive role in mentally handicapped children.

The question then is this: When is an equivalent minimal level of linguistic competence attained in the moderately and severely retarded individual? This general question must immediately be rephrased in terms of a set of more specific questions bearing on the various components of the language system.

The data organized in Table 1 supply the general context from which it is possible to give hypothetical answers to these questions.

As to the way moderately and severely mentally retarded children and adolescents acquire language (i.e., they acquire it much like normal children do but for rate of acquisition and ultimate level of development attained [delay position] or otherwise [difference position]), it is not easy to give a simple answer.

The findings are not fully in agreement either with a delay or a difference position. At a relatively superficial level of analysis and particularly for the phonological, lexical, and semantic aspects of language, it is possible to compare the retarded to younger normal children. However, when finer grained analyses are made, particularly as to the morphosyntactic aspect of language, the same comparison is far less satisfactory.

As to articulation and coarticulation, the studies indicate that a level of so-called phonological competence corresponding approximatively to that of the normal 5-year-old child cannot be expected in the moderately and severely retarded child before age 9 or 10 and very likely later in many cases. The picture is even worse in Down's syndrome subjects. In terms of the lexicon, the performance of retarded individuals on a variety of tasks (understandig lexical items, basic vocabulary of use, responses on word association tasks, lexical diversity of speech) indicate that the levels reached are, in general, comparable to those attained by normal children around 5 or 6 years of age. Table 2, adapted from Bartel, Bryan, and Keehn (1973), gives more detailed information on the mental ages at which a variety of lexical structures are acquired (or have not been acquired yet) by nonretarded and severely and moderately mentally retarded children on the Carrow Test of Linguistic Comprehension. It should be added that in order for the retarded subjects to attain the MA levels indicated in the table they have to be between 9 and 13 years in chronological age (see table 1).

TABLE 2

Mental ages at which 60% of nonretarded (X) and moderately and severely retarded children (O) comprehend lexical items on the Carrow Test of Linguistic Comprehension (adapted after Bartel, Bryan, & Keehn, 1973).

Language component	3.0	3.6	4.0	4.6	5.0	5.6	6.0	6.6	7.0	Not acquired
Nouns										
coat, glass, ball, car, tree,										
chair, dog, bicycle, baby,										
table, man, piano, pencil,										
mother, boy, paint, spoon,										
bird, shoe, book, hand, cat,										
fish, girl,	XO									
farm	X		O							
box	X	O								
sheep	X	O								
pair			X							O
half							O	X		
Verbs										
jump, run	X	O								
hit		XO								
catch			X				O			
give				O	X					
Adjectives										
little/big	X				O					
fast/slow	X				O					
big/little	X		O							
tall/short		XO								
alike/different								X		O
red	X	O								
black/yellow		XO								
two		X			O					
some, many, middle						X	O			
more, four						XO				

155

Table 2 (continued)

Language component	3.0	3.6	4.0	4.6	5.0	5.6	6.0	6.6	7.0	Not acquired
few							XO			
fourth							X			O
left/right			XO							
Demonstratives										
these/those			XO							
that/this			X			O				
Interrogatives										
who/what	X					O				
when/where			X							O
Prepositions										
up/down	X	O								
on	X	O								
in	X		O							
under	X									O
by		X		O						
between		X	O							
in front of			X							O

As can be seen in the table, the lexical level reached by the retarded children at MA-3 years (which is probably already beyond the level the majority of these children have reached around CA-5 years) is still very low. It takes a long time before additional words fill in (though they never do so completely) the lexical classes that these children can understand.

An even more discouraging picture emerges from the data gathered on the acquisition of grammatical morphology and syntax by the retarded subjects. The average level reached by normal children in the receptive and productive use of grammatical inflexions around 5 years is certainly not approached (if it is ever reached) before 14 or 15 years in severely and moderately retarded individuals. The results reported suggest they are somewhat better able to acquire a number of syntactic structures. But the competence levels reached by the retarded subjects around 12 years or later are often if not always below those of normal 5-year-olds. More detailed information and examples are available in Bartel, Bryan, and Keehn's data (1973) obtained with the Carrow Test of Linguistic Comprehension (Table 3).

156

TABLE 3

Mental ages at which 60% of nonretarded (X) and moderately and severely retarded children (O) comprehend morphosyntactical items on the Carrow Test of Linguistic Comprehension (adapted after Bartel, Bryan, & Keehn, 1973).

Language component	3.0	3.6	4.0	4.6	5.0	5.6	6.0	6.6	7.0	Not acquired
Derivational suffixes										
farm/farmer				XO						
paint/painter			O	X						
catch/catcher						XO				
tall/taller				O	X					
piano/pianist										XO
bicycle/bicyclist										XO
Gender and number pronouns										
he, she, they		X		O						
her, him, them		X				O				
his, her, their			X							O
Number, nouns and verbs										
chair/chairs			O	X						
ball/balls			X							O
coats/coat				O	X					
tables/table					X					O
is/are			X							O
Tense, verbs										
is riding, rode, will ride	X	O								
painted, paints, will paint			X							O
will jump, jumps, jumped				X						O
has eaten, is eating, will eat							X			O
Voice, verbs										
the car bumps the train, the train bumps the car	X			O						
the boy pushes the girl, the girl pushes the boy	X			O						
the man is hit by the boy, the boy is hit by the man								X		O
the boy is chased by the dog, the dog is chased by the boy							X			O
Negation										
the baby is crying, the baby is not crying	XO									
the girl isn't running, the girl is running		X					O			

Table 3 (continued)

Language component	3.0	3.6	4.0	4.6	5.0	5.6	6.0	6.6	7.0	Not acquired
neither the boy nor the girl is jumping, the boy and the girl are jumping										XO
Syntactic structure Predication, noun-verb number agreement										
the cat plays	X		O							
the boys jump					X					O
Complementation, direct-indirect object										
show me the ball	X	O								
she showed the girl the boy				X						O

CONCLUSIONS AND IMPLICATIONS

It seems clear that language acquisition in retarded children, particularly in the moderately and severely retarded, is a very slow process. Years are needed before the retarded child starts speaking even short utterances. It is not before 10 or 12 years or even later, depending on the child and on the linguistic aspect under consideration, that a receptive and/or a productive competence roughly comparable to that of the average normal 4- of 5-year-old child is established. It could be argued, however, that such a comparison between older retardates and younger normal children is far from satisfactory: the older retarded subjects cannot really be likened to younger normal ones in many respects. I have adopted this comparative approach for the sake of discussion and not to try to prove or to disprove its intrinsic validity.

It would seem that the implications regarding bilingual education in the retarded children are straightforward. It may be acceptable and perhaps useful to start bilingual education with mildly retarded children only a few years later than with normally developing children (say around a chronological age of 8 or 9 years). The situation, however, looks completely different when moderately and severely retarded individuals are taken into consideration. For these subjects, first-language acquisition is a strenuous, lengthy, and difficult endeavour, and it requires many years and much effort before they can attain a restricted productive and receptive capacity. So it would be extremely hazardous to risk systematic second-language training - let alone a complete immersion program - before late adolescence and without a favourable environment and maximum help from family and school. If bilingual education is not rendered compulsive or felt to be highly necessary, one might as well dispense with it among moderately and severely retarded individuals due to the danger of destabilizing their meager linguistic accomplishments. Applying Cummins' threshold hypothesis to this problem, it could safely be predicted that few, if any, linguistic and cognitive benefits accrue from bilingual education for these retarded subjects. For the threshold level necessary for such benefits is not reached (if it ever is) until quite late in the child's development.

This is not to say that, if social circumstances make second-language learning necessary, a number of useful and functional vocabulary items and simple idiomatic structures could not be learned by moderately and severely retarded children - if teaching started early in life and made use of the intervention techniques that have proved efficient with these subjects (cf. Rondal & Lambert, 1983 for a review). In this case the only additional thing to teach the retarded subjects would be to discriminate between those situations that call for using items $X_{i...j}$ from language X and those calling for the use of items $Y_{i...j}$ from language Y. This represents a simple case of discriminative learning of which most moderately and severely retarded subjects should be quite capable.

159

EARLY BILINGUALS:
HOW MONOLINGUAL - LIKE ARE THEY?*

Molly Mack

INTRODUCTION

One of the central and abiding questions implicit in the study of bilingualism has been the following: Is the linguistic performance of fluent early bilinguals indistinguishable from that of monolinguals? It has largely been assumed that there is a strong correlation between age at the onset of L_2 acquisition and subsequent L_2 fluency, but the extent to which early bilingualism results in monolingual-like performance has not fully been determined.

On one hand, it seems clear that early L_2 acquisition is a powerful predictor of L_2 fluency. For example, Larew (1961) administered an articulation test to a group of English-speaking school children aged 7-11 and 14 in order to assess the children's ability to imitate Spanish sounds. She found that the 7-year-old students achieved the greatest accuracy. Asher and García (1969) also found that age correlated with degree of accent, for the youngest children in their study of Cuban immigrants to the U.S. were the least likely to possess strong Spanish accents. Similar findings have been presented by Seliger et al. (1975), Oyama (1976), and Tahta et al. (1981a, 1981b). And in a study of both perception and production of voice-onset time in 72 Spanish-speaking children acquiring English, Williams (1979) found that the younger the children were, the more similar their English pronunciation and perceptual functions were to those of English monolinguals. As Lenneberg (1964) states, "It seems as if the degree of accent correlates fairly well with the age during which a second language is acquired" (pp. 594-595).

Early L_2 acquisition also seems to correlate with proficient syntactic performance. Patkowski (1980) examined the English sentences of 67 immigrants, whose length of residence in the US varied from 6 to over 35 years. Sentences were rated by two trained ESL teachers. The highest (best) scores correlated inversely with a subject's age upon arrival to the US, rather

* This project was funded by an Ellen Swallow Richards Endowed Fellowship from the American Association of University Women.

than length of residence in the US or amount of formal or informal training in English.

An interesting semantically based experiment designed to tap the processing of lexical items was undertaken by Genesee et al. (1978) who examined three groups of 18 French-English bilinguals who had demonstrated equal proficiency in both of their languages. The three groups consisted of those who had begun to acquire French and English in infancy, those who had begun to acquire their L_2 around the ages of 4 to 6, and those who had acquired their L_2 after the age of 12. EEG activity over the two cerebral hemispheres of each subject was monitored during monaural presentation of French and English words. The bilinguals who had acquired their L_2 after age 12 revealed a pattern of electroencephalic responses which differed from that of the other two groups, leading the authors to speculate that "the infant and childhood bilinguals were prone to adopt a left hemisphere-biased, semantic-type strategy, whereas the adolescent bilinguals were prone to adopt a more right hemisphere-biased, phonetic-acoustic-type strategy" (p. 10). They also proposed that "the phonetic, syntactic, and semantic components of the adolescent bilingual's language processing system may be more differentiated neurophysiologically than those of the infant and childhood bilingual" (p. 10).

Clinical work with monolingual children also suggests that there is a difference in the ability of children and adults to acquire language. For example, Lenneberg (1967) indicates that a child between the ages of 4 and 10 who becomes aphasic may recover with few or no residual effects, while adults with comparable impairment may have a worse prognosis. Too, there is the now-famous case of "Genie," a child upon whom nearly complete isolation was enforced from shortly after her birth until the age of 14. During this period, she received almost no linguistic input. Upon her arrival at a medical-research facility, it was determined that she had virtually no language skills. Even after years of effort on the part of Genie to learn English, she retained abnormal patterns in her speech production and perception (Curtiss, 1977).

Clearly then, there seems to be something special about the relationship between age and language acquisition ability. As Lenneberg (1967) observes,

the disequilibrium state called language-readiness is of limited duration. It begins around two and declines with cerebral maturation in the early teens. At this time, apparently a steady state is reached, and the cognitive processes are firmly structured, the capacity for primary language synthesis is lost, and cerebral reorganization of functions is no longer possible (p. 377).

It is probable that, if the capacity to acquire the first language declines with the age of the learner, the capacity to acquire the second language will likewise. As Lamendella (1977) suggests, "The immature neurolinguistic systems of children may have an intrinsically greater potential for complete and efficient acquisition of second languages than the mature systems of adults" (p. 165).

Thus, evidence from psycholinguistics and neurolinguistics provides support for the notion that, in areas of phonetics, syntax, and semantics, younger children appear to outperform older children in their acquisition of the first language as well as in the acquisition of the second. It is evidence such as this that has led linguists to apply the term "critical period" to that time in a child's development when language *must* be acquired if the child is to have eventual native-like fluency.

Yet, even if it is agreed that "earlier is better," there remains empirical evidence which suggests the following: The early acquisition of a second language probably does correlate positively with subsequent L_2 proficiency. But it may also result in or encourage interference between the L_1 and L_2. Or it may yield L_2 structures that differ from those of monolinguals. That is, it is possible for a monolingual norm to be *approximated* without being *achieved*, and this may be an inevitable consequence of exposure to an L_2.

For example, in Asher and García's study, even those Spanish-English bilinguals who had entered the US between the ages of 1 and 6 and who had lived in the US for 5 to 8 years had some accent: Not one of these children was judged to sound like a native speaker of English.

And in an experiment conducted by Lambert and Rawlings (1969), French-English bilinguals were required to search for core concepts in a mixed-language set of associations (e.g., to search for a word such as "table" when presented with the words "chaise," "food," "desk," "bois," "manger," etc.). The authors divided their subjects into two groups - compound and coordinate. The primary criterion for determining membership in one group or the other was age at onset of L_2 acquisition. The compound bilinguals had acquired both languages in infancy, and the coordinate bilinguals had acquired one language after age 6. Lambert and Rawlings hypothesized that, for the former group, the mixed-language test condition would not be as "distracting and confusing" as it would be for the latter group who would, presumably, have "greater functional independence of languages" (p. 607). And in fact, they found that the compound (early) bilinguals were more successful at extracting core concepts from mixed-language lists than were the coordinate (late) bilinguals. They concluded that there was less functional separation of the two languages of the compound (early) bilinguals than of the coordinate (late) bilinguals.

163

The assumption underlying results of tests such as this is that functional interdependence correlates with (or is a feature of) linguistic interference (although it is, in theory, possible to keep distinct the notions of linguistic interdependence and linguistic interference). It is, in fact, largely maintained that if a bilingual's two languages are closely (or inextricably) related, then that bilingual will experience more interference - or will be more likely to experience interference - than will a bilingual whose languages are more or less functionally separate. As Paradis (1980) states in reference to the organization of the semantic system, "To the extent that [bilinguals'] semantic system is compound [interdependent], they will exhibit bidirectional interference and behave inappropriately in both languages" (p. 424).

So it cannot readily be assumed that the early acquisition of two languages assures native-like performance in both. Therefore, in order to further explore the question of whether early bilingualism results in monolingual-like proficiency, the author conducted four experiments designed to compare monolinguals' and early bilinguals' performance in English tests tapping the phonetic, syntactic, and semantic components.

EXPERIMENTS

Subjects were 10 English monolinguals aged 18 to 27, and 10 French-English bilinguals, aged 19 to 32. At the time of testing, all subjects were, or had recently been, students at Brown University. The English monolinguals had had an average of 2 years of foreign language training and none spoke or understood any foreign language well. The bilinguals had all learned French and English before the age of 8 and all claimed to be fluent in both languages. The bilinguals' manner of L_2 acquisition varied - as did their dialectal and geographical backgrounds. (They had lived in France, Canada, Belgium, or Switzerland, as well as in the United States.)

To determine that the bilinguals were fluent in both French and English, they were administered a fairly detailed language-background questionnaire and a 13-question self-evaluation fluency questionnaire. They were also recorded reading an English and a French paragraph of approximately 150 words apiece and speaking extemporaneously in English and French in response to questions posed in English and French. Their English reading and speaking were judged by a trained linguist (not the experimenter) who rated the subjects' accent and fluency on a 10-point scale with a score of 10 being the best - i.e., the score which a native and monolingual speaker of English would be expected to receive. The bilinguals' average score for fluency in speaking was 9.5 while it was 10.0 for accent in speaking. Their average score for fluency in reading was 8.4 while it was 9.7 for accent in reading. The bilinguals' French reading and speaking were judged by three native and highly dominant speakers of French. All three judges had been raised in France and two still resided there. These judges used the same 10-point rating scale as the English judge did. Averages of their ratings were derived for each subject. The bilinguals' average score for fluency in speaking was 7.1 while it was 7.5 for accent in speaking. Their average score for fluency in reading was 6.3 while it was 7.0 for accent in reading. Overall, the bilinguals received higher scores in English than in French.

In addition to these scores, scores based upon the bilinguals' self-evaluation were tabulated. Results of this evaluation appear in Figure 1. The

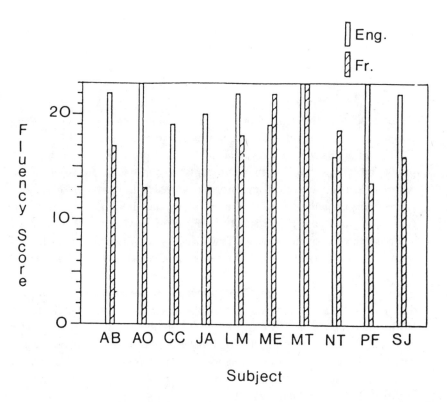

Fig. 1 The bilinguals' self-evaluation fluency scores in English and French. The maximum score attainable in either language was 23. Only one bilingual (MT) rated himself perfectly and equally fluent in both languages and only two (ME and NT) rated themselves as more fluent in French than in English.

165

maximum number of points any subject could receive in either language was 23. Only one subject (MT) considered himself equally and completely fluent in both French and English and only two subjects (ME and NT) considered themselves somewhat more fluent in French than in English.

As is apparent, the judges' ratings and the bilinguals' self-evaluation fluency scores revealed that, in general, the bilinguals were more fluent in English than in French. To this extent, the experiments were biased in favor of the bilinguals' English: Based upon their high ratings in English and their consistently lower ratings in French, it was considered possible that they would prove indistinguishable from the English monolinguals in their performance on a variety of psycholinguistic tests in English.

Experiment I was a phonetics experiment consisting of production and perception tests involving voice-onset time - a phonetic feature which has been used in the analysis of acoustic correlates of accent (Caramazza et al., 1973; Obler, 1982; Williams, 1979). For it has been shown that voice-onset time (VOT) differs cross-linguistically (Lisker & Abramson, 1964). VOT is a temporal measure based upon the timing relation between consonant release and the onset of phonation. It is a highly salient, though not sole, cue for distinguishing the class of voiced and voiceless consonants in English. For example, the average VOT of a voiced stop consonant in English is about + 20 msec (it has a "short-lag" VOT) while the average VOT of a voiceless stop consonant in English is about + 70 msec (it has a "long-lag" VOT). In English, voiced consonants may also be prevoiced, in which case phonation begins prior to the release of the consonant. However, the difference between prevoiced and short-lag voiced consonants is allophonic rather than phonemic in English. On the other hand, in French, voiced stop consonants may be prevoiced or they may have very short VOTs, while voiceless stop consonants have VOTs which are somewhat longer but which are nonetheless still "short-lag" VOTs (Caramazza et al., 1973; Caramazza and Yeni-Komshian, 1974).

Moreover, it has been found that bilinguals whose two languages have different VOT distributions may produce, in at least one of their languages, VOTs intermediate in value to those of monolingual speakers of each language (Caramazza et al., 1973). Furthermore, bilinguals whose two languages have different VOT categories tend to perceive VOT differently from the way in which monolingual users of the two languages do (Caramazza et al., 1973; Williams, 1979).

Thus, it was believed possible that, in producing and/or perceiving VOT in English, the bilinguals in the present study might not perform like English monolinguals.

166

Subjects were recorded on high-quality equipment as they read 54 mono-syllabic CVC words twice. All words began with the alveolar stop /d/ or /t/ and had one of nine medial vowels. Subjects were also presented with two perception tapes (for discrimination and identification) of computer-synthesized and randomized syllables consisting of a /da-ta/ continuum with VOTs ranging from —60 msec to +90 msec in 10-msec increments. In the discrimination task, subjects were required to discriminate between two members of a pair whose VOTs differed by 20 msec while in the identification task they were required to label (identify) each stimulus they heard as /da/ or /ta/.

All utterances from the speech production task were transferred to a PDP 11/34 computer, and VOT measurements, with a computer accuracy of within .05 msec, were made from the waveform display. Results indicated that, in production, the monolinguals and bilinguals performed nearly identically. There was no significant difference in the number of prevoiced utterances they produced, and their prevoicing durations were similar. The average VOT for /d/ (excluding prevoicing) was +20.09 msec for the monolinguals and +21.45 msec for the bilinguals, while the average VOT for /t/ was +84.76 msec for the monolinguals and +80.62 msec for the bilinguals.

In their perception of VOT, the groups also performed nearly identically. In the discrimination task, both groups exhibited strong peaks on pairs having VOTs of 0 and +20 msec and VOTs of +10 and +30 msec. And in the identification task, there was no significant difference between the groups' crossover boundary between /da/ and /ta/.

Thus, in the production and perception of a specific consonantal feature, the bilinguals performed essentially identically to the monolinguals, suggesting that their early acquisition of French and English had not resulted in a difference in the production and perception of VOT in English.

Another experiment was conducted to evaluate the two groups' production and perception of the vowels /i/ and /I/. In English, these vowels are distinguished from one another by virtue of their formant frequencies, durations, an degree of diphthongization - with /i/ being more "acute," longer, and more diphthongized than /I/ (Heffner, 1950; Peterson & Barney, 1952; Peterson & Lehiste, 1960). In French, however, /i/ is more acute than it is in English, its duration may be shorter, and it is less diphthongized (Heffner, 1950; Delattre, 1964; O'Shaughnessy, 1981). Further, in at least some French dialects, the vowel /I/ is non-occurrent.

It is also known that vowel production is closely related to vowel identification such that the vowel categories used by a speaker structure the way

167

in which he or she labels vowels (Christensen et al., 1981; Stevens et al., 1969). Moreover, Garnes (1977) found that, in the identification of phonemic vowel duration, Icelandic-English bilinguals performed differently from Icelandic monolinguals. For the bilinguals, presumably due to the influence of their English, seemed to display greater uncertainty in their responses than did the Icelandic monolinguals.

Thus, it seemed possible that the French-English bilinguals might produce and/or perceive the vowels /i/ and /I/ differently from the English monolinguals due to differences in the acoustic correlates of the vowel /i/ in French and English and due to differences in the structure of the two vowel systems.

Subjects were recorded as they read 10 CVC words twice. All vowels were preceded by a consonant and were followed by /d/. Subjects were also presented with two perception tapes (for discrimination and identification) of computer-synthesized and randomized vowels in an /i-I/ continuum. The formant frequencies of the synthesized stimuli varied, although their overall durations did not.

All utterances from the speech production task were transferred to a PDP 11/34 computer, and the vowel formant frequencies (of F2), vowel durations, and degree of vowel diphthongization were measured and analyzed. Results indicated that no significant differences emerged between the two groups with respect to any of these three parameters. For example, the average duration of /i/ was 251.84 msec for the monolinguals and 244.33 msec for the bilinguals, while the average duration of /I/ was 175.25 msec for the monolinguals and 173.51 msec for the bilinguals. In their discrimination of the /i-I/ continuum, the two groups also performed nearly identically. This was not especially surprising, given that other researchers have found that language background seems to have little effect upon vowel discrimination (e.g., Stevens et al., 1969). However, the two groups did label the vowel continuum significantly differently. That is, the bilinguals identified significantly fewer stimuli as /i/ than the monolinguals did. Such a result points to the effect of French upon the bilinguals' English vowel system. For, based upon what is known about the acoustic properties associated with the French /i/, it would be predicted that, for a monolingual speaker of French, only the most acute of the vowel stimuli (i.e., only those vowels at the /i/ end of the continuum) would be labelled as acceptable exemplars of /i/. Thus, it appears that, with respect to their identification of the vowels /i/ and /I/, the bilinguals' evinced effects of their knowledge of the French vowel system.[1]

1. It is reasonable to ask why interference emerged in the bilinguals' perception of vowels but

A third experiment was designed to assess speed and accuracy of grammaticality judgments in a reaction-time test of syntactic processing. It is well known that grammatical sentences are recalled and recognized more accurately than ungrammatical ones (Marks & Miller, 1964; Miller & Isard, 1963; Slamecka, 1969).

Yet little research has been conducted to assess this finding in view of bilingual linguistic performance. Nonetheless, a recent study by Blair and Harris (1981) does suggest that monolinguals and bilinguals do respond differently to grammatical and ungrammatical sentences - at least when the ungrammatical sentences contain structures literally translated from one of the bilinguals' languages. In their comparative study of English monolinguals and Spanish-English bilinguals, these researchers found that English monolinguals responded significantly slower to sentences containing literal translations of Spanish phrases than they did to normal English sentences; however, the bilinguals did not respond significantly slower to such sentences. Blair and Harris attributed this finding to "some form of interlingual interaction" (p. 466) in the bilinguals' comprehension of English.

Thus, the present experiment was conducted to determine whether the English monolinguals and French-English bilinguals would exhibit the same pattern of RTs and/or the same number of errors in response to these sentence types.

There was a total of 60 sentences, half of which were grammatical and half of which were not. Sentences were of three types: grammatical in English (e.g., "Almost all the reports were good"), ungrammatical in English due to scrambled word order (e.g., "Most of the funny are stories"), and ungrammatical in English due to the presence of a structure translated literally from French (e.g., "Nearly all the news were bad" [from "Presque

Footnote continued

> not consonants. This may have been due to the fact that vowels are processed somewhat differently from consonants. For example, steady-state vowels are perceived less categorically than consonants (Fry et al., 1962; Pisoni, 1973; Stevens et al., 1969); their discrimination is less affected by listeners' language background than is the discrimination of consonants (Stevens et al., 1969); and they are less strongly left-lateralized in tests of dichotic listening than consonants (Cutting, 1974; Shankweiler & Studdert-Kennedy, 1967).
>
> In addition to this sound-class distinction, there was a modality-dependent distinction. For, in their *production* of the vowels /i/ and /I/, the bilinguals performed almost identically to the monolinguals while in their *identification* of these vowels, they performed significantly differently. This may point to an inherent dichotomy between production and perception. Indeed, in analyzing VOT production and identification in the L_1 (French) of Canadian French-English bilinguals, Caramazza et al. (1973) found that the bilinguals' production of VOT in French was nearly identical to that of Canadian French monolinguals, but that their identification of VOT was not.

169

toutes les nouvelles étaient mauvaises"]). Computer-randomized sentences appeared one at a time on a video terminal screen, and subjects responded to each sentence by pressing one of two keys - a "yes" key if the sentence was grammatical and a "no" key if it was not.

Data analysis revealed that there was a marginally significant difference in the overall reaction times (RTs) for the two groups, with the monolinguals responding faster to all sentence types. The monolinguals' average RT for the grammatical (GR) sentences was 2.005 sec, while the bilinguals' was 2.253 sec; the monolinguals' average RT for the ungrammatical scrambled (SC) sentences was 1.761 sec, while the bilinguals' was 2.217 sec; and the monolinguals' average RT for the ungrammatical sentences with literally translated French structures (FR) was 1.812 sec, while the bilinguals' was 2.123 sec. A significant difference also emerged between the two groups in terms of their error rates - but only on the FR sentences. In response to these sentences, the bilinguals' error rate (18.67%) was over twice that of the monolinguals' (7.33%). In fact, in response to each of three FR sentences, three or four bilinguals erred while no monolinguals did. These sentences were the following: *"Explain me the meaning of this exercise"; *"She is used to jog every day"; and *"It has finally stopped to rain."

Results of this syntactic processing experiment suggest that the bilinguals' possession of French quite clearly affected their responses to English sentences, especially when those sentences were syntactically similar to sentences found in French.

A fourth experiment was designed to assess speed and accuracy of word-acceptability judgments in a lexical-decision test of semantic processing. It has been found that, if a real word (a prime word) is followed by a semantically related word (a target word), RTs for the target word are faster than if the target word is semantically unrelated to the prime word or if the target word is a nonsense word (Becker, 1980; Meyer & Schvaneveldt, 1971; Tweedy et al., 1977). For example, Becker (1980) found that the average RT for related pairs of words was 550 msec and for unrelated pairs, 630 msec.

In order to assess reaction-times among bilinguals, Mägiste (1979) conducted an experiment with Swedish-German bilinguals. She found that, in naming common objects and two-digit numbers, the bilinguals were consistently slower than Swedish monolinguals. She proposed that the bilinguals' slower RTs could be attributed to "an effect of interference of the competing language systems" (p. 87).

So a semantic (or, more properly, a lexico-semantic) experiment was conducted to determine whether the same pattern of RTs emerged among the monolinguals and bilinguals in their responses to various word-pair

170

types, and whether the same speed and accuracy of response did as well.

Stimuli consisted of 104 English word pairs, half of which had real-word targets and half of which did not. There were three word-pair types: real-word prime and related real-word target (RR); real-word prime and unrelated real-word target (RU); and real-word prime and nonsense-word target (RN). The nonsense words were orthographically and phonetically acceptable but nonoccurrent in English, and none was a real word in French. An example of each word-pair type is as follows: "dark"-"light" (RR), "moon"-"truck" (RU), "log"-"shome" (RN). All pairs were computer-randomized. Each prime word appeared on a video terminal screen for 500 msec. It then disappeared and, 500 msec later, the target word appeared. As in the syntax experiment, subjects responded "yes" or "no" by key press.

Results revealed that the bilinguals were significantly slower than the monolinguals in response to all three pair types. The monolinguals' average RT for the RR pairs was 570 msec, while the bilinguals' was 685 msec; the monolinguals' average RT for the RU pairs was 636 msec, while the bilinguals' was 775 msec; and the monolinguals' average RT for the RN pairs was 678 msec, while the bilinguals was 854 msec. As is apparent, the same pattern of facilitation held for both groups, with RTs for the RR pairs being the fastest and RTs for the RN pairs the slowest. There was no significant difference in the two groups' error rate for any of the word-pair types.

It would seem, then, that the bilinguals' possession of two lexico-semantic systems affected their ability to respond as rapidly as the monolinguals did to target words. A possible explanation for this finding is that in the course of accessing their English lexico-semantic system the bilinguals accessed their French as well.

DISCUSSION

Before discussing the relevance of the above findings to early bilingualism, it is necessary to clarify the concept "bilingual linguistic interference." It was assumed from the outset of these experiments that, if differences emerged between the performance of the English monolinguals and the French-English bilinguals, these differences could be attributed to the effect of linguistic interference - i.e., to the effect of the bilinguals' French upon their English, such that linguistic features or structures characteristic of French were manifested in the bilinguals' production, perception, or processing of linguistic features or structures characteristic of English. Such interference is here termed direct "intrusive" interference.

But there is another broader interpretation of bilingual linguistic interference. This interpretation is predicated upon the notion that a bilingual's linguistic system (in one or both of the languages) may be different from a monolingual's system because the bilingual has acquired two languages. Thus, interference in this sense is not directly attributable to the "intrusion" of aspects of one language on another; rather, it arises because one (or both) of the languages has been internalized differently by bilinguals than by monolinguals. It would be predicted that, in some tests of bilingual ability, intrusive interference may be apparent while, in others, the effect of two languages resulting in a differently internalized linguistic system may be apparent. As Makkai (1978) notes,

> On the morphophonemic level ... errors are frequently quite unrelated to any native language patterns, and are based instead on the imperfect learning of target language morphophonemic alternation patterns. Thus, 'he /duwz/' and 'he /seyz/' result from not having learned to make the proper morphophonemic transformations (p. 49).

This is viewed as the nonintrusive type of interference. For the problem here arises because the bilingual has two language systems and may attempt (especially in the early stages of second-language acquisition) to simplify the language being acquired.

Although the distinction between these two types of interference (intrusive and nonintrusive) is theoretically valid, it may be difficult to ascertain which is involved (or to what extent each one is involved) if bilinguals are found to perform differently from monolinguals in a given psycholinguistic test. For example, the French-English bilinguals' relatively high error rate on the FR sentences seems to point clearly to the presence of interference from French (i.e., the bilinguals may have inadvertently accessed their French syntactic component while attempting to access their English). Yet, it could also point to the presence of interference from their bilingualism - which interference has resulted in the internalization of an English grammar which is organized differently from that of English monolinguals. That is, the bilinguals might actually have, as part of their English grammar, rules generating (or permitting) such sentences as "Explain me the meaning of this exercise." Such a sentence - ungrammatical for monolingual speakers of English - might be especially likely to be part of the bilinguals' grammar since other apparently analogous phrases such as "tell me," "show me," and "read me" are acceptable in English and since the phrase "expliquez-moi" is perfectly acceptable in French.

To reiterate: It may not always be possible to determine which type of

172

interference is involved if bilinguals are found to differ from monolinguals. Nonetheless, it is believed that a distinction should be maintained between interference due to specific features or structures of a given language and interference due to bilingualism itself.

In response to the question raised in the introduction to this chapter ("Is the linguistic performance of fluent early bilinguals indistinguishable from that of monolinguals?"), the answer is no. It is obvious that, at least to some extent, the bilinguals responded significantly differently from the monolinguals to tests tapping the phonetic, syntactic, and semantic components.

It might be asked whether the finding of differences between the monolinguals' and bilinguals' English invalidates the notion of a critical period for second-language acquisition. For it could be argued that if the linguistic system of bilinguals who have acquired two languages well before puberty is not monolingual-like, then the concept of "perfect" bilingualism may be based upon a desired ideal, rather than upon a linguistic reality. However, it is believed that the results of the present study do not undermine the critical-period hypothesis. For there is a considerable body of evidence that early L_2 acquisition is a powerful facilitator of L_2 proficiency. Conclusions drawn from neurolinguistic studies should be kept in mind here as well. For when reports are made that the linguistic performance of brain-damaged children is potentially or actually superior to that of adults with comparable damage (e.g., Lenneberg, 1967), this is often interpreted as strong evidence of a critical period for language acquisition - even if the children are not able to perform, linguistically, exactly as normal children do. It seems only logical to extend such reasoning to the linguistic performance of the bilinguals in the present study. That is, the linguistic system of fluent early bilinguals may approximate the system of monolinguals, but it will not be indistinguishable from it.

To conclude, the four experiments conducted revealed systematic differences between a group of English monolinguals and a group of French-English bilinguals. These differences were attributed to the presence of linguistic interference in the English of the bilinguals - interference from their French and/or from their bilingualism. That these bilinguals did not perform essentially the same as the monolinguals did provide support for the notion that there is a valid and fundamental difference between the linguistic behavior of bilinguals and monolinguals. Such a difference may be an inevitable consequence of bilingualism. That is, it may emerge *regardless* of how young bilinguals are when they acquire their two languages or how fluent they ultimately become.

VISUAL, PHONETIC, AND SEMANTIC PROCESSING IN EARLY AND LATE BILINGUALS

Jyotsna Vaid

Psychological research on the repercussions of knowing more than one language has recently entered the domain of neuropsychology (see Galloway, 1983; Paradis, 1977, 1983; Vaid & Genesee, 1980; Vaid, 1982; for reviews). As in the cognitive literature, researchers in the neuropsychology of bilingualism are beginning to probe more closely the context of second-language acquisition, or what McLaughlin (this volume) terms "the conditions of presentation" of the two languages. In particular, the variable of age of second-language acquisition appears to influence language processing both cognitively and cortically.

Age of Second-Language Acquisition: Cognitive Studies
The cognitive literature on bilingualism has for the most part focused on childhood bilinguals as compared to their monolingual counterparts. It has been noted that early bilingualism confers certain cognitive advantages in mental flexibility, concept formation, and the like, which are not entirely attributable to such factors as IQ, social class, and degree of bilingualism, although these may modify the size of the advantage (Cummins & Gulutsan, 1974; Duncan & DeAvila, 1979; Peal & Lambert, 1962; see also McLaughlin, this volume).

Numerous studies have also reported distinct linguistic repercussions of childhood bilingualism, especially as regards an earlier dissociation of particular sound/meaning correspondences. That is, early exposure to two languages appears to accelerate awareness of the arbitrary relationship between sound and meaning (Ben-Zeev, 1977a, b; Cummins, 1978; Ianco-Worrall, 1972). This in turn may foster a more analytic approach to language structure, thereby leading to superior performance on sentence disambiguation tasks (Cummins & Mulcahy, 1978) or on word meaning generation (Balkan, 1970). According to Ben-Zeev (1977a), increased sensitivity to structural regularities of linguistic input among bilingual as compared to monolingual children develops as a way of coping with the task of mastering two separate linguistic systems.

Much of the emphasis of psychological studies on the cognitive repercussions of bilingualism has been on second-language acquisition in infancy or in early childhood. Yet it is of interest to ascertain whether the cognitive consequences of early bilingualism extend into adulthood, and whether second-language acquisition in early adulthood has repercussions of its own.

A body of literature that is relevant to an understanding of early/late bilingual differences in linguistic or cognitive functioning is the work of W. E. Lambert and colleagues in the 1950's and 1960's on compound and coordinate forms of bilingualism (Lambert, 1969). This distinction refers to differences in internal representation of word meanings in bilingual linguistic memory, a compound system being one in which words from the two languages are stored in a single system and a coordinate form of bilingualism being one in which the two languages have separate lexicons (see Ervin & Osgood, 1954; Weinreich, 1953). Compound bilingualism is thought to arise when both languages are learned simultaneously (i.e., in early bilingualism) and coordinate bilingualism is thought to characterize successive acquisition of the two languages (i.e., late onset of bilingualsm). Indeed, the criterion used for classifying bilinguals as compound or coordinate was age of onset of bilingualism. As such, Lambert's findings are of interest inasmuch as they indicate that age of language acquisition influences performance on verbal learning and verbal memory tests.

Age of Second-Language Acquisition: Neuropsychological Studies
Age may be an important factor influencing hemispheric specialization of language insofar as the maturational state of the brain differs during early versus late language acquisition. Similarly, differences in cognitive maturity associated with age may also contribute to differences in brain organization of early vs. late bilinguals.

By now there are over a dozen studies comparing cerebral lateralization of language in early and late bilinguals (see Vaid, 1983; Vaid & Lambert, 1979 for a review). In almost all of these studies, different patterns of hemispheric involvement have been noted for early as compared to late bilinguals, generally in the direction of greater right-hemisphere (RH) participation among late bilinguals, unless the second language of late bilinguals had been learned in a formal setting (Carroll, 1980).

Hemisphere differences are also determined by the particular linguistic requirements of a given task, as suggested by a recent study by Kotik (1981). Kotik observed that late Polish-Russian bilinguals showed faster neural responses in their RH on a task of language recognition, and, as such, performed similarly to the French-English late bilinguals studied by Genesee, Hamers, Lambert, Mononen, Seitz, and Starck (1978) on the same task. However, when the task called for judgments of word animacy, Kotik's subjects now showed faster neural responses in their left hemisphere (LH).

Neuropsychological research with monolinguals has now developed to the point where investigators are concerned with devising reliable ways of comparing hemispheric specialization for different types of linguistic judgments. The available clinical evidence suggests that phonological and syntactic judgments are primarily mediated by the left hemisphere, and that visuospatial or acoustic judgments may be mediated by the right hemisphere; semantic judgments may call on either of the two hemispheres, depending on whether the input is processed by recourse to a phonological recoding (see Zaidel, 1978).

THE PRESENT STUDY

In light of evidence indicating that early and late bilinguals differ in language functioning and that the two hemispheres differ in which aspects of language they primarily subserve, the aim of the present study was to assess bilingual subgroup differences in neuropsychological processing of various aspects of language. Specifically, the study examined the performance of early and late French-English bilinguals and monolingual controls on speeded word pair comparisons on the basis of orthographic, phonetic, and semantic criteria. The tasks involved judgments of rhyme (Experiments 1, 2), semantic category (Experiment 1), and synonymity (Experiment 3), within a tachistoscopic procedure.

With regard to visual field asymmetries, it was anticipated that orthographic judgments would differentially engage the RH while phonological judgments would be favored in the LH. Semantic judgments were expected to involve either of the two hemispheres.

With regard to bilingual subgroup differences, it was hypothesized that early bilinguals would be more inclined to adopt semantic response strategies. Late bilinguals were expected to be more responsive to surface properties of the input, as these properties are more salient markers of language of the input, and thus, would aid in keeping the two languages functionally segregated. Thus, whenever the preferred response strategy of a particular group (e.g., semantic, for early bilinguals) matched the optimal strategy for performing a particular task (e.g., synonym judgment), group differences in speed of response were expected. Whether group differences in task performance would interact with task differences in hemisphere performance was of particular interest.

GENERAL METHOD

Subjects

Subjects were paid volunteers from McGill University who responded to notices asking for fluent French/English bilinguals and English monolinguals. Bilinguals were subdivided according to when they had acquired proficiency in their second language. In each of the three experiments, one group consisted of bilinguals who had acquired both French and English before the age of 4 years. These subjects were considered "early" bilinguals. Another group comprised individuals who had become proficient in their second language after the age of 10 years. These subjects were considered "late" bilinguals. Half of the late bilinguals in each study spoke French as a first language while the remainder were native speakers of English. The third group consisted of English monolinguals who had had little if any exposure to another language. Within each group there were an equal number of males and females. A different set of subjects was used in each experiment.

All subjects reported normal or corrected-to-normal vision and were strongly right-handed, with a very low incidence of familial sinistrality. Handedness was assessed by a questionnaire adapted from Oldfield (1971) and Crovitz and Zener (1975). A detailed account of subjects' language acquisition histories and current language usage was also obtained. Fluency in their two languages was assessed in the bilinguals by the following measures: (1) self-ratings of the ability to speak, read, write, and understand each language, on a 7-point scale where 7 indicated native-like competence. Persons who did not rate themselves as at least 4 on three of the four measures were not included in any of the experiments. Bilinguals were also asked to compare their proficiency in their two languages for each of the language modalities on a 3-item scale where the items were "same as", "better than" or "worse than" the other language. To qualify for the experiment subjects were to have indicated "same as" for reading and general comprehension. (2) In addition to the self-rating information, most of the bilinguals were briefly interviewed over the phone or in person to gauge their oral fluency in the two languages. (3) A speeded reading measure adapted from the Stroop Color Naming Test (Stroop, 1935) was

178

also used to screen subjects on language fluency (see also Lambert, 1969). Bilinguals' speed of naming aloud in each language a random series of colored lines was measured. Colors used were blue, brown, red, and green, as both English and French terms are monosyllabic. As an additional check on pronunciation skills, only those subjects were used whose accent in each language, judged while they were engaged in color-naming, was native-like.

Apparatus

A Gerbrands three-channel tachistoscope was used to present the stimuli at a viewing distance of 57 cm. Responses were recorded in milliseconds (msecs) by a Hunter digital timer which was triggered upon presentation of the test stimulus and was deactivated by the subject's pressing of either of the two response keys.

Stimuli

In each experiment stimulus pairs were successively presented, the interval between the first and second member of the pair being approximately 1 second. The first word of a pair was always presented bilaterally and the second unilaterally.

Bilinguals were tested in both their languages in Experiments 1 and 3. In Experiment 2, a lack of sufficient French words that met the criteria for stimulus selection in that study made it necessary to use English stimuli only. Monolinguals in all three studies were only tested in English.

Test stimuli across languages were matched as closely as possible on such dimensions as number of letters, number of syllables, and frequency of occurrence in written text.

Procedure

A baseline reaction time measure was first administered, after which instructions for the experiment were presented, in either English or French, depending on the particular condition. For the bilinguals, order of presentation of English and French stimuli was counterbalanced such that half of the bilinguals per subgroup were tested in English first and the remainder were tested in French first.

Latency of response was recorded from the timer by a blind experimenter. Errors of commission (where the wrong key was pressed) and/or of omission (where no response was made or where response exceeded 2 seconds) were replaced, so that only accurate responses were entered into the RT data analysis.

179

Data Analysis
An analysis of variance was performed on the data. Separate analyses were conducted to compare, on the one hand, the performance of early and late bilinguals and monolinguals in English and, on the other, the performance of early and late bilinguals on each of their languages. Only the first of these analyses is reported here, in the interest of brevity, although results were generally comparable in the second analysis (see Vaid, 1981, for further details).

EXPERIMENT 1

Hemisphere differences in rhyme and semantic category matching
This experiment sought to compare patterns of visual field asymmetries in early and late bilinguals and monolingual controls on a task involving sensory and semantic processing. Subjects were to decide, as quickly as possible, whether successively presented words rhymed or were from a common semantic category (e.g., NOSE: ROSE/LEGS). Rhyme pairs were orthographically similar and same semantic category pairs were orthographically dissimilar. Thus, spelling provided a reliable cue for rhyme as well as for meaning responses.

To determine whether meaning pairs were encoded at a semantic rather than a surface level, an incidental free recall test was administered at the end of the experiment. Since semantic properties of words are believed to undergo more extensive processing than graphemic or phonemic properties (Craik & Lockhart, 1972), it was predicted that if rhyme and meaning stimuli in the present study were coded differently, meaning words would be better recalled than rhyme. By the same token, since word comparisons on the basis of visual and/or phonological criteria are faster than semantic comparisons (Cohen, 1968; Leiber, 1977), rhyme judgments were expected to be faster than judgments of semantic category.

With regard to hemisphere differences, a RVF superiority for semantic category matching was expected on the basis of evidence from laterality studies with monolinguals for LH specialization in this task (Eling, Marshall, & Van Galen, 1981; Gross, 1972; Urcuioli, Klein, & Day, 1981). Rhyme judgments in the present study were expected to be facilitated by orthographic similarity of the rhyme pairs. To the extent that rhyme decisions were visually mediated, a LVF superiority was expected on the basis of evidence for RH participation in visual comparisons of letter or word pairs (Cohen, 1972; Gibson et al., 1972).

180

It was further expected that early bilinguals would show better recall of meaning than rhyme words as compared to late bilinguals if, as hypothesized earlier, early bilinguals are more predisposed towards semantic components of linguistic input. Similarly, late bilinguals were expected to be generally faster given that they would be more inclined to process rhyme *and* meaning words on a surface level, which would yield overall shorter response latencies.

METHOD

Subjects
A total of 48 university students participated in the experiment. There were 16 early bilinguals (mean age of 21.1 yrs), 16 late bilinguals (mean age of 22.3 yrs) and 16 monolinguals (mean age of 22.5 yrs).

Stimuli
Stimuli were 24 English and 24 French high frequency, monosyllabic words selected from Eaton's (1940) word frequency count. Per language, 8 words were designated as target words and were each paired with a rhyming and a same semantic category item. A nonrhyming, semantically unrelated word (FIRE and FEU) was also paired with each of the target words. Six additional words per language served as practice items. Four of the same category pairs per language referred to the category of body parts (e.g., NOSE/LEGS; DENT/OEIL) while the remaining four pairs referred to miscellaneous categories. All rhyme pairs were orthographically identical except in the initial letter. Test stimuli were presented at a visual angle of 2° to the left or right of center.

Procedure
On each trial, subjects were first shown a target word, in free vision, followed by the central fixation digit shown in the tachistoscope. Immediately upon offset of the fixation field, a test item was flashed in either the right or left visual field at a constant exposure duration of 120 msecs. Subjects were to decide as quickly as possible whether the test word rhymed with the target word or whether the two words were from the same semantic category. In cases where the stimulus neither rhymed nor was semantically related, subjects were to refrain from responding. Each test word was presented twice per visual field in a fixed, random sequence.

Immediately following the experiment, an incidental free recall test was

181

administered in which subjects were asked to write down as many of the test and/or target words as they could remember. They were allowed as much time as they needed.

RESULTS

A 3x2x2x2 way analysis of variance with repeated measures on subjects was performed on the mean response latencies for English stimuli. The factors were group (early vs. late bilingual vs. monolingual), sex (male vs. female), visual field (right vs. left) and response type (rhyme vs. nonrhyme), respectively. As no significant sex differences were obtained, this factor was removed from the analysis.

The results revealed significant main effects for all three remaining factors. The group effect, $F(2,45) = 3.38, p < .05$, indicated that mean response time of late bilinguals (718 msecs) was faster than that of monolinguals (873 msecs) but not early bilinguals (807 msecs); Tukey's $hsd = 146$, $p < .05$. Monolinguals and early bilinguals did not differ from one another. See Figure 1. The main effect of visual field, $F(1,45) = 6.01, p < .05$, indicated that words presented in the LVF were recognized faster than those

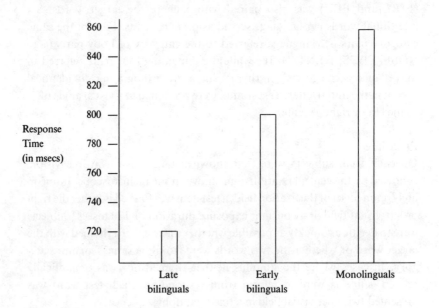

Figure 1. Group differences in overall response time in Experiment 1.

182

shown in the RVF (mean RTs were 787 and 811 msecs, respectively). Finally, mean responses to rhyme (762 msecs) were significantly faster than those to same semantic category (836 msecs); $F(1,45) = 25.65, p < .01$.

Analysis of Recall Scores

An analysis of variance as a function of group (early vs. late bilingual vs. monolingual), sex (male vs. female), and response type (rhyme vs. meaning) was performed on the percentage of rhyme and meaning test words recalled by each subject. For bilinguals, this value was obtained by collapsing across language of the stimulus. A main effect of sex was found, $F(1,42) = 6.86$, $p < .05$, whereby females showed a higher level of recall than males (55.5% vs. 44.9%, respectively). Moreover, recall was generally higher for meaning (57.7%) than for rhyme words (43.49%); $F(1,42) = 22.83, p < .01$.

Although the group by response type interaction did not reach significance, an analysis of the number of subjects per group who recalled more meaning than rhyme words revealed group differences. A significant majority (81.2%) of early bilinguals recalled more meaning than rhyme words, $\chi^2(1) = 6.25, p < .05$, as compared to a nonsignificant percentage of late bilinguals (68.8%) and monolinguals (50%).

DISCUSSION

The finding that semantic pairs yielded longer response times but better recall than rhyme pairs indicates that meaning words were processed more thoroughly, or more "deeply" than rhyme words (Craik & Lockhart, 1972). This finding appears to have characterized early bilinguals more so than the other two groups, who showed greater variability in their processing of rhyme and meaning. Thus, a superior recall of meaning versus rhyme words was most consistently observed in early bilinguals. Moreover, late bilinguals were faster than monolinguals, who did not differ in their speed of response from early bilinguals. These results support the hypothesis that late bilinguals are more inclined to process input at a surface level.

The finding of a LVF superiority for rhyme judgments is consonant with previous laterality studies that report a LVF superiority in the matching of visually identical word pairs (Gibson et al., 1972; Levy & Trevarthen, 1977). It would appear that orthographic criteria were instrumental in mediating rhyme decisions in the present experiment. However, simultaneous phonological matching of the words cannot be ruled out. A more controlled examination of the phonological and orthographic components of rhyme

183

judgments is undertaken in Experiment 2, to follow.

Contrary to expectation, a RVF superiority was not obtained for semantic category matching. The greater difficulty of the semantic task as compared to the rhyme task, given that in the semantic task the subject had first to generate two superordinate categories and then compare them while in the rhyme task only a matching process was necessary, may be one explanation for the results. However, it is not a satisfactory explanation, for greater task difficulty might at most result in overall slower response latencies, and not, as was observed, in a LVF advantage.

Alternatively, RH participation in semantic category judgments in the present experiment could simply reflect a visual matching strategy, inasmuch as "same category" pairs were always spelled differently, while "different category" (or rhyme) pairs were always spelled similarly. To the extent that RH involvement in the rhyme task was interpreted to reflect the use of visual matching, RH involvement in the meaning task might be similarly interpreted. The fact that all word pairs were highly concrete, and were visually presented may have contributed to the use of a visual strategy for response. According to this interpretation, one could attribute the observed superior recall of meaning as compared to rhyme words to semantic processing *following* a given response. Experiment 3 was undertaken to sort out the possible contributions of the above mentioned factors.

EXPERIMENT 2

Hemisphere Differences in Rhyme Monitoring

Whereas the rhyme task in the previous experiment was designed so as to encourage reliance on orthographic cues, rhyme judgments could still, or in addition, have been based on phonological properties of the words. In Experiment 1, there was no way of ascertaining which criteria – orthographic, phonological, or some combination of the two – had actually been used to arrive at decisions about rhyme, and, thus, what the observed patterns of hemispheric asymmetries reflected. The present rhyme experiment was designed so as to discourage reliance on orthography. In this study nonrhyme as well as rhyme pairs were similarly spelled (e.g., LINT-MINT, PINT). Thus, unlike Experiment 1 where it was optional, phonological matching in the present study was mandatory. Moreover, the extent to which individuals might, nevertheless, make use of orthography to mediate rhyme judgments could be assessed through their error scores, since reliance on orthography would result in a greater number of false positive errors (that is, responding "rhyme" to nonrhyming though orthographically similar words).

The design of the present study requires that the words be phonologically recoded and lexically accessed before decisions about rhyme can be made. Lexical access is necessary in order to decide whether the phonological rendition of the test word (e.g. PINT as/pInt/) to match the target word (/mInt/) is in fact a word in the lexicon. A LH superiority was therefore expected in the present study, in light of similar findings in the clinical (Zaidel, 1978) and experimental literature (Barry, 1981).

Group differences in proclivity to process semantic vs. surface properties of input were also expected in the form of more errors made by late than by early bilinguals. Late bilinguals might be more misled by orthographic cues inasmuch as late bilinguals might be less likely to go through lexical search to verify whether their test word in fact had an entry in the lexicon.

METHOD

Subjects
Subjects included 8 early bilinguals (mean age of 19.9 yrs.), 8 late bilinguals (mean age of 21.4 yrs.) and 16 monolinguals (mean age of 24.2 yrs.).

Stimuli
Stimuli consisted of 24 monosyllabic English words adapted from Meyer, Schvaneveldt, and Ruddy (1974). As in Experiment 1, stimuli included a set of target items paired with rhyming and nonrhyming test items. Unlike Experiment 1, rhyme *and* nonrhyme pairs were similar in spelling, but were not related semantically.

Stimuli were prepared from 28-point white Letraset capitals and were positioned vertically on black Mayfair cards to eliminate possible reading scan biases arising from horizontal presentation (White, 1973). Target words were centered on the cards whereas test words were displaced at a visual angle of 2.2° to the left or right of center.

Procedure
The procedure was the same as that used in Experiment 1 with the exception that stimulus exposure duration was reduced from 120 to 80 msecs since a larger Letraset size was used in Experiment 2 as compared to that in Experiment 1.

Preliminary analysis revealed no significant sex differences. The data were reanalyzed with sex removed as a factor, the remaining factors being group (early vs. late bilingual vs. monolingual), visual field (right vs. left) and response type (rhyme vs. nonrhyme).

A main effect of response type, $F(1,29) = 39.3, p < .01$, indicated faster responses to rhyming than nonrhyming pairs on the order of 118 msecs. An interaction of visual field by response type, $F(1,29) = 13.86, p < .01$, revealed that the rhyme/nonrhyme difference was larger in the RVF than in the LVF and that rhyme words in the RVF were recognized significantly faster than those in the LVF, $F(1,51) = 9.07, p < .01$. See Table 1.

Table 1

Mean Performance (in msecs) in Experiment 2
as a Function of Visual Field and Response Type

	Response Type	
Visual Field	Rhyme	Nonrhyme
Right	760	927
Left	819	890

Commission Errors

A comparison of bilinguals and monolinguals using the Wilcoxon matched pairs signed rank test indicated that bilinguals had a significantly higher error rate than monolinguals (12% vs. 8%, respectively); $T(16) = -5$, $p < .01$.

A three-way analysis of variance was performed on the bilinguals' error scores as a function of group (early vs. late), visual field (right vs. left) and stimulus type (rhyme vs. nonrhyme). A main effect of stimulus type, $F(1,14) = 6.67, p < .05$, indicated that the majority of errors were of the false positive variety. Moreover, late bilinguals made more errors than early bilinguals, $F(1,14) = 7.15, p < .05$. A group by visual field interaction, $F(1,14) = 5.96, p < .05$, further revealed that more errors were made by late than by early bilinguals for words shown in the LVF especially (2.4 vs. 0.6 errors, respectively); $F(1,21) = 22.4, p < .01$.

The results indicate that when rhyme decisions require phonological matching they are mediated by the LH in all individuals. However, group differences were present in the extent to which rhyme decisions were based on the words' spelling: late bilinguals were more susceptible to interference produced by orthographic similarity, as compared to early bilinguals. This was especially evident for words presented in the LVF. When input is directed to the RH, decisions about rhyme cannot be based on phonological characteristics; at the same time, the words' visual characteristics alone do not provide sufficient cues for response. Successful response on the task requires a lexical search to verify if the candidate item is a valid word or not. The fact that early bilinguals were better able to resist the misleading influence of the words' orthography suggests that they were more likely than late bilinguals to process the words at a further level than simply on the basis of their orthographic characteristics.

EXPERIMENT 3

Hemisphere Differences in Synonym Recognition

This experiment examined hemisphere asymmetries in semantic processing under different conditions than those characterizing Experiment 1 in order to assess the generalizability of the findings obtained in that experiment. First, while stimuli in Experiment 1 were concrete words, those in the present experiment were abstract, although otherwise comparable in frequency of use. Secondly, RH involvement in semantic category judgments in Experiment 1 could have arisen because of orthographic regularities of the input predisposing a visual matching strategy. To minimize visual cues in the present experiment, word pairs were not orthographically matched and the first word of each pair was spoken rather than presented visually. Finally, to make the semantic task more comparable to the rhyme task in terms of processing effort, a synonym judgments task was used instead of a semantic category matching task.

If the nature of the stimuli (concrete vs. abstract) or the nature of the modality of the target word (visual vs. auditory) influenced the laterality effects observed for the semantic task in Experiment 1, then in the present study one would expect a different laterality effect for semantic judgments, namely, a RVF superiority. However, if the nature of the linguistic processing (semantic) is an important determinant of hemisphere differences,

187

then one should find evidence for bilateral hemispheric involvement, as found in other studies using similar semantic tasks (Dennis, 1980).

Whatever the outcome with respect to visual field asymmetries, early bilinguals should be faster than late bilinguals in making synonym judgments if, as previously hypothesized, they are more readily inclined to adopt a semantic response strategy.

METHOD

Subject
Subjects included 8 early bilinguals (mean age of 23 yrs.), 8 late bilinguals (mean age of 25.7 yrs.) and 8 monolinguals (mean age of 23.3 yrs.).

Stimuli
A total of 48 abstract, high frequency English nouns were selected from Toglia and Battig's (1978) *Handbook of Semantic Word Norms.* Of these, 24 words served as the English stimuli and French equivalents of the other 24 served as the French stimuli. In each language, stimuli were grouped into 12 triads consisting of a target word (e.g., OBLIGATION), its synonym (i.e., DUTY) and a nonsynonym (e.g., TRADE). Each nonsynonym was itself a synonym for another target word (e.g., COMMERCE). Moreover, the nonsynonym associated with COMMERCE was used as a synonym for the target word OBLIGATION (i.e., DUTY).

Target words were presented auditorily. Test words were positioned vertically on grey cards using 28-point black Letraset capitals and were displaced 2.24° to the left or right of center.

Procedure
While subjects fixated on center, they heard the target word which was followed by a test word presented in either visual field for a constant exposure duration of 100 msecs. Subjects were to press a particular response key with the index finger of one hand if the two words were synonyms and another key with the other hand if the words were not synonyms. Each of the 12 test stimuli was presented twice per visual field – once as a synonym and once as a nonsynonym of the target word – yielding a total of 48 trials per language.

As no significant sex differences were found in a preliminary analysis, the data were reanalyzed removing the factor of sex. The remaining factors were group (early vs. late bilingual vs. monolingual), visual field (right vs. left), and response type (synonym vs. nonsynonym).

A significant main effect of group, $F(2,21) = 5.16, p < .05$, was obtained. Mean RT's of monolinguals, early bilinguals and late bilinguals were 754, 898 and 951 msecs., respectively. Post hoc comparisons revealed that the only significant difference was between monolinguals and late bilinguals, Tukey's $hsd = 160, p < .05$. See Figure 2. A main-effect-of-response type,

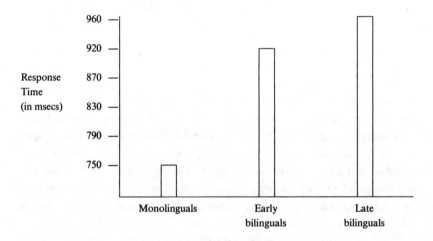

Figure 2. Group differences in overall response time in Experiment 2.

$F(1,21) = 39.04, p < .01$, revealed that synonyms were identified faster than nonsynonyms (812 vs. 923 msecs., respectively). A group-by-visual-field interaction approached significance, $F(2,21) = 3.364, p < .054$. Interaction breakdown revealed a significant LVF superiority among early bilinguals, $F(1,21) = 5.74, p < .05$; no significant visual field differences were obtained among late bilinguals and monolinguals. Moreover, while monolinguals were faster than late bilinguals in both visual fields, early bilinguals were significantly faster than late bilinguals in the LVF only, $F(2,24) = 8.52$, $p < .01$. See Table 3.

Table 3

Mean Performance (in msecs) in Experiment 3 as a Function of Group and Visual Field

| | Visual Field | |
Group	Right	Left
Early bilinguals	927	869
Late bilinguals	944	957
Monolinguals	743	766

DISCUSSION

As expected, early bilinguals were faster than late bilinguals in matching words on the basis of synonymity. Furthermore, despite the fact that stimuli were abstract and target words were auditorily presented, evidence for bilateral hemispheric involvement was obtained, consistent with findings in the monolingual literature (Marcel & Patterson, 1978; Martin, 1978). Finally, a group-by-visual-field interaction indicated that the faster responses of early bilinguals as compared to late bilinguals were especially prominent for words presented in the left visual field. It would appear that early bilinguals are not only more skilled at making semantic discriminations, but that they are especially skilled when the input is initially directed to the right hemisphere. Late bilinguals and monolinguals, on the other hand, partake of both hemispheres in making semantic judgments.

CONCLUSIONS

The evidence presented in these experiments suggests that differences in cerebral lateralization of language among early and late bilinguals and monolinguals primarily reflect task-related processing demands. Where group differences in lateralization occur, these may reflect differences in choice of response strategy (where the task allows for a choice) or differences in speed of response.

Furthermore, it would appear that early onset of bilingualism predisposes a semantic mode of processing linguistic input while late onset of bilingualism induces a greater sensitivity to surface features of the input.

190

The relative salience of meaning for early bilinguals may have arisen from their early exposure to different forms conveying a single referent. The relative salience of surface features for late bilinguals may in turn have developed as a byproduct of a tendency to keep their two languages apart; surface features of language, being better markers of language-of-input, may thus be more readily processed than semantic features. Monolinguals, like early bilinguals, tend to process for meaning; however, like late bilinguals, they are bound to particular sound/meaning correspondences.

At the neuropsychological level, differences among the groups may be hypothesized with respect to the manner in which semantic information is accessed: early bilinguals may tend to access meaning directly from the visual representation while late bilinguals and monolinguals may engage in phonological recoding to a greater extent. Thus, when the task calls for phonological processing, a RVF superiority was found in all groups; however, semantic processing gave rise to individual differences in visual field preferences.

It remains for further cognitively oriented research on bilingualism to document and explore the implications of the above findings for early vs. late bilingual differences in reading processes.

THE DEVELOPMENT OF THE BODY PERCEPT AMONG WORKING- AND MIDDLE-CLASS UNILINGUALS AND BILINGUALS*

Bruce Bain and Agnes Yu

Based on a cursory history, it would be understandable if a neophyte student of bilingualism were to get a feeling of *plus ça change, plus c'est la même chose.* The pre-WWII literature was rather clear in its conclusions: learning a second (preferably classical) language for reasons of *Haute Culture* was desirable, indeed the defining characteristic of upper-class pretentions to intellectualism; while learning an everyday *lingua communis* for reasons of economic survival by working-class immigrants resulted (in the language of those times) in deformed intellect and character. As the upper classes faded into history, the middle classes inherited their prejudices about language purity, and their preferences for learning them in reified institutions. The working classes were still to learn their languages in the streets. By the 60's and 70's the conclusions were again clear: in countries like Canada where it is mandated that preferred incumbents of senior civil service positions shall be bilingual, it was (perhaps not coincidentally) found (via the St. Lambert project and its imitators) that middle-class children with adequate mother-tongue development (in one official language) could comfortably become bilingual through immersion in school (in the other official language). The street-school arena of the working-class immigrants still hadn't changed, but now, they were told, their heritage languages were to be treated with "sympathetic understanding."

As far as this overview of some trends in bilingual studies goes it is not without credibility. The problem with it, however, is that it is based on

* This research was supported by Grant Nos.: W70454 & S761001 from the Canada Council; 5527072, 451780504, 45278080 & 452792153 from the Social Science and Humanities Research Council of Canada; 5532525 from the University of Alberta. Sincere appreciation for various assistances is acknowledged to R. Bauer, A. M. Fantino, M. & L. Frison, G. Grube, E. & S. Jonas, A. Salviani, E. Spadafora, Gerold Zaner, and especially R. Haymond.

remarkably few empirical studies of a cross-cultural nature. A major problem in this field of inquiry is the dearth of studies conducted cross-nation, cross-social class, cross-language within a unified methodology. Researchers concerned with the cognitive consequences of bilingualism have been particularly lax in this regard. Much cognitive-type research has been conducted in parochial, socio-economically biased contexts using test materials that were equally biased. A favorite procedure has been to compare local bilingual and unilingual subjects, of the same social (usually middle) class, on standardized tests or local school materials, and to assume or even suggest that the findings were generalizable cross-class, cross-nation, etc. Another popular procedure has been to survey these studies and, without always noting their parochial nature, to draw universal conclusions. There is no doubt that important insights can accrue from well-conducted local research (e.g., Rondal, 1973) and from critical literature reviews (e.g., Paulston, 1975). But, in addition to the arguments about the epistemological and social limitations of local studies and literature reviews (see Dittmar, 1976), there remains our feeling that a comprehensive, cross-cultural study is the most fruitful way of distinguishing etic from emic phenomena. With the aim of clarifying or at least qualifying some of the findings in (cognitive aspects of) bilingual studies, our general purpose was to conduct the necessary unified study using test materials that had some measurable claim to being class and culture fair.

It should be made clear that it is not our intention to critically address the myriad theoretical, political, and ideological conflicts which criss-cross the field of bilingual studies. For example, the conflict of theory, practice, and purpose between (certain) social scientists and (other) educators is legendary (see Skutnabb-Kangas & Toukomaa, 1976). The conflict concerns those social scientists who recognize the complete integration of all semiotic means with the individual's objectively real social context versus those educators who recognize the individual's need to master the language of the school to meet the demands of a standardized curriculum. Resolving these contradictions necessitates a historical critique along lines suggested by Habermas (1979), Hymes (1982), and Apple (1982). The warp and woof of national politics, economic power relations, school curriculum, and research findings requires a similar critique. We do not, at this time, intend to address these critiques. Rather, it is the recognition of their importance which makes it imperative that comprehensive, unified studies be conducted. A prior condition for a critical analysis of these vital social contradictions is sound, trans-national data on ego or individual development under similar social constraints.

194

Toward this end, our empirical goal was to study the development of the body percept (as a substantive measure of central determinants in individual cognition), in relation to middle-class bilingualism and working-class immigrant bilingualism, with appropriate unilingual comparison groups in Italy, (The Federal Republic of) Germany, and Canada. Our theoretical goal was to further the understanding of the traditional problem of the individual, language, and society.

Sociogenesis of the body percept

The notion that the body percept (referred to variously as body schema, corporeal image, self-concept, etc.) is a self-contained concept, independent of a person's socio-historical environment, and measurable through pencil and paper tests of "self-image", is not the object of this study. Those approaches are *pars pro toto;* they assume a static, Descartean ego blissfully unrelated to the surrounding world. Those specious notions are adequately dealt with by Giorgi (1970).

The view of the body percept adopted in this study stems from the philosophical works of Merleau-Ponty (1962) and the psychological works of Wapner and Werner (1965). Their view is that a theory of the body *is* a theory of perception. This is to say, that object perception and self-perception are not mutually exclusive; that the body percept is not reducible to the perception of the body; that in perceiving the world the body perceives itself, and the conditions of this self-perception, general or individual, are in a dialectic interchange with the world. This dynamic reciprocity between object perception and the perceiving self are described by Merleau-Ponty:

> There is consciousness in the body *itself*. In my touching I am aware of my touching, otherwise how could I adapt the movement of my hand to the thing I am going to touch... Similarly we can see things because we move our eyes in the right way, the movement of our eyes conditions our vision. (This is crucial) we do not adjust our hand, move our eyes or adapt any part of our body in light of our ideas... Our body moves its hands, eyes, etc., in the right way in a dialectical interchange with the things it is going to touch, to see, etc. ... (This is to say) the consciousness I have of my body is not the consciousness of an isolated mass, it is a body schema. It is the perception of my body's position in relation to the vertical, the horizontal, the haptic, the visual, and the other axes of its world (1962, p. 117).

The ontogenesis of the body percept in relation to the various "axes of its world" is a particular concern of Wapner and Werner (1965, *et passim*). They studied the developmental differentiation of body and world through experimentally controlled estimations of verticality as a function of: (1) modification of the position of the body itself, i.e., tilting chair studies; (2) modification of visual perceptual indices and of external reference systems,

195

i.e., rod-and-frame studies; (3) modification of both at the same time, i.e., tilting chair and rod-and-frame studies. Unlike earlier studies of perception which were not usually concerned with more than judgements about what was seen, the Wapner and Werner studies demanded a physical involvement while exploring perceptual functions. Moreover the results were not dependent on "conversations about one's self" or on inferences from nonbody perception. A well-documented conclusion of the Wapner and Werner studies is that measurements of the body percept are powerful guiding categories for analysis of pertinent changes in ontogenesis (Stone & Church, 1980). The centrality of these measures for understanding personality (Witkin et al., 1954), pathology (Critchley, 1957) ego dynamics, psychosomatic disorders, psychoses (Fisher & Cleveland, 1958) led Wapner and Werner to reaffirm:

> ...that there is no perception of objects "out there" without a frame of reference, and
> conversely, there can be no perception of the body-as-object without an environmental
> frame of reference. In all cases the variability or stability of the psycho-biological unit
> "body:world" reflects itself in body perception as well as object perception (1965, p. 10).

There are two lacunae in body percept research to date, one theoretical, one empirical. The theoretical necessity is to envision the development of the body percept in a sociogenetic context (cf., Vygotsky, 1978). The empirical necessity is to analyze the changes in the ontogenesis of the body percept as a function of particular social/educational/language experiences. Significant theoretical work has already begun by Titone (1982, et passim). Titone's purpose, like ours, is to get closer to the problem of the individual, language, and society. The starting point of his analysis is Nuttin's (1968) "relational theory of personality". Personality is, for Nuttin, an oscillation between two poles, the ego and the world, in which the ego is not only internally structured, but is schematically dependent on the lived world (physical, social, historical). Thus the world of people, objects, and intentions is not only situated in front of the ego, but constitutes the very content of individual psychological life. Titone's crucial contribution to Nuttin's theory (as it is also to Merleau-Ponty's, and Wapner & Werner's) is the recognition of the role of language in these dynamics. Titone insists, along with Bruner, Oliver, and Greenfield (1967), Luria (1976), and Bain and Yu (1980), that perception is a complex cognitive activity involving the intimate participation of language. He states:

> ...that language as communication and expression is the very marrow of personality...
> furthermore, first language acquisition and second language learning each represent a
> particular mode of existence: a definite way of self-assertion in front of the world – a
> symbolic act of recognition of the Existant (Titone, 1982, p. 8).

196

A theoretical extension of the views of Merleau-Ponty, and Wapner and Werner by way of Titone is to suggest, first, that the body percept is basically a product of objective historical and cultural conditions; second, that language as it reflects the world of the Existant effects pertinent changes in the course of development of the body percept.

The empirical necessity is to test relevant hypotheses in the field of bilingual studies guided by the proposed theoretical model. As stated above, to our knowledge, such a venture has not been tried in the past. Witkin et al. (1954), Wober (1969), Dawson (1973), Yu (1981) and others have done extensive work in the cross-cultural study of cognitive style. Cognitive style is a related aspect of the general issue of psychological differentiation. Unlike our own theoretical model, however, cognitive style studies tend to eschew notions about language as part of that complex of central determinants. We have nonetheless drawn heavily on this cross-cultural research tradition, especially from Berry (1976), in the formulation of the research questions and methodology.

Summary

Reliable information about cognitive comparisons of bilinguals and unilinguals have suffered from: the need to integrate these studies with the general problem of the individual, language, and society; the need for unified, trans-national studies; the need for more basic, less biased measures of cognitive consequences of first- and second-language experience. Titone's appreciation of the sociogenesis of the body percept, coupled with a standard methodology from cross-cultural psychology, was suggested as a way of meeting these needs. If we are even modestly successful in providing the desired information, there is the hopeful prospect of getting some further closure on the problem of language, and providing direction toward resolving the ideological conflicts that confound bilingual studies.

The worlds of the existants: social-educational climates

In Canada and West Germany the reason for the presence of working-class immigrant labourers is, in Galbraith's phrase (1978, p. 10) "to turn the wheels of the economies of these industrialized nations". Canada and West Germany differ in one significant respect, however: in Canada these labourers are *immigrants;* in West Germany they are *guest workers (Gastarbeiter).* This one fact – in Canada in due course the immigrants can become citizens, whereas in West Germany when "the wheels of industry turn too slowly" the migrants are sent home – gives the Canadian immigrant something to hope for in the future. This hope undoubtedly influences long-term aspira-

197

tions, but in the short-term, the social/economic/educational world of Canadian and West German immigrant workers is characteristically impoverished (on Canada, see, Case, 1977; on West Germany, see Dittmar et al., 1978). This "culture of the immigrant" is also coloured by a love/hate, crude assimilationist/social rejection ambivalence which reigns undisturbed from previous eras (on Canada, see Kallen, 1982; on West Germany, see Böhning, 1972). With regard to the pupil populations of this study, the relationship between economic-structural conditions and education policy bear many similarities. In Canada and West Germany educational policy is tempered by economic – not humanistic – goals. Although of different historical origins, both countries have adopted similar, class-based policies toward bilingual education.

There are a number of systematized ways of classifying types of bilingualism (cf., Fishman, 1967; McLaughlin, 1978). The immediate concern is with only two types: middle-class élite bilingualism (MCEB); and, working-class immigrant bilingualism (WCIB). The social-educational climate, or, lived worlds of MCEB and WCIB pupils are well delineated (Greenfield, 1976; Paulston, 1975; Yu & Bain, 1980). MCEB programmes are immersion programmes *de facto* and *de jure*. Into these programmes, socially established parents voluntarily chose to send their children to be educated through the medium of a (particular) foreign language. WCIB programmes are *"in fact"* immersion programmes, albeit claiming to be foreign-language training programmes comparable to those established for the middle-class. Into these latter programmes, socially unsettled immigrant parents, with no choice as to the language of instruction, send their children to be educated in the *lingua communis* of the host country. MCEB programmes stress curriculum subjects, with the foreign language (which the teacher simply expects the pupils to acquire) used as the medium of communication and expression. WCIB programmes stress the linguistic features of the foreign language as an end in itself (not as a means to communicate and learn curriculum subjects). The majority of the MCEB formal school day is conducted in the foreign language, but, for obvious social and pedagogical reasons, the mother-tongue is taught as a curriculum subject for a period of the day. The totality of the WCIB formal school day is conducted in the foreign language; (the social and pedagogical reasons for not including their mother-tongue as curriculum subjects can only be surmized). MCEB teachers are usually bilingual, can conduct dialogues in the stronger and weaker languages, and can understand the communicative intent of their pupils. WCIB teachers are usually unilingual, can conduct monologues in the *lingua communis,* and, apart from obvious practical problems, can under-

198

stand little of the communicative intent of their pupils. MCEB children are a self-perceived part of the broader community, and recipients of normal institutionalized forms of individual and collective support. WCIB children perceive themselves (as they are symbolically recognized) as outsiders, and recipients of various degrees of neglect or hostility. The goal of MCEB immersion programmes is to develop and maintain the first and second languages. The goal of WCIB immersion programmes is to replace the first with the second.

The middle-class élite bilingual (MCEB) and the working-class immigrant bilingual (WCIB) types of immersion programmes are both very effective in achieving their implicit and explicit goals. For example, Stern et al. accurately report the cognitive-educational consequences of "immersion", but fail to mention that they are describing MCEB immersion:

> (In the Canadian, anglophone context) ... the repeated findings of immersion studies indicate that from the point of view of French, *immersion* is the most effective program wherever it occurs in the school system... (1976, p. 124).

Masemann, on the other hand, although well aware of the distinctions between "immersion" for the middle-class and "immersion" for the working-class fails to report explicit cognitive-educational consequences of WCIB immersion (mostly because the few studies which do exist are methodologically or ideologically suspect), but accurately describes the final outcome of the WCIB process:

> (In the Canadian, immigrant context) ... the low prestige level of parents' jobs and the lack of general respect among Canadian-born students for Italian, Greek, or Portuguese culture ... are evidence to the student that he is an outsider. The students' responses to these many varied messages are that they ardently wish to master English, even if they are willing to speak their mother-tongue at home or in church... Is is only in high school or while working that the immigrants come to realize what opportunities they have missed. They bear the scars of having been taunted by their Anglo-classmates for not being proficient in spoken English (and from newly arrived immigrants from their homeland for the deteriorated state of their mother-tongue), and finish with the stigma of having attended a school that "slow learners" also attended (1975, p. 120).

MCEB and WCIB constitute two types of lived worlds, two types of social-educational contexts, one "constructive immersion," one "destructive immersion." In both countries the middle classes have the freedom to choose between a MCEB programme or a standard programme in the *lingua communis* of their respective countries. In theory the indigenous working classes have the same choice. But, as Bain noted elsewhere (1982, p. 7) "that freedom is an illusion. The indigenous working classes of Canada and West Germany receive considerable social and political pressure to keep their children functionally unilingual in the *lingua communis.*" In the final analysis, the middle classes and working classes of Canada and West Germany are intertwined in historical and cultural conditions that have many common threads – and separate outcomes.

METHODOLOGY

General

This study was designed to answer two empirical questions. First, what are the general developmental regularities between the body percept (measured via the Uznadze Haptic-Kinesthetic Test) and object perception (measured via microgenetically timed tachistoscopic exposures of Fields Expressive Faces Test)? Second, what are the developmental relationships between performance on these measures of body percept and object perception, and (6- to 9-year-old) MCEB, WCIB, middle-class unilingual, and working-class unilingual school children in Canada, West Germany, and Italy?

The starting point of this study was Witkin et al.'s (1974) cross-cultural analysis of cognitive styles (i.e., field dependence/field independence) of school children of villagers in Holland, Mexico, and Italy. Following in their footsteps, we designed a two-fold study, one ideographic, one nomothetic. The ideographic study consists of a series of ethnomethodological studies of small numbers of children (and their families) from each village at various stages in their lives. Of particular concern are the children who have spent their formative years in these villages, but who, at school age, had emigrated with their parents to industrialized cities and nations. Because of its longitudinal, case study nature these ideographic profiles are still being compiled. We will continue (as we have done thus far), however, to use some of this pertinent information for description or interpretation in the present nomothetic study. In this latter instance, we began with five industrialized cities (Calgary, Edmonton, and Vancouver, Canada; Bremen and Hamburg, West Germany) which have large Italian immigrant populations, and all the other social groups, language programmes, and related criteria. And for what in effect became an important control group, we selected samples from among their peers in the Italian villages from which they had originally emigrated.

Like Witkin et al. (1974) and Berry (1976) we confronted that issue of selection bias and comparability which hobbles many cross-cultural (and cross-class) studies by getting local assistants to facilitate practical arrangements, to translate and back translate test instructions, to conduct test procedures – albeit with the principal investigators in close proximity.

200

Subjects: common information

The final subject population consisted of 660 pupils, 330 in grade 1, 330 in grade 3, equally divided by sex. All subjects were living in intact families, were mentally and physically healthy, and were free of specific haptic-kinesthetic and eye sight problems. All subjects were attending public schools. Each subject was attending the same school in which he/she began his/her academic career, and none were chronic absentees. At the time of testing: grade-1 subjects were not less than 6y0mos nor more than 7y0mos; grade-3 subjects were not less than 8y0mos nor more than 9y0mos. Testing was done in the second to last month of the school year. The subjects had thus (virtually) completed 1 or 3 years of schooling. Each subject participated in a test of "communicative competency." This consisted of holding two independent, everyday conversations with two judges (adult, native speakers). One conversation was held in the school (with teacher as judge), the other was held in the local playground, streetcorner, etc. (with research assistant as judge). In the case of the bilingual subjects these dialogues were repeated in each language. Using the age/grade expectations as the general criteria of communicative fluency, subjects were classified according to three categories: *competent* (native-like or near native-like conversational ability); *partially competent* (could mostly comprehend, and limited speaking ability); *noncompetent* (very little or no comprehension, and no speaking ability or could use only single words). Prescriptive norms of pronunciation, grammar and syntax were not a consideration. For subjects to be included in the study there had to be agreement between judges. Interjudge reliability was $r = .76$.

Italian subjects

Group A These consisted of 50 grade 1 and 50 grade 3, Italian-born unilingual (Italian) pupils attending semi-urban schools in the Lombardy region of Italy. Witkin et al. (1974) characterizes this region as low in social conformity and generally better educated than certain other regions of Italy. The material well-being of these subjects' families was that of skilled and semi-skilled working-class labourers. The language of the home and school was Italian. All subjects were *competent in Italian*.

Group B These consisted of 50 grade 1 and 50 grade 3, Italian-born immigrant pupils attending city centre schools in Canada. Grade 1 subjects were in English-as-a-second language programmes. Grade 3 subjects were in regular classrooms, with one period a day in concentrated English. The families were native to the Lombardy region of Italy. Their material well-being was that of skilled and semi-skilled working-class labourers. The

201

language of the home was Italian. The language of the school was English. The grade 1 subjects were *competent in Italian* and *noncompetent in English*. The grade 3 subjects were *partially competent in Italian* and *partially competent in English*.

Group C The profile of group C is similar to group B with the following exceptions: the schools were located in West Germany; the language of the home was Italian; the language of the school was German; the grade 1 subjects were *competent in Italian* and *noncompetent in German;* the grade 3 subjects were *partially competent in Italian* and *partially competent in German*.

Note: the families of groups B and C had emigrated within 1 year of their children starting school in grade 1. Groups A, B, and C had thus spent their early formative years in a similar social-psychological climate in Italy. All these children were *competent in Italian* when they started in their respective schools in grade 1.

Canadian subjects

Group D These consisted of 30 grade 1 and 30 grade 3, Canadian-born unilingual (Anglophone) pupils attending city centre schools in Canada. These subjects were in regular classrooms. The material well-being of these subjects' families was that of skilled and semi-skilled working-class labourers. The language of the home and school was English. All subjects were *competent in English*.

Group E These consisted of 30 grade 1 and 30 grade 3, Canadian-born unilingual (Anglophone) pupils attending suburban schools in Canada. These subjects were in regular classrooms. The material well-being of these subjects' families was that of middle-class professionals and semi-professionals. The language of the home and school was English. All subjects were *competent in English*.

Group F These consisted of 30 grade 1 and 30 grade 3, Canadian-born (Anglophone) pupils in a French immersion programme in suburban schools in Canada. The material well-being of these subjects' families was that of middle-class professionals and semi-professionals. The language of the home was English. The language of the school was French. The grade 1 subjects were *competent in English* and *noncompetent in French*. The grade 3 subjects were *competent in English* and *partially competent in French*.

German subjects

Group G The profile of group G is similar to Canadian Group D with the following exceptions: the subjects were German-born; the language of the home and school was German; all subjects were *competent in German*.

Group H The profile of group H is similar to Canadian Group E with the following exceptions: the subjects were German-born; the language of the home and school was German; all subjects were *competent in German.*

Group I The profile of group I is similar to Canadian Group F with the following exceptions: these German pupils were in an English immersion programme; the language of the home was German; the language of the school was English; the grade 1 subjects were *competent in German* and *noncompetent in English;* the grade 3 subjects were *competent in German* and *partially competent in English.*

Subjects: summary

The final sample consisted of representatives of three nations (Italy, Canada, West Germany), two social classes (working, middle), three types of school language programmes (unilingual, WCIB, MCEB), two age/grade levels (6-7y/grade 1; 8-9y/grade 3) for a total of 18 subgroups. At each age/grade level there were: *5 working-class groups* (Italian-born schooled in Italian; Italian-born schooled in English; Italian-born schooled in German; Canadian-born schooled in English; German-born schooled in German); and *4 middle-class groups* (Canadian-born schooled in English; Canadian-born schooled in French; German-born schooled in German; German-born schooled in English).

Socio-economic class

Blishen's Socio-Economic Index (Blishen & McRoberts, 1976) was used to determine the material well-being of subjects' families. Although this index was designed in Canada, it is sufficiently specific yet flexible enough to be used in the Italian and West German contexts relevant to this study (Blishen & McRoberts, 1976; Yu, 1981). The Blishen Index is based upon the educational and income characteristics of each occupation, and not on its prestige or perceived social characteristics. It is useful in the present study because the Index is based upon relatively objective and sociological divisions rather than upon subjective or psychological divisions. General equivalence and not identity of education/occupation was used as the criteria for "working" or "middle" class designation. Families which fell outside of those parameters were rejected.

Test battery and procedures

The Uznadze Haptic-Kinesthetic Test (Uznadze, 1966) was administered as the measure of the body percept. This was selected for three reasons. First, the hands, posture and motor apparatus (i.e., the body) when used as a perceptual object is unique in that it is simultaneously that which is perceived and also a part of the perceiver. Thus, when an individual holds the Uznadze spheres, he/she concurrently has a sensation of touching and being touched. No other (type of) perceptual object ever occupies such a dual position or participates so intimately in the perceptual process. Second, in a pilot study, we found reliable correlations between the Uznadze Haptic-Kinesthetic Test, and Wapner and Werner's tests of the body percept: rod-and-frame, $r = .74$; tilting chair; $r = .71$; rod-and-frame and tilting chair, $r = .67$. This scale of correlations is in essential agreement with Hritzuk (1968). The Uznadze Haptic-Kinesthetic Test has also been used in a wide range of studies, general and individual, of central determinants in perception (e.g., Feignberga & Zhuravleva, 1977; Asmolov, 1979). Third, the instruments are simple to administer and score, and readily packagable to move from site to site. The apparatus consists of three spheres of equal volume (88 mm), two of equal weight (190 g), one of unequal weight (69 g).

Apparatus used to measure the body percept demand that subjects focus on the tension between the self and some external object(s). In this instance the procedure is to haptically-kinesthetically prepare a subject to "touch/judge" a pair of spheres of equal size and weight. Following repeated applications of the "like size/weight" spheres (during which the subject comes to anticipate a certain size/weight), one sphere is surreptitiously switched to "like size/unequal weight." From the number of trials it takes a subject to recognize that a switch has occurred, the examiner makes claims about the subject's body percept. The examiner feels justified in doing so because the subject is required to perceive his/her body-as-object in terms of two conditions of haptic-kinesthetic environmental frame of reference, one condition in which he/she was perceptually habituated, immediately followed by another condition which is haptically identical but kinesthetically different. *Uznadze Haptic-Kinesthetic test procedure.* This procedure was designed by Hritzuk (1968) for use with children. *Note:* Subjects did not see the spheres prior nor subsequent to testing. Each subject was blindfolded, seated, arms bent, forearms parallel to tights, palms upward, and instructed:

> I am going to place a ball in each hand. I'll leave them there for a brief moment and remove them. Each time I do this I want you to tell me if they weight the same or different. And if they are different, which one is heavier.

Instructions were repeated and clarified as required. The like size/weight spheres were applied 10 times; then without breaking the cadence (1 sec. on, 2 secs. off) one like size/unequal weight sphere was switched. The number of trials taken to perceive the changed conditions (i.e., equilibrium of size and weight) was the criterion measure.

204

A word about microgenesis. Faced with a novel problem (e.g., Fields' expressive faces), individuals approach them through a developmental sequence of actions that range from their most primitive to most sophisticated. In other words, earlier modes of action are continually present as the basis of all mental life. This microgenetic process is so rapid that it must be slowed down mechanically to be empirically observed. Through use of the tachistoscope, this normally rapid unfolding of action systems is, in effect, stretched out over time and thus made available to empirical observation. Microgenetic processes occur at all stages of ontogenesis (cf., Angyal, 1941; Goldstein, 1939; Werner, 1948). The inclusion of this procedure is not only important to the theoretical study of central determinants in perception; it was also to ensure reliability of the body percept measure. The scope of this study necessitated this abundance of caution.

The Fields Expressive Faces Test (Fields, 1953, et passim) was administered as the measure of object perception. This use of the Fields test has a number of advantages: it avoids the problem of locally biased test materials; in Titone's terms (see above) it assesses subjects' perceptions of "the world of people, objects and intentions that must be integral to the study of the individual, language and society"; and when administered tachistoscopically, it provides a reliable complement to the Uznadze test approach to the body percent (Bain, 1973). The Fields Expressive Faces Test materials consist of 30 matched pairs of photographed (Caucasian) faces. Each pair is matched in terms of affective intention (i.e., different faces with identical "looks on their faces"). One of each pair was mounted on a slide for tachistoscopic presentation; the other was enlarged to 6 x 16 (cm) and mounted on cardboard. The tachistoscope was a Phi-electric, Portable Model, no. V-09597. Luminance levels, with no stimuli on the screen, were adjusted to 21.58 cd/m^2. The slides were shown at the three microgenetic exposure times originally suggested by Sander (1930): 1 sec. (Aktualgenese); 5 secs. (Vorgestalt); 10 secs. (Gestaltgerüst). These exposure times were replicated by Findley and Frenkel (1972; cf., Flavell & Draguns, 1957). The cognitive demands become less endogenous and more exogenous over the ascending order of exposure time.

Microgenesis of perception of Fields Expressive Faces procedure. This procedure for use of the tachistoscope with children was designed by Findley and Frenkel (1972). The subjects were encouraged "to play with 'the video machine', to see what it did, to look inside to see samples, etc...." The faces which were mounted on cardboard were placed immediately beside the tachistoscope. The subjects were instructed to familiarize themselves with "the expression, the look, the grimace, etc." on each mounted face. To ensure familiarity, games of "who does this look like" were played with each face. Five practice trials (using matched pairs that were not part of the formal test) at each of the three exposure levels were conducted. The subjects were instructed to:

> Look in the machine and see the expression on the face. Then look at these (mounted) faces and point to the one which has the same expression (During the practice trials the specific wording was changed until individual subjects understood instructions.).

The formal testing consisted of presenting 10 expressive faces at each of the three exposure times. The criterion measure was the number of (mounted) matched expressive faces correctly identified. No specific time was designated for pointing to the matched face. No repeated exposure (on the tachistoscope) were permitted. Exposure times were randomized. Following each subject, the tachistoscopic slides were randomized.

General procedures. All subjects were tested individually. Order of body percept and object percept measures was randomized. Communication between subjects and examiners was in the appropriate language. Candies and pop were available. Care was taken to ensure a conductive ambience.

Note: In as much as we are dealing with processes and not properties, with epistemological demands that are not biased in favour of a particular socio-economic or parochial context, and given the interwoven nature of the historical lived-worlds of this subject population, it can be claimed that these procedures are culture and class fair (cf., Fields, 1953; Uznadze, 1966; Wapner & Werner, 1965; Cole & Schribner, 1974; Triandis & Lambert, 1980; Boucher, in press).

RESULTS

Figure 1 shows that performance on the Uznadze Haptic-Kinesthetic test follows a developmental progression from more to less trials by age/grade for all groups. Progressive perceptual differentiation of this order has been found elsewhere (e.g., Piaget & Lambercier, 1944; Langer, 1969; Stone & Church, 1980). At the grade 1/6-7-y level, there were, however, two revealing findings: (1) there were no significant differences between groups A, B, C, D, E, G, H – nor between groups F, I; (2) there were significant differences between groups F, I and A, B, C, D, E, G, H ($p<.01$). Thus, at the grade 1/6-7-y level, the two MCEB groups performed the haptic-kinesthetic test in significantly less trials than did the two WCIB groups and the five unilingual groups. At the grade 3/8-9-y level, the two revealing findings were: (1) there were no significant differences between groups A, D,

206

Groups

A - Italian, working class, unilingual, in Italy.
B - Italian, working-class immigrant, bilingual, in Canada.
C - Italian, working-class immigrant, bilingual, in West Germany.
D - Canadian, working class, unilingual, in Canada.
E - Canadian, middle class, unilingual, in Canada.
F - Canadian, middle class, bilingual, in Canada.
G - German, working class, unilingual, in West Germany.
H - German, middle class, unilingual, in West Germany.
I - German, middle class, bilingual, in West Germany.

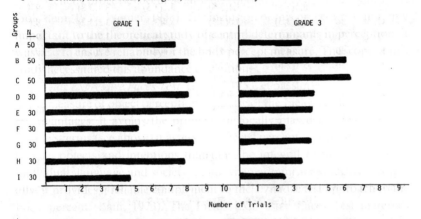

Figure 1. Number of trials on Uznadze Haptic-Kinesthetic Test by 9 groups of Grade 1/6-7
year olds, and 9 groups of Grade 3/8-9 year olds.

Note: Fewer trials implies more differentiated body percept.

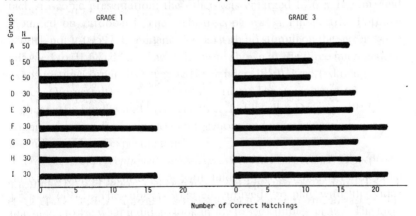

Figure 2. Number of correct matchings (total scores only) of Fields Expressive Faces Test by 9
groups of Grade 1/6-7 year olds, and 9 groups of Grade 3/8-9 year olds.

Note: Greater number of correct matchings implies more differentiated object perception.

207

TABLE 1

Means and standard deviations on Uznadze Haptic-Kinesthetic Test and Fields Expressive Faces Test for 9 groups of Grade 1/6-7 year olds

Groups	N	Uznadze Test M(SD)	Fields Test, Tachistoscope exposures 1 sec. M(SD)	5 secs. M(SD)	10 secs. M(SD)	Total Correct
A	50	7.6(3.3)	3.2(3.4)	3.5(3.0)	3.3(3.4)	10.0
B	50	8.1(3.8)	3.1(3.6)	3.2(3.5)	3.1(3.8)	9.4
C	50	8.3(3.5)	3.0(3.5)	3.4(3.7)	3.2(3.2)	9.6
D	30	7.9(4.2)	3.0(4.4)	3.2(4.5)	3.5(4.7)	9.7
E	30	8.2(4.6)	3.4(4.7)	3.4(4.6)	3.2(4.6)	10.0
F	30	5.1(2.6)	5.2(2.6)	5.7(2.5)	5.7(2.5)	16.3
G	30	8.2(4.5)	3.1(4.1)	2.9(4.3)	3.6(3.8)	9.6
H	30	7.9(4.5)	3.4(4.3)	3.5(4.6)	3.0(4.5)	9.9
I	30	4.8(2.4)	5.3(2.5)	5.6(2.6)	5.5(2.3)	16.4

TABLE 2

Means and standard deviations on Uznadze Haptic-Kinesthetic Test and Field's Expressive Faces Test for 9 groups of Grade 3/8-9 year olds

Groups	N	Uznadze Test M(SD)	Fields Test, Tachistoscope exposures 1 sec. M(SD)	5 secs. M(SD)	10 secs. M(SD)	Total Correct
A	50	3.8(3.7)	5.4(3.5)	5.5(3.2)	5.7(3.4)	16.6
B	50	6.1(4.5)	3.6(4.1)	3.4(4.6)	3.3(4.4)	10.3
C	50	6.2(4.7)	3.3(4.5)	3.5(4.8)	3.4(4.3)	10.2
D	30	3.9(3.8)	5.5(3.0)	5.6(3.6)	5.7(3.1)	16.8
E	30	3.7(3.5)	5.6(3.2)	5.4(2.7)	5.4(3.6)	16.4
F	30	2.2(1.2)	7.6(2.6)	7.5(2.2)	7.6(2.8)	22.7
G	30	4.0(3.5)	5.5(2.9)	5.7(3.4)	5.8(3.3)	17.0
H	30	3.6(3.4)	5.8(3.1)	5.6(3.4)	5.7(3.5)	17.1
I	30	2.4(1.4)	7.4(2.0)	7.6(2.0)	7.5(2.4)	22.5

E, G, H – nor between groups B, C – nor between groups F, I; (2) significant differences occurred between groups F, I and groups A, B, C, D, E, G, H ($p < .01$) – and between groups A, D, E, G, H and groups B, C ($p < .01$). The extent of the difference between groups F, I and groups B, C was significant ($p < .001$). Thus, at the grade 3/8-9-y level, the two MCEB groups required significantly fewer trials than did the four unilingual and two WCIB groups; while the four unilingual groups required significantly fewer trials than did the two WCIB groups. Figure 2 shows that performance on tachistoscopic exposures of Fields Expressive Faces Test follows a developmental progression from less to more correct matchings by age/grade for all groups (cf., Bruner & Tagiuri, 1961; Boucher, in press). The pattern of "no differences" and "significant differences" on the Fields Test is identical with the pattern of performance on the Uznadze Test (cf., Figs. 1 and 2). This can be explicitly seen on Tables 1 and 2. The symmetry of these findings suggests a holistic relationship between the body percept (measured via the Uznadze Haptic-Kinesthetic Test) and object percept (measured via the Fields Test of Facial Expression exposed at Aktualgenese, Vorgestalt and Gestaltgerüst levels of microgenesis). The findings further suggest that social-educational climate and school-language programmes play differential roles in influencing central determinants in perception.

DISCUSSION

This study was designed to reveal the course of ontogenetic evolution (and microgenetic unfolding at each stage of ontogenesis) of the body percept – as it is schematically dependent on working- and middle-class unilingual lived-worlds, and, on working- and middle-class, bilingual lived-worlds – in Canada, West Germany, and Italy. To paraphrase Merleau-Ponty, Wapner and Werner, and Titone: the evidence of this study suggests that the lived-worlds of the Existants are schematically mirrored in the developmental regularities of the body percept. This is to say, first, that behind the body percept stand real relations among people; second, that language as it reflects the nature of those relationships effects the ontogeny of the body percept. Because the evidence was based on a trans-national cross-class, cross-language, unified study these views merit serious consideration.

There are four interrelated issues to be discussed here: the dialectical nature of object perception and self-perception; the unity of microgenetic and ontogenetic unfolding of the body percept; the specific effects of social-educational climate and school-language programmes; the problem of the individual, language, and society. We will discuss the first two issues together, and the last two separately.

The evidence of this study suggests a constant reciprocity between object perception and the perceiving self. They further suggest (as originally predicted by Angyal, 1941; Goldstein, 1939; Werner, 1948) that at all stages of ontogenesis there is a homologous microgenetic unfolding. The microgenetic and ontogenetic processes are "two faces" of the general developmental thrust. They are inextricably united in the evolution of perceptual differentiation (cf., Chaplin & Krawiec, 1979; Flavell & Draguns, 1957; Merleau-Ponty, 1962). This holistic relationship, this joint unfolding of the perception of one's own body in relation to the various axes of the external world, substantiates two of Merleau-Ponty's, and Wapner and Werner's theoretical stances. First, that a theory of the body *is* a theory of perception. The developmental regularities and irregularities of the psycho-biological unit "body:world" were mutually reflected in self-perception and object perception. Second, that lower (endogenous) mental processes are transformed or integrated as subordinates in the higher (exogeneous) mental processes which comprise the more complex organization of later individuality. The evidence also supports Titone's position that the very marrow of personality and the lived-world of the Existant constitute a unified whole.

The theoretical importance of these claims notwithstanding, it would be empirically imprudent to suggest that this evidence represents etic or universally valid claims about the nature of human development. Wober (1967) found, for example, that with adult Nigerians there was an absence of a correlation between performance on the rod-and-frame test and performance on the Embedded Figures test. These standard tests of central determinants in perception, with that subject population, did not seem to reflect a common, underlying psychological process. Wober's findings do not contradict the findings of this study. His findings seem to a product of what Berry (1976, p. 1) refers to as "the Ss' human ecology", or, what we would call "the objective historical and cultural conditions." What Wober's findings do do, however, is affirm the empirical necessity of conducting unified, cross-cultural studies in order to distinguish etic from emic phenomenon. In the short run, the empirical evidence of the present study should not be generally outside *its* particular sociogenetic context. The theoretical claims nonetheless retain their heuristic value.

Social-educational climate (or, more narrowly, social class) and school-language programme produced differential effects on the course of body percept development. Regardless of nation or *lingua communis*, the working and middle classes, throughout both age/grade levels, showed a similar developmental progression. One implication of this finding is that contrary to Bernstein (1964, et passim) and some of his less cautious advocates (e.g., Olim, 1970; Schatzmann & Strauss, 1955), there is no automatic correlation between social class and speech type (at least in Canada, Italy, and West Germany) with regard to general cognitive consequences. The procedures used in this study do not permit statements about "elaborate and restricted speech codes", "class or racial dialects", and the like. However, our selection criterion was communicative competency not normative usage. This (functional) criterion permits only the claim that between working- and middle-class Italian, Anglophone Canadian and West German unilingual children there were no differences in central determinants in perception.

The course of body percept development between WCIB children and MCEB children on the one hand, and between these bilingual children and the unilingual children on the other hand, resulted in provocative contrasts. At the younger level, the WCIB children (in Canada and West Germany) performed similarly to the five unilingual groups (in Italy, Canada, and West Germany). Recall that the WCIB children at this time were *competent* in Italian, and *noncompetent* in Canadian English or German. By the older level, the WCIB children showed no appreciable change in body percept development (reminiscent of Piaget's notion of "décalage"). By the older level, the five unilingual groups had shown a significant developmental change. In other words, compared to their unilingual counterparts who remained in Italy, and compared to the other four unilingual groups in Canada and West Germany, the WCIB children had reached a developmental plateau, while the unilingual children had proceeded in a regular course of developmental change. Recall that the WCIB children at this time (after three years in a "destructive immersion" programme) had become only *partially competent* in Italian and had acquired only *partial competence* in Canadian English or German (reminiscent of Hansegård's notion of "double semilingualism"). It is our contention that the language dysfunction acquired by the WCIB children was instrumental in arresting the process of perceptual differentiation.

There is another facet to this contention. At the younger and older levels, the MCEB children showed an accelerated body percept development compared to their unilingual and WCIB peers. Recall, too, that while the WCIB children went from *competent* to *partially competent* in their mother tongue, and from *noncompetent* to *partially competent* in their respective *lingua communis,* the MCEB children maintained *competency* in their respective *lingua communis,* while proceeding from *noncompetent* to *partially competent* in their respective target languages. It seems that as long as there is communicative competency in *a* historical language (i.e., a mother tongue of historical origin that is culturally transmitted) the body percept evolves along progressively more in a regular differentiated continuum. Although there are promising signs (e.g., Ekstrand & Finnocchiaro, 1977), vital research is necessary to determine the nature of body percept development when working-class immigrant children are permitted to maintain

211

communicative competency in their mother tongue while learning a *lingua communis*. This of course necessitates a radically different social-educational climate and school-language programme than host countries have politically encouraged to date.

It is our second contention that in the case of middle-class children, school-language programme plays a larger role in accelerating body percept development than does social-educational climate. With social-educational climate/material well-being held constant, the children in the "constructive immersion" programme showed a qualitative difference in performance compared to their peers in a "mother tongue" programme. It seems that when children are (in Titone's terms) "self-assertive in front of a world that provides emotional and cultural support", the intellectual demands of "learning another mode of existence" results in accelerated differentiation of object percept and self-percept.

In conclusion, we are in agreement with Titone that the problem of the individual, language, and social relations constitutes an indivisible whole. The parts of the problem are conceptually distinct and phenomenally irreducible. Bilingual studies are central to the resolution of the problem because of the emphasis they place on the dynamics of the whole. Bilingual studies are also important for another reason, namely, they are the Ariadne's thread for unravelling the politics and ideologies which have enmeshed contemporary social science. Our neophyte student's cursory overview of the history of bilingual studies contained certain oversimplified facts. What was missed in that overview, and hopefully revealed to some extent in this study, was the recognition that behind the lived worlds of the Existants stands real relations among people – mediated by language.

212

YES, BUT...

Yvan Lebrun and Michel Paradis

As the contents of this volume reflect, the question of early bilingualism can be investigated from a variety of perspectives. From a linguistic perspective, one may examine the simultaneous acquisition of two systems; the ability to keep them separate, to switch between them, and to translate; the involuntary use of elements of one language (phonetic, phonological, morphological, syntactic, and/or semantic) when using the other; and the possible internalization of hybrid grammars. From a cognitive perspective, one may explore the effects of simultaneous acquisition of two linguistic systems on cognitive development, concept formation, reasoning, and one's world view. From a neuropsychological perspective, one may consider the effect of simultaneous acquisition of two linguistic systems on cerebral mechanisms involved in the processing of language and communication. From a psychosocial perspective, one may inquire into the effect of early bilingualism on sociolinguistic and psychosocial behaviors; reactions in the face of two linguistic and cultural groups and problems of identification with one or the other of these groups, or the absence of identification with a particular linguistic and cultural group; and personality development in a bilingual context.

In addition, the sociopolitical dimension cannot be ignored. It is for sociopolitical reasons that choices are made, after the pros and cons of other aspects have been considered (when indeed they are). The decision, for instance, that for a language-handicapped child of English background in the Province of Quebec it is better to acquire whatever French he can at the expense of some possible lack of improvement in English, his mother tongue, is based on a sociopolitical value judgment. Another judgment might be that it is better for the child to receive as much stimulation as possible in his English mother tongue at the expense of whatever French he might acquire in an immersion situation in school. Such choices are best made when the linguistic, cognitive, and sociopsychological aspects have been fully considered.

Over the years, bilingualism (and early bilingualism in particular) has alternately been considered a disease by some and a panacea by others. It would be surprising if there were benefits at no cost, or only costs without benefit. On the other hand, one may question to what extent the simultaneous acquisition of two languages produces a seesaw effect in reducing competence in one language in proportion to increasing competence in the other (Epstein, 1915; Macnamara, 1966, p. 9-38; van Overbeeke, 1972, p. 86-88), resulting in the "semilingualism" of the "equilingual", or in a shift of dominance in the unbalanced bilingual as proficiency in the other language improves.

Each chapter comprising the present volume adduces, in its own way, new evidence in support of the view that early bilingualism is not as dreadful as some have depicted it. Under certain circumstances the young child benefits from having to learn more than one language. Indeed, if a number of conditions are fulfilled, early exposure to a second language reflects favorably on the child's verbal, intellectual, and psychological development.

It is difficult to compare these studies with those found in the previous literature because of the wide range of methodologies that have been used in the past in collecting data, from diary case studies to longitudinal studies with repeated measurements, and cross-sectional studies, as well as because of the diversity of subjects, from socioeconomically deprived emigrant children to affluent middle-class culturally enriched language-majority children.

Hence, despite numerous investigations, the factors which influence the outcome of early bilingualism are not yet fully understood. Our knowledge of these determinants is to some extent still conjectural. Nonetheless, a number of features may be mentioned which have repeatedly appeared to be associated with the success or failure of bilingual education.

Balanced bilingualism seems difficult to achieve if the two languages are not equally liked and equally valued by the child. A positive attitude towards each of the languages to be mastered appears to be a prerequisite for bilingual proficiency. For example, although his mother tongue was American English, Julien Green never felt quite at home in it and chose to write his novels in French, which was his second language. As a child, he definitely preferred French to English, as he himself reports (1941): "I could not bring myself to believe that English was a real language; rather did I take it to be a jumble of meaningless sounds which grown-ups made to pretend they were carrying on a conversation.... To me the real names of things were French; other names were fancy and unreal." This attitude probably

214

explains why Green as an adult felt more at ease in French.

The parents' attitude towards bilingualism also seems an important factor, and their contribution to the development of the language spoken at home is often decisive. In many cases it is necessary for them to help the child acquire the verbal competence without which it seems difficult to achieve adequate command of a second language, or indeed to avoid negative consequences of bilingualism. Bruck (this volume p. 98) is careful to point out that the language-impaired children whom she studied and who proved to benefit from immersion were members "of a dominant prestigious culture which places primary emphasis on the development of first-language skills." Her findings would probably have been different, had she examined minority-language children who received little parental support in their efforts to achieve verbal proficiency.

Another important factor seems to be the opportunity for the child to use both languages actively in conversation with adults and peers. As McLaughlin states at the end of his contribution (this volume, p. 49) children need to be constantly encouraged to express their desires, ideas and intentions in either of the languages they are exposed to. In other words, the outcome of early bilingualism appears to depend to a nonnegligible extent on whether or not the child is motivated to acquire and use two languages and is praised for doing so.

On the other hand, it appears advisable to keep the two languages as distinct as possible. Mixed bilingualism does not seem to lead to as high a level of verbal competence as a learning situation in which the two languages are separated.

More debatable is the influence of age on the acquisition of second-language skills. Some people, and notably Penfield (see the introduction to the present volume), contend that the first 10 or 12 years of life form a critical period for language learning; if one does not learn the second language during this period, the acquisition of that language will be laborious and will remain incomplete. On the contrary, others maintain that youth does not confer any advantage in learning foreign languages. Evidence pertaining to this issue is sparse and inconclusive. On the one hand, it has been shown that in a laboratory situation adults and adolescents outperform young children in learning to understand commands given in a foreign language (Asher, 1969) or in imitating foreign words (Snow & Hoefnagel-Höhle, 1977). It has also been demonstrated that preschoolers do not make quicker progress than older subjects during the first year of exposure to a foreign language in a naturalistic environment (Snow & Hoefnagel-Höhle, 1977 and 1978). On the other hand, perfor-

215

mance of 7-year-olds in imitating foreign words has been found to exceed that of adults in a laboratory setting (McCrae Cochrane & Sachs, 1979). Thus, experimental findings are divergent. But, even if all such investigations showed young children to be inferior to adolescents and adults, this still might not falsify Penfield's view that there is a critical period for language learning between birth and puberty. Obviously, if the young child is to prove superior to the adolescent and the adult in verbal acquisition, this can only be in the long run. That is, not until he has had several years of exposure is the child likely to develop a better command of the language. At the beginning of the learning period the adolescent and the adult, because they are generally better motivated and have a longer attention span and better developed cognitive capacities, are likely to surpass the toddler and the preschooler. Moreover, the child's ultimate superiority may consist mainly in the ability to use the language for a longer time without fatigue, i.e., without degradation of the verbal output. The main drawback of acquiring a language after puberty is not so much, it would seem, that one cannot achieve mastery, but rather that one cannot maintain that standard for several hours on end. He who learned a language after, say, 12 years of age, appears to use much more mental energy when speaking that language than he who acquired it in early childhood. Accordingly, the former will become tired more quickly, and errors or deviations (articulatory, grammatical, or semantic) will occur in his speech. Indeed, it looks as if linguistic habits formed after puberty never reach the same degree of automaticity as linguistic habits formed early in life. One might hypothesize that language acquired in adolescence or adulthood remains essentially bound to the cortex and, in contradistinction to languages learned in early childhood, can hardly benefit from the facilitatory intervention of subcortical systems (see Lamendella, 1977).

In summary, some early bilinguals have been shown to perform better than monolinguals on some tests. Bilingual children seem to acquire symbol substitution sooner, and they seem to do better on tests of originality and cognitive flexibility. They also show greater metalinguistic awareness, earlier discrimination between facial symbolisms, earlier acquisition of object constancy, earlier proficiency in rule discovery and problem solving, and earlier reliance on meaning (as opposed to sound). But they also tend to show, at least initially in some contexts, a more limited vocabulary in each language.

All this seems to justify the conclusion that early bilingualism is advisable whenever the child does not have a marked first-language delay (possibly associated with mental retardation), when he can be given adequate verbal

216

support and stimulation in either language, and when the two languages are kept sufficiently distinct. In other words, early bilingualism is to be encouraged as long as it can satisfy a number of requirements. If such conditions are met, acquisition of more than one language in childhood is possible without detriment to the child's verbal, cognitive, and psychological development. To be successful, bilingual education, like any other kind of learning, must be adequately planned and properly implemented. Most young plants can only thrive in well-kept gardens.

REFERENCES

ALBERT M., OBLER L. (1978) *The bilingual brain: Neuropsychological and neuro-linguistic aspects of bilingualism.* New York, Academic Press.

ANDERSON T., BOYER M. (1978) *Bilingual schooling in the United States (2nd Edition).* Austin, National Education Laboratory Publishers.

ANGYAL A. (1941) *Foundations for a science of personality.* New York, Commonwealth Fund.

APPLE M. (1982) *Education and power.* London, Routledge and Kegan Paul.

ARNBERG L. (1981) *The effects of bilingualism on development during early childhood: A survey of the literature.* Linköping University, Linköping Studies in Education Reports, No. 5.

ARONSSON K. (1981a) *The bilingual preschooler as grammarian: Children's paraphrases of ungrammatical sentences.* Psychological Research Bulletin, Lund University, Sweden, 21: 1-26.

ARONSSON K. (1981b) *Nominal realism and bilingualism: A critical review of the studies on word: Referent differentiation.* Osnabrücker Beiträge zur Sprachtheorie, 20.

ARTHUR G. (1947) *Point scale of performance tests. Revised Form II. Manual for administering and scoring the tests.* New York, Psychological Corporation.

ASHER J. (1969) *The total physical response techniques of learning.* The Journal of Special Education 3: 253-262.

ASHER J., GARCIA R. (1969) *The optimal age to learn a foreign language.* Modern Language Journal 53: 334-341.

ATTWELL A., ORPET R., MEYERS C. (1967) *Kindergarten behavior ratings as a predictor of academic achievement.* Journal of School Psychology 6: 43-46.

ASMOLOV A. (1979) *Deiatel 'nost' i ustanovka.* Moskva, Izd-vo Moskovskogo universiteta.

BAIN B. (1973) *Toward a theory of perception.* Journal of General Psychology 89: 157-296.

BAIN B. (1982) *The illusion of choice in ethnic bilingual education.* In PANNU R., HIRABAYSHI G. (eds.) *Ethnic education.* Edmonton, University of Alberta Press.

BAIN B., YU A. (1980) *Cognitive consequences of raising children bilingually: One parent, one language.* Canadian Journal of Psychology 34: 304-313.

BALKAN L. (1970) *Les effets du bilinguisme français-anglais sur les aptitudes intellectuelles.* Brussels, AIMAV.

BARBLAN L. CHIPMAN H. (1978) *Temporal relationships in language: A comparison between normal and language retarded children.* In DRACHMAN G. (ed) *Salzburger Beiträge zur Linguistik.* V. Salzburg, W. Neugebauer.

BARIK H. (1975) *French comprehension test.* Toronto, Ontario Institute for Studies in Education.

BARIK H., SWAIN M. (1974) *English-French bilingual education in the early grades: The Elgin study.* Modern Language Journal 58: 392-402.

BARIK H., SWAIN M. (1975a) *Three-year evaluation of a large scale early French immersion program: The Ottawa study.* Language Learning 25: 1-30.

BARIK H., SWAIN M. (1975b) *Early grade French immersion classes in a unilingual English Canadian setting: The Toronto study.* Scientia Paedagogia Experimentalis 12: 153-177.

219

BARIK H., SWAIN M. (1976a) *Primary-grade French immersion in a unilingual English-Canadian setting: The Toronto study through grade 2.* Canadian Journal of Education 1/1: 39-58.

BARIK H., SWAIN M. (1976b) *Update to French immersion: The Toronto study through grade three.* Canadian Journal of Education 1/4: 33-42.

BARKMAN L. (1969) *Some psychological perspectives on bilingualism and second language teaching.* McGill Journal of Education 4: 45-58.

BARRY C. (1981) *Hemispheric asymmetry in lexical access and phonological encoding.* Neuropsychologia 19: 473-478.

BARTEL N., BRYEN D., KEEHN S. (1973) *Language comprehension in the moderately retarded child.* Exceptional Children 39: 375-382.

BATEMAN B., WETHERELL J. (1965) *Psycholinguistic aspects of mental retardation.* Mental Retardation 3: 8-13.

BECKER C. (1980) *Semantic context effects in visual word recognition: An analysis of semantic strategies.* Memory and Cognition 8: 493-512.

BEN ZEEV S. (1977a) *Mechanisms by which childhood bilingualism affects understanding of language and cognitive structures.* In HORNBY P. (ed.) *Bilingualism: Psychological, social and educational implications.* New York, Academic Press, 29-55.

BEN ZEEV S. (1977b) *The influence of bilingualism on cognitive strategy and cognitive development.* Child Development 48: 1009-1018.

BERGMAN C. (1976) *Interference vs. independent development in infant bilingualism.* In KELLER G., TESCHNER R., VIERA S. (eds.) *Bilingualism in the bicentennial and beyond.* New York, Bilingual Press/Editorial Bilingue.

BERNSTEIN B. (1964) *Elaborated and restricted codes: Their social origins and some consequences.* American Anthropologist 66: 55-69.

BERRY J. (1967) *Human ecology and cognitive style.* New York, Sage.

BHATNAGAR J. (1980) *Linguistic behaviour and adjustment of immigrant children in French and English schools in Montreal.* International Review of Applied Psychology 29: 141-158.

BILOVSKY D.,SHARE J. (1865) *The ITPA and Down's syndrome: An exploratory study.* American Journal of Mental Deficiency 70: 78-83.

BLAIR D., HARRIS R. (1981) *A test of interlingual interaction in comprehension by bilinguals.* Journal of Psycholinguistic Research 10: 457-467.

BLISHEN B., McROBERTS H. (1976) *A revised socioeconomic index for occupations in Canada.* Canadian Review of Sociology and Anthropology 13: 71-78.

BÖHNING R. (1972) *Educational plight of immigrant children in West Germany.* In DEAKIN N. (ed.) *Immigrants in Europe.* Fabian Research Series 306: 18-24.

BOUCHER J. (in press) *Emotion and culture.*

BROWN R. (1973) *A first language.* Cambridge, Mass., Harvard University Press.

BRUCK M. (1978) *The suitability of early French immersion programs for the language disabled child.* Canadian Journal of Education 3: 51-72.

BRUCK M. (1982) *Language impaired children's performance in an additive bilingual education program.* Applied Psycholinguistics 3: 45-60.

BRUCK M., LAMBERT W., TUCKER G. (1974) *Bilingual schooling through the elementary grades: The St. Lambert project at grade seven.* Language Learning 24: 183-203.

BRUCK M., LAMBERT W., TUCKER G. (1976) *Cognitive and attitudinal consequences of bilingual schooling: The St. Lambert project through grade six.* International Journal of Psycholinguistic Research 5-6: 6-13.

BRUCK M., RABINOVITCH M., OATES M. (1975) *The effects of French immersion programs on children with language disabilities - a preliminary report.*

220

Working Papers on Bilingualism 5. Toronto, Ontario Institute for Studies in Education.

BRUNER J., TAGIURI R. (1961) *The perception of people.* In LINDZEY G. (ed.) *Handbook of social psychology, vol. 1.* Cambridge, Addison-Wesley.

BRUNER J., OLIVER R., GREENFIELD P. (1967) *Studies in cognitive growth.* New York, John Wiley & Sons, Inc.

BUBENIK V. (1978) *The acquisition of Czech in the English environment.* In PARADIS M. (ed.) *Aspects of bilingualism.* Columbia, S.C., Hornbeam Press.

BURLING R. (1959) *Language development of a Garo and English speaking child.* Word 15: 45-68.

BURSTALL C., JAMIESON M., COHEN S., HARGREAVES M. (1974) *Primary French in the balance.* Slough, Berks., National Foundation for Educational Research.

CARAMAZZA A., YENI-KOMSHIAN G. (1974) *Voice onset time in two French dialects.* Journal of Phonetics 2: 239-245.

CARAMAZZA A., YENI-KOMSHIAN G., ZURIF E., CARBONE E. (1973) *The acquisition of a new phonological contrast: The case of stop consonants in French-English bilinguals.* The Journal of the Acoustical Society of America 54: 421-428.

CARROLL F. (1980) *Neurolinguistic processing of a second language: Experimental evidence.* In SCARCELLA R., KRASHEN S. (eds.) *Research in second language acquisition.* Rowley, MA, Newbury House, 81-86.

CARROLL J. (1969) *Psychological and educational research into second language teaching to young children.* In STERN H. (ed.) *Languages and the young school child.* London, Oxford University Press, 56-68.

CARROLL J. (1975) *The teaching of French as a foreign language in eight countries.* New York, Wiley & Sons.

CARROW E. (1957) *Linguistic functioning of bilingual and monolingual children.* Journal of Speech and Hearing Disorders 22: 371-380.

CARROW E. (1971) *Comprehension of English and Spanish by preschool Mexican-American children.* Modern Language Journal 55: 299-307.

CATFORD J. (1971) *Learning a language in the field: Problems of linguistic relativity.* In LUGTON R., HEINLE C. (eds.) *Toward a cognitive approach to second language acquisition.* Philadelphia, Center for Curriculum Development.

CASE F. (1977) *Racism and national consciousness.* Toronto, Plowshare Press.

CELCE-MURCIA M. (1978) *The simultaneous acquisition of English and French in a two-year-old child.* In HATCH E. (ed.) *Second language acquisition: A book of readings.* Rowley, Mass., Newbury House.

CHAFE W. (1970) *Meaning of the structure of language.* Chicago, The University of Chicago Press.

CHAPLIN J., KRAWIEC T. (1979) *Systems and theories of psychology.* New York, Holt, Rinehart and Winston.

CHIPMAN H. (1979) *Understanding language retardation: A developmental perspective.* Paper presented at the 5th I.A.S.S.M.D. Conference, Jerusalem, August 1979.

CHOMSKY N. (1965) *Aspects of the theory of syntax.* Cambridge, Mass., The M.I.T. Press.

CHRISTENSEN J., RYALLS J., LIEBERMAN P. (1981) *The 'universal phonetic level' and transcriptions of children's speech.* Brown University Working Papers in Linguistics 4: 122-123.

CIRCUS (1974) *An assessment program for pre-primary children.* Princeton, N.J. Educational Testing Service.

CLARK E. (1973) *What's in a word? On the child's acquisition of semantics in his first language.* In MOORE T. (ed.) *Cognitive development and the acquisition of language.* New York, Academic Press.

COAN R., CATTELL R. (1972) *Manual for the early school personality questionnaire. Form A.* Champaign, Ill., Institute for Personality and Ability Testing.

COHEN A., FATHMAN A., MERINO M. (1976) *The Redwood City bilingual education project, 1971-74: Spanish and English proficiency, mathematics and language use over time.* Working Papers on Bilingualism 8: 1-29.

COHEN A., SWAIN M. (1976) *Bilingual education: The immersion model in the North American context.* TESOL Quarterly 10: 45-53.

COHEN G. (1968) *A comparison of semantic, acoustic, and visual criteria for matching word pairs.* Perception and Psychophysics 4: 203-204.

COHEN G. (1972) *Hemispheric differences in a letter classification task.* Perception and Psychophysics 11: 139-142.

COLE M., SCRIBNER S. (1974) *Culture and thought: A psychological introduction.* New York, John Wiley & Sons.

NERS C. (1969) *A teacher rating scale for use in drug studies with children.* American Journal of Psychiatry 126: 152-156.

CONNERS C. (1970) *Symptom patterns in hyperkinetic, neurotic, and normal children.* Child Development 41: 667-682.

COOK N. (1977) *Semantic development in children with Down's syndrome.* Communication presented at the 85th Annual Convention of the American Psychological Association, San Francisco, August 1977.

CORNEJO R. (1973) *The acquisition of lexicon in the speech of bilingual children.* In TURNER P. (ed.) *Bilingualism in the Southwest.* Tucson, University of Arizona Press.

COWAN J., SARMED Z. (1976) *Reading performance of bilingual children according to type of school and home language.* Working Papers on Bilingualism 11: 74-114.

CRAIK F., LOCKHART R. (1972) *Levels of processing: A framework for memory research.* Journal of Verbal Learning and Verbal Behavior 11: 671-684.

CRITCHLEY M. (1957) *Observations on anosodiaphoria.* L'Encéphale 6: 540-546.

CROVITZ H., ZENER K. (1962) *A group test for assessing hand-and-eye dominance.* American Journal of Psychology 75: 271-276.

CUMMINS J. (1976) *The influence of bilingualism on cognitive growth: A synthesis of research findings and explanatory hypotheses.* Working Papers on Bilingualism 9: 1-9.

CUMMINS J. (1978a) *Bilingualism and the development of metalinguistic awareness.* Journal of Cross-Cultural Psychology 9: 139-149.

CUMMINS J. (1978b) *Educational implications of mother tongue maintenance in minority-language groups.* Canadian Modern Language Review 34: 395-416.

CUMMINS J. (1979) *Linguistic interdependence and the educational development of bilingual children.* Review of Educational Research 49: 222-251.

CUMMINS J. (1980) *The cross-lingual dimensions of language proficiency: Implications for bilingual education and the optimal age issue.* TESOL Quarterly 14: 175-188.

CUMMINS J. (1981a) *Age on arrival and immigrant second language learning in Canada: A reassessment.* Applied Linguistics 2: 132-149.

CUMMINS J. (1981b) *The role of primary language development in promoting educational success for language minority students.* In California State Department of Education, *Schooling and language minority students: A theoretical framework.* Los Angeles, National Dissemination and Assessment Center.

222

CUMMINS J. (1981c) *Bilingualism and minority language children.* Toronto, Ontario Institute for Studies in Education.

CUMMINS J. (1984) *Bilingualism and special education: Issues in assessment and pedagogy.* Cleveden, Avon, Multilingual Matters.

CUMMINS J., GULUTSAN M. (1974) *Bilingual education and cognition.* The Alberta Journal of Educational Research 20: 259-269.

CURTISS S. (1977) *Genie.* New York, Academic Press.

CZIKO G. (1976) *The effects of language sequencing on the development of bilingual reading skills.* Canadian Modern Language Review 32: 534-539.

DALE P. (1977) *Syntactic development in Down's syndrome children.* Communication at the 85th Annual Convention of the American Psychological Association, San Francisco, August 1977.

DAMICO J., OLLER J. (1980) *Pragmatic vs. morphological/syntactic criteria for language referrals.* Language Speech and Hearing Services in the School 11: 85-94.

DARCY N. (1953) *A review of the literature on the effects of bilingualism upon the measurement of intelligence.* Journal of Genetic Psychology 82: 21-58.

DARCY N. (1963) *Bilingualism and the measurement of intelligence: A review of a decade of research.* Journal of Genetic Psychology 103: 259-282.

DAWSON J. (1973) *Culture and perception.* New York, Wiley.

DELATTRE P. (1964) *Comparing the vocalic features of English, German, Spanish and French.* International Review of Applied Linguistics 2: 71-97.

DENNIS M. (1980) *Language acquisition in a single hemisphere: Semantic organization.* In CAPLAN D. (ed.) *Biological studies of mental processes.* Cambridge, Mass.: The M.I.T. Press, 159-185.

DEWART H. (1979) *Language comprehension processes of mentally retarded children.* American Journal of Mental Deficiency 84: 177-183.

DIMITRIJEVIC N. (1965) *A bilingual child.* English Language Teaching 20: 23-18.

DITTMAR N. (1976) *Sociolinguistics.* London, Edward Arnold Ltd.

DITTMAR N., HABERLAND H., SKUTNABB-KANGAS T., TELEMAN U. (eds.) (1978) *Papers from the first Scandinavian-German Symposium on the language of immigrant workers and their children.* Roskilde, Roskilde Universitets-Centre Linguistgruppen.

DODD B. (1972) *Comparison of babbling patterns in normal and Down's syndrome infants.* Journal of Mental Deficiency Research 16: 35-40.

DODD B. (1975) *A comparison of the phonological systems of mental age matched normal, severely subnormal and Down's syndrome children.* British Journal of Disorders of Communication 11: 27-42.

DOLL E. (1965) *Vineland social maturity scale: Condensed manual of directions. 1965 edition.* Circle Pines, Minn., American Guidance Service.

DONALDSON M. (1978) *Children's minds.* Glasgow, Collins.

DOWNING J. (undated) *Bilingualism and learning to read: A cross-cultural approach.* Unpublished paper, University of Victoria, Canada.

DOYLE A., CHAMPAGNE M., SEGALOWITZ N. (1978) *Some issues in the assessment of bilingual consequences of early bilingualism.* In PARADIS M. (ed.) *Aspects of bilingualism.* Columbia, S.C., Hornbeam Press.

DUCHAN J., ERICKSON J. (1976) *Normal and retarded children's understanding of semantic relations in different verbal contexts.* Journal of Speech and Hearing Research 19: 767-776.

DUNCAN S., DE AVILA E. (1979) *Bilingualism and cognition: Some recent findings.* National Association of Bilingual Education Journal 4: 15-50.

223

DUNN L. (1965) *Peabody picture vocabulary test (expanded manual).* Circle Pines, Minn., American Guidance Service.

EATON H. (1940) *Semantic frequency list for English, French, German and Spanish.* Chicago, The University of Chicago Press.

EDWARDS D. (1973) *Sensory-motor intelligence and semantic relations in early child grammar.* Cognition 2: 395-434.

EDWARDS H., COLLETTA S., FU L., McCANAY B., McLAUGHLIN B. (1978) *Evaluation of the federally and provincially funded extension of the second language programs in the schools of the Ottawa Roman Catholic Separate Board.* Annual Report.

EDWARDS H., SMYTH F. (1976) *Evaluation of second language programs and some alternatives for teaching French as a second language in grades five to eight.* Toronto, Ontario Ministry of Education.

EKSTRAND L., FINNOCCHIARO M. (1977) *Migration today: Some social and educational problems.* In BURT M., DULAY H., FINNOCCHIARO M.(eds.) *Viewpoints on English as a second language.* New York, Regents.

ELING P., MARSHALL J., VAN GALEN G. (1981) *The development of language lateralization as measured by dichotic listening.* Neuropsychologia 19: 767-774.

ELWERT W. (1960) *Das zweisprachige Individuum: Ein Selbstzeugnis.* Wiesbaden, Steiner.

ENGEL W. VON RAFFLER (1966) *Linguaggio attivo e linguaggio passivo.* Orientamenti Pedagogici 13: 893-894.

ENGLE P. (1975) *The use of vernacular languages in education.* Arlington, Virginia, Center for Applied Linguistics.

EPSTEIN I. (1916) *La pensée et la polyglossie.* Paris, Payot.

ERVIN S., OSGOOD C. (1954) *Second language learning and bilingualism.* Journal of Abnormal and Social Psychology 49: 139-146.

FEIGNBERGA I., ZHURAVLEVA G. (1977) *Veroiatnostnoe prognozirovanie i deiatel' nosti cheloveka.* Moskva, Izd-vo Moskovskogo universiteta.

FELDMAN C., SHEN M. (1971) *Some language-related cognitive advantages of bilingual 5-year-olds.* Journal of Genetic Psychology 118: 235-244.

FIELDS S. (1953) *Discrimination of facial expression and its relation to social adjustment.* Journal of Social Psychology 38: 63-71.

FILLMORE C. (1967) *The case for case.* In BACH E., HARMS R. (eds.) *Universals in linguistic theory.* New York, Holt, Rinehart and Winston, 1-88.

FINDLEY G., FRENKEL O. (1972) *Children's tachistoscopic recognition thresholds for recall of words which differ in connotative meaning.* Child Development 43: 1098-1103.

FISHER S., CLEVELAND S. (1958) *Body image and personality.* New York, D. van Nostrand Company.

FISHMAN J. (1967) *Bilingualism with and without diglossia.* In McNAMARA J. (ed.) *Problems of bilingualism.* Journal of Social Issues 2.

FLAVELL J., DRAGUNS J. (1957) *A microgenetic approach to perception and thought.* Psychological Bulletin 54: 197-217.

FOX B., ROUTH D. (1975) *Analyzing spoken language into words, syllables and phonemes: A developmental study.* Journal of Psycholinguistic Research 4: 331-342.

FRITH U. FRITH C. (1974) *Specific motor disabilities in Down's syndrome.* Journal of Child Psychology and Psychiatry 15: 293-301.

FROSTIG M., LEFEVER W., WHITTLESEY J. (1966) *Administration and scoring manual*

224

for the Marianne Frostig developmental test of visual perception (Revised). Palo Alto, Cal., Consulting Psychologists Press.

GALBRAITH J. (1978) *The new industrial state.* New York, Houghton Mifflin.

GALLOWAY L. (1983) *Etudes cliniques et expérimentales sur la participation de l'hémisphère droit au traitement du langage chez les bilingues: modèles théoriques.* Langages 72: 79-114.

GARDNER R., LAMBERT W. (1959) *Motivational variables in second language acquisition.* Canadian Journal of Psychology 13: 266-272.

GARDNER R., SMYTHE P. (1973) *The integrative motive in second language acquisition.* Research Bulletin 275. London, University of Western Ontario.

GARNES S. (1977) *Some effects of bilingualism on perception.* Papers in Psycholinguistics and Sociolinguistics, Ohio State University, 1-10.

GEISSLER H. (1938) *Zweisprachigheit deutscher Kinder im Ausland.* Stuttgart, Kohlhammer.

GENESEE F. (1976) *The suitability of immersion programs for all children.* Canadian Modern Language Review 32: 494-515.

GENESEE F. (1978) *A longitudinal evaluation of an early immersion school program.* Canadian Journal of Education 3: 31-50.

GENESEE F., HAMAYAN E. (1980) *Individual differences in second language learning.* Applied Psycholinguistics 1.

GENESEE F., HAMERS J., LAMBERT W., MONONEN L., SEITZ M., STARCK R. (1978) *Language processing in bilinguals.* Brain and Language 5: 1-12.

GEZI K. (1974) *Bilingual-bicultural education: A review of relevant research.* California Journal of Educational Research 25: 223-239.

GIBSON A., DIMOND S., GAZZANIGA M. (1972) *Left field superiority for word matching.* Neuropsychologia 10: 463-446.

GIORGI A. (1970) *Psychology as a human science.* New York, Harper and Row.

GLOVSKY L. (1970) *A comparison of two groups of mentally retarded children on the I.T.P.A.* Training School Bulletin 67: 4-14.

GOLDSTEIN K. (1939) *The organism.* New York, American Book Co.

GOLICK M. (1977) *Language disorders in children: A linguistic investigation.* Unpublished Ph.D. thesis, McGill University.

GORDON W., PANAGOS J. (1976) *Developmental transformational capacity of children with Down's syndrome.* Perceptual and Motor Skills 43: 967-973.

GRAY V., CAMERON C. (1980) *A follow-up evaluation of the fifth year of early French immersion.* Unpublished manuscript, Psychology Department, University of New Brunswick.

GREEN J. (1941) *An experiment in English.* Harper's Magazine 183: 397-405.

GREENFIELD T. (1976) *Bilingualism, multiculturalism and the crisis of purpose in Canadian culture.* In SWAIN M. (ed.) *Bilingualism in Canadian education: C.S.S.E. yearbook, 1976.* Edmonton, Western Industrial Research Centre.

GUMPERZ J. (1970) *Verbal strategies in multilingual communication.* Monograph Series on Languages and Linguistics 23: 129-143.

GUMPERZ J., HERNANDEZ-CHAVEZ E. (1972) Bilingualism, bidialectalism and classroom interaction. In CAZDEN C., JOHN V., HYMES D. (eds.) *Functions of language in the classroom.* New York, Teachers College Press.

HABERMAS J. (1979) *Communication and the evolution of society.* New York, Beacon Press.

HAKUTA K., DIAZ M. (in press) *The relationship between degree of bilingualism and cognitive ability.* In NELSON K. (ed.) *Children's language,* vol. 6.

HECAEN H., ALBERT M. (1978) *Human neuropsychology.* New York, Wiley.

225

HEFFNER R. (1950) *General phonetics.* Madison, The University of Wisconsin Press.

HRITZUK J. (1968) *A comparative and experimental application of the psychology of set.* Unpublished Ph.D. thesis, University of Alberta, Canada.

HYMES D. (1982) *Report from an underdeveloped country: Toward linguistic competence in the United States.* In BAIN B. (ed.) *The sociogenesis of language and human conduct.* New York. Plenum.

IANCO-WORRALL A. (1972) *Bilingualism and cognitive development.* Child Development 43: 1390-1400.

IMEDADZE N. (1967) *On the psychological nature of child speech formation under conditions of exposure to two languages.* International Journal of Psychology 2: 129-132.

JAHN F. (1808) *Deutsches Volkstum.* Reprinted in HIRT's *Deutsche Sammlung.* Breslau, 1930.

JANKY J. (1978) *A critical review of some developmental and predictive precursors of reading disabilities.* In BENTON A., PEARL D. (eds.)*Dyslexia.* New York, Oxford University Press.

JASTAK J., JASTAK S. (1965) *The wide range achievement test. Manual of instructions.* Wilmington, Dela., Guidance Associates.

JONES W. (1966) *Bilingualism in Welsh education.* Cardiff, University of Wales Press.

KALEN E. (1982) *Multiculturalism: Ideology, policy and reality.* Journal of Canadian Studies 17: 51-63.

KEANE V. (1972) *The incidence of speech and language problems.* Mental Retardation 10: 3-8.

KIMURA D. (1961) *Some effects of temporal-lobe damage on auditory perception.* Canadian Journal of Psychology 15: 156-165.

KIRK S., McCARTHY J., KIRK W. (1968) *Examiner's manual: Illinois test of psycholinguistic abilities.* Revised edition. Urbana, Ill., University of Illinois Press.

KOTIK B. (1981) *An evoked potential study of Polish-Russian bilinguals.* Unpublished manuscript, Rostov State University.

KRASHEN S. (1973) *Lateralization, language learning and the critical period. Some new evidence.* Language Learning 23: 63-74.

KRASHEN S. (1975) *The development of cerebral dominance and language learning: More new evidence.* In DATO D. (ed.) *Developmental psycholinguistics: Theory and application.* Washington, Georgetown University Round Table on Languages and Linguistics.

LACKNER J. (1968) *A developmental study of language behavior in retarded children.* Neuropsychologia 6: 301-320.

LAMBERT J. (1978) *Introduction à l'arriération mentale.* Bruxelles, Mardaga.

LAMBERT W. (1969) *Psychological studies of interdependencies of the bilingual's two languages.* In PUHVEL J. (ed.) *Substance and structure of language.* Los Angeles, University of California Press, 99-126.

LAMBERT W. (1974) *Culture and language as factors in learning and education.* Presented at 5th Annual Learning Symposium on Cultural Factors in Learning, November 1973, Washington; and TESOL Meeting, March, Denver.

LAMBERT W. (1975) *Culture and language as factors in learning and education.* In WOLFGANG A. (ed.) *Education of immigrant students.* Toronto, Ontario Institute for Studies in Education.

LAMBERT W. (1977) *The effects of bilingualism on the individual: Cognitive and sociocultural consequences.* In HORNBY P. (ed.) *Bilingualism.* New York, Academic Press, 15-27.

226

LAMBERT W., RAWLINGS C. *(1969) Bilingual processing of mixed-language associative networks.* Journal of Verbal Learning and Verbal Behavior 8: 604-609.

LAMBERT W., TUCKER G. (1972) *Bilingual education of children: The St. Lambert experiment.* Rowley, Mass., Newbury House.

LAMBERT W., TUCKER G., d'ANGLEJAN A. (1973) *Cognitive and attitudinal consequences of bilingual schooling: The St. Lambert project through grade five.* Journal of Educational Psychology 65: 141-159.

LAMENDELLA J. (1977) *General principles of neurofunctional organization and their manifestation in primary and nonprimary language acquisition.* Language Learning 27: 155-196.

LANCE D. (1969) *A brief study of Spanish-English bilingualism: Final report.* Research Project Orr-Liberal Arts - 15504. College Station, Texas, Texas A & M.

LANDRY R. (1974) *A comparison of second-language learners and monolinguals on divergent thinking tasks at the elementary school level.* Modern Language Journal 58: 10-15.

LANGER J. (1969) *Theories of development.* New York, Holt, Rinehart and Winston, Inc.

LAREW L. (1961) *The optimum age for beginning a foreign language.* Modern Language Journal 45: 203-206.

LAYTON T., SHARIFI H. (1979) *Meaning and structure of Down's syndrome and nonretarded children spontaneous speech.* American Journal of Mental Deficiency 83; 439-445.

LEBRUN Y. (1967) *Schizophasie et bégaiement.* Acta Neurologica et Psychiatrica Belgica 67: 939-945.

LEBRUN Y. (1978a) *Vroegtijdige meertaligheid.* Streven (July issue), 887-889.

LEBRUN Y. (1978b) *Warum sprach Victor aus Aveyron nicht?* Zeitschrift für Kinderund Jugendpsychiatrie 6: 396-408.

LEBRUN Y. (1980) *Victor of Aveyron. A reappraisal in light of more recent cases of feral speech.* Language Sciences 2: 32-43.

LEBRUN Y., BUYSSENS E. (1982) *Metalanguage and speech pathology.* British Journal of Disorders of Communication 17: 21-25.

LEIBER L. (1977) *Visual, acoustic, and semantic processing of word pairs.* Neuropsychologia 15: 217-229.

LENNEBERG E. (1964) *The capacity for language acquisition.* In FODOR J., KATZ J. (eds.) *The structure of language: Readings in the philosophy of language.* Englewood Cliffs, New Jersey, Prentice-Hall, Inc.

LENNEBERG E. (1967) *Biological foundations of language.* New York, Wiley and Sons.

LEONARD L. (1979) *Language impairment in children.* Merrill-Palmer Quarterly 25: 205-232.

LEOPOLD W. (1939) *Speech development of a bilingual child: A linguist's record.* Vol. 1: *Vocabulary growth in the first two years.* Evanston, Ill., Northwestern University Press.

LEOPOLD W. (1947) *Speech development of a bilingual child: A linguist's record.* Vol. 2. *Sound learning in the first two years.* Evanston, Illinois, Northwestern University Press.

LEOPOLD W. (1949) *Speech development of a bilingual child: A linguist's record.* Vol. 3: *Grammar and general problems in the first two years.* Evanston, Ill., Northwestern University Press.

LEVY J., TREVARTHEN C. (1977) *Perceptual semantic and phonetic aspects of elementary language processes in split-brain patients.* Brain 100: 105-118.

227

LIEPMANN D., STAEGERT J. (1947) *Language tagging in bilingual free recall.* Journal of Experimental Psychology 103: 1137-1141.

LINDHOLM K., PADILLA A. (1977) *Language mixing in bilingual children.* Journal of Child Language 5: 327-335.

LINDHOLM K., PADILLA A. (1978) *Child bilingualism: Report on language mixing, switching, and translations.* Linguistics 16: 23-44.

LISKER L., ABRAMSON A. (1964) *A cross-language study of voicing in initial stops: Acoustical measurements.* Word 20: 384-422.

LOPEZ M., HICKS R., YOUNG R. (1947) *Retroactive inhibition in a bilingual A-B, A-B' paradigm.* Journal of Experimental Psychology 103: 85-90.

LOWIE R. (1945) *A case of bilingualism.* Word 1: 249-259.

LOZAR B., WEPMAN J., HAAS W. (1972) *Lexical usage of mentally retarded and non-retarded children.* American Journal of Mental Deficiency 76: 534-539.

LURIA A. (1976) *Cognitive development: Its cultural and social foundations.* Cambridge, Harvard University Press.

MACCOBY E., JACKLIN C. (1974) *The psychology of sex differences.* Stanford, Stanford University Press.

MACKEY W. (1965) *Bilingual interference: Its analysis and measurement.* Journal of Communication 15: 239-249.

MACKEY W. (1967) *The lesson to be learned from bilingualism.* In LEON P. (ed.) *Applied linguistics and the teaching of French.* Montréal, Centre Educatif et Culturel, 53-62.

MACNAB G. (1979) *Cognition and bilingualism: A reanalysis of studies.* Linguistics 17: 231-255.

MACNAMARA J. (1966) *Bilingualism and primary education.* Edinburgh, Edinburgh University Press.

MACNAMARA J. (1975) *Comparisons between first and second language learning.* Working Papers on Bilingualism 7: 71-95.

MÄGISTE E. (1979) *The competing language systems of the multilingual: A developmental study of decoding and encoding processes.* Journal of Verbal Learning and Verbal Behavior 18: 79-89.

MAKAI V. (1978) *Bilingual phonology: Systematic or autonomous?* In PARADIS M. (ed.) *Aspects of bilingualism.* Columbia, S.C., Hornbeam Press.

MARCEL A., PATTERSON K. (1978) *Word recognition and production: Reciprocity in clinical and normal studies.* In REQUIN J. (ed.) *Attention and performance, Vol. 7.* Hillsdale, N.J., Erlbaum, 209-226.

MARKS L., MILLER G. (1964) *The role of semantic and syntactic constraints in the memorization of English sentences.* Journal of Verbal Learning and Verbal Behavior 3: 1-5.

MARTIN M. (1978) *Hemispheric asymmetries for physical and semantic selection of visually presented words.* Neuropsychologia 16: 717-724.

MASEMANN V. (1975) *Immigrant students' perceptions of occupational programmes.* In WOLFGANG A. (ed.) *Education of immigrant students.* Toronto, Ontario Institute for Studies in Education.

McCARTHY D. (1930) *Language development of preschool child.* Institute of Child Welfare Monograph Series No. 4, Minneapolis, University of Minnesota Press.

McRAE COCHRANE R., SACHS J. (1979) *Phonological learning by children and adults in a laboratory setting.* Language and Speech 22:145-149.

McDOUGALL A., BRUCK M. (1976) *English reading within the French immersion program: A comparison of the effects of the introduction of English reading at different grade levels.* Language Learning 26/1: 37-43.

McINNIS C., DONOGHUE E. (1980) *A comparative study of the relative effectiveness of two different second language training programs.* Canadian Journal of Psychology 34/4: 314-327.

McLAUGHLIN B. (1977) *Second language learning in children.* Psychological Bulletin 84/3: 438.

McLAUGHLIN B. (1978) *Second language acquisition in childhood.* New York, John Wiley and Sons.

MERCER J. (1973) *Labelling the mentally retarded.* Berkeley, University of California Press.

MERLEAU-PONTY M. (1962) *Phenomenology of perception.* London, Routledge and Kegan Paul.

MEYER D., SCHVANEVELDT R. (1971) *Facilitation in recognizing pairs of words: Evidence of a dependence between retrieval operations.* Journal of Experimental Psychology 90: 227-234.

MEYER D., SCHVANEVELDT R., RUDDY M. (1974) *Functions of graphemic and phonemic codes in visual word recognition.* Memory and Cognition 2: 309-321.

MEYER-EPPLER W., LUCHSINGER R. (1955) *Beobachtungen bei der verzögerten Rückkopplung der Sprache* (Lee-Effekt). Folia Phoniatrica 7: 87-97.

MIKES M. (1967) *Acquisition des catégories grammaticales dans le langage de l'enfant.* Enfance 20: 289-298.

MILLER G. (ed.) (1973) *Linguistic communication: Perspectives for research.* Newark, Dela., International Reading Association.

MILLER G., ISARD S. (1963) *Some perceptual consequences of linguistic rules.* Journal of Verbal Learning and Verbal Behavior 2: 217-228.

MILNER B. (1954) *Intellectual function of the temporal lobes.* Psychological Bulletin 51: 42-61.

MILNER B. (1958) *Psychological defects produced by temporal lobe excision.* Proceedings of the Association for Research in Nervous and Mental Disease. The Brain and Human Behavior 36. Baltimore, Williams and Wilkins.

MODIANO N. (1968) *National or mother language in beginning reading: A comparative study.* Research in the Teaching of English 2: 32-43.

MORRISON J. (1958) *Bilingualism: Some psychological aspects.* The Advancement of Science 56: 287-290.

MUELLER M., WEAVER S. (1964) *Psycholinguistic abilities of institutionalized and institutionalized trainable mental retardates.* American Journal of Mental Deficiency 68: 775-783.

MURRELL M. (1966) *Language acquisition in a trilingual environment: Notes from a case study.* Studia Linguistica 20: 9-35.

MYKLEBUST H. (1971) *The pupil behavior rating scale.* New York. Grune & Stratton.

NUTTIN J. (1968) *La structure de la personnalité.* Paris, Presses Universitaires de France.

NYGREN-JUNKEN L. (1977) *The interaction between French and English in the speech of four bilingual children.* Master's thesis, Ontario Institute for Studies in Education, Toronto, Ontario.

OBLER L. (1982) *The parsimonious bilingual.* In OBLER L., MENN L. (eds.) *Exceptional language and linguistics.* New York, Academic Press.

O'CONNOR N., HERMELIN B. (1963) *Speech and thought in severe subnormality.* New York, McMillan.

OJEMANN G., WHITAKER H. (1978) *The bilingual brain.* Archives of Neurology 35/7: 409-412.

OKSAAR E. (1970) *Zum Spracherwerb des Kindes in zweisprachiger Umgebung.* Folia Linguistica 4: 330-358.

229

OLDFIELD R. (1971) *The assessment and analysis of handedness: The Edinburgh Inventory.* Neuropsychologia 9: 97-113.

OLIM E. (1970) *Maternal language styles and cognitive development of children.* In WILLIAMS F. (ed.) *Language and poverty.* Chicago, University of Chicago Press.

ORTIZ A. (1982) *Special education in bi-lingual/bi-cultural communities.* Paper presented at the Sixth International Congress of the International Association for the Scientific Study of Mental Deficiency; August, Toronto.

O'SHAUGHNESSY D. (1981) *A study of French vowel and consonant durations.* Journal of Phonetics 9: 385-406.

OYAMA S. (1976) *A sensitive period for the acquisition of a nonnative phonological system.* Journal of Psycholinguistic Research 5: 261-283.

PADILLA A., LIEBMAN E. (1975) *Language acquisition in a bilingual child.* Bilingual Review 2: 34-55.

PARADIS M. (1977) *Bilingualism and aphasia.* In WHITAKER M., WHITAKER H. (eds.) *Studies in neurolinguistics, Vol.3.* New York, Academic Press, 65-121.

PARADIS M. (1980) *Language and thought in bilinguals.* In IZZO J., McCORMACK W. (eds.) *The Sixth LACUS Forum.* Columbia, S.C., Hornbeam Press.

PARADIS M. (ed.) (1983) *Readings on aphasia in bilinguals and polyglots.* Montreal, Didier.

PATKOWSKI M. (1980) *The sensitive period for the acquisition of syntax in a second language.* Language Learning 30: 449-472.

PATTEN B. (1973) *Visually mediated thinking: A report of the case of Albert Einstein.* Journal of Learning Disabilities 6: 415-420.

PAULSTON C. (1974) *Ethnic relations and bilingual education: Accounting for contradictory data.* Working Papers on Bilingualism 6. Toronto, Ontario Institute for Studies in Education.

PAVLOVITCH M. (1920) *Le langage enfantin: Acquisition du serbe et du français par un enfant serbe.* Paris, Champion.

PEAL E., LAMBERT W. (1962) *The relation of bilingualism to intelligence.* Psychological Monographs 76: 546.

PENFIELD W. (1953) *A consideration of the neurophysiological mechanisms of speech and some educational consequences.* Proceedings of the American Academy of Arts and Sciences 85/5: 201-214.

PENFIELD W. (1964) *The uncommitted cortex.* The Atlantic (July), 77-81.

PENFIELD W. (1965) *Conditioning the uncommitted cortex for language learning.* Brain 88: 787-798.

PENFIELD W., ROBERTS L. (1959) *Speech and brain mechanisms.* Princeton, N.J.,Princeton University Press.

PETERSON G., BARNEY H. (1952) *Control methods used in a study of the vowels.* The Journal of the Acoustical Society of America 24: 175-184.

PETERSON G.,LEHISTE I. (1960) *Duration of syllabic nuclei in English.* The Journal of the Acoustical Society of America 32: 693-703.

PIAGET J. (1954) *The construction of reality in the child.* New York, Basic Books.

PIAGET J., LAMBERCIER M. (1944) *Recherches sur le développement des perceptions.* Archives de Psychologie, Genève 30: 139-196.

PICHON E. (1936) *Le développement psychique de l'enfant et de l'adolescent.* Paris, Masson.

PICHON E., BOREL-MAISONNY S. (1937) *Le bégaiement.* Paris, Masson.

PIMSLEUR P., STOCKWELL R., COMREY A. (1962) *Foreign language learning ability.* Journal of Educational Psychology 53: 15-26.

230

PROVONOST W., DUMBLETON C. (1953) *A picture-type speech sound discrimination test.* Journal of Speech and Hearing Disorders 18: 258-266.
RAVEN J. (1960) *Guide to the standard progressive matrices.* London, Lewis.
RAVEN J. (1965) *The colored progressive matrices.* London, Lewis.
REISE A. (1931) *Albert Einstein.* New York, Boni.
RENFREW C. (1971) *Action picture test manual.* Oxford, The Churchill Hospital.
RONDAL J. (1973) *Le rôle du langage dans la régulation du comportement moteur chez l'enfant.* Journal de Psychologie 3: 289-324.
RONDAL J. (1975) *Développement du langage et retard mental: Une revue critique de la littérature en langue anglaise.* L'Année Psychologique 75: 513-547.
RONDAL J. (1978a) *Maternal speech to normal and Down's syndrome children matched for mean length of utterance.* In MEYERS C. (ed.) *Quality of life in severely and profoundly mentally retarded people: Research foundations for improvement.* Washington, D.C., American Association on Mental Deficiency, 193-265.
RONDAL J. (1978b) *Developmental sentence scoring procedure and the delay-difference question in language development of Down's syndrome children.* Mental Retardation 16: 169-171.
RONDAL J. (1978c) *Patterns of correlation for various language measures in mother-child interactions for normal and Down's syndrome children.* Language and Speech 21: 242-252.
RONDAL J., LAMBERT J. (1983) *Langage et communication chez les handicapés mentaux.* Théorie, évaluation et intervention. Neuchâtel, Delachaux et Niestlé.
RONDAL J., SERON X. (eds.) (1982) *Troubles du langage. Diagnostic et rééducation.* Brussels, Mardaga.
RONDAL J., LAMBERT J., CHIPMAN H. (eds.) (1981) *Psycholinguistique et handicap mental.* Brussels , Mardaga.
RONJAT J. (1913) *Le développement du langage observé chez un enfant bilingue.* Paris, Champion.
RUDEL R. (1981) *Residual effects of childhood reading disabilities.* Bulletin of the Orton Society 31: 89-102.
RUKE-DRAVINA V. (1967) *Mehrsprachigheit im Vorschulalter.* Lund, Gleerup.
RUMELHART D., LINDSAY P., NORMAN D. (1972) *A process model for long-term memory.* In TULVING E., DONALDSON W. (eds.) *Organization of memory.* New York, Academic Press.
RYAN J. (1975) *Mental subnormality and language development.* In LENNEBERG E., LENNEBERG E. (eds.) *Foundations of language development: A multidisciplinary approach* (Vol.2). New York, Wiley, 269-277.
SANDER F. (1934) *Seelische Struktur und Sprache.* Reprinted in SANDER F., VOLKELT H. (1962) *Ganzheitspsychologie.* München, Beck: 447-453.
SANDER F. (1930) *Structures, totality of experience and Gestalt.* In MURCHISON C. (ed.) *Psychologies of 1930s.* Worchester, Clark University Press.
SCHATZMANN L. STRAUSS A. (1955) *Social class and modes of communication.* American Journal of Sociology 60: 329-338.
SCHMIDT-ROHR G. (1933) *Mutter-Sprache.* Jena, Diederich.
SCHUMANN J. (1975) *Affective factors and the problem of age in second language acquisition.* Language Lerrning 25/2: 209-235.
SELIGER H., KRASHEN S., LADEFOGED P. (1975) *Maturational constraints on the acquisition of second language accent.* Language Science 36: 20-22.
SERSEN E., ASTRUP E., FLOIDSTAD I., WORTIS J. (1970) *Motor conditioned reflexes and word association in retarded children.* American Journal of Mental Defi-

ciency 74: 495-591.

SIGUAN M., SERRA M. (1981) *Bilinguisme et arriération mentale.* In RONDAL J., LAMBERT J., CHIPMAN H. (eds.) *Psycholinguistique et handicap mental.* Brussels, Mardaga, 230-237.

SKUTNABB-KANGAS T. (1978) *Semilingualism and the education of migrant children as a means of reproducing the caste of assembly line workers.* In DITTMAR N., HABERLAND H., SKUTNABB-KANGAS T., TELEMAN V. (eds.) *Papers from the First Scandinavian-German Symposium on the language of immigrant workers and their children.* Roskilde, Denmark, Universitetscenter.

SKUTNABB-KANGAS T., TOUKOMAA P. (1976) *Teaching migrant children's mother tongue and learning the language of the host country in the context of the socio-cultural situation of the migrant family.* Helsinki, Finland, The Finnish National Commission for Unesco.

SLAMECKA N. (1969) *Recognition of word strings as a function of linguistic violations.* Journal of Experimental Psychology 79: 377-378.

SLOBIN D. (1971) *On the learning of morphological rules: A reply to Palermo and Eberhart.* In SLOBIN D. (ed.) *The ontogenesis of grammar.* New York, Academic Press.

SMITH B. (1977) *Phonological development in Down's syndrome children.* Communication presented at the 85th Annual Convention of the American Psychological Association, San Francisco, August.

SMITH B., OLLER K. (1981) *A comparative study of pre-meaningful vocalizations produced by normally developing and Down's syndrome infants.* Journal of Speech and Hearing Disorders 46: 46-51.

SMITH M. (1949) *Measurement of vocabularies of young bilingual children in both of the languages used.* Journal of Genetic Psychology 74: 305-310.

SMITH M. (1957) *Word variety as a measure of bilingualism in preschool children.* Journal of Genetic Psychology 90: 143-150.

SMYTHE P., STENNET R., GARDNER R., (1976) *Children and adults as foreign language students.* Canadian Modern Language Review 32: 10-21.

SNOW C., HOEFNAGEL-HÖHLE M. (1977) *Age differences in the pronunciation of foreign sounds.* Language and Speech 20: 357-365.

SNOW C., HOEFNAGEL-HÖHLE M. (1978) *The critical period for language acquisition: Evidence from second language learning.* Child Development 49: 1114-1128.

SPRADLIN J. (1963) *Language and communication of mental defectives.* In ELLIS N. (ed.) *Handbook of mental deficiency: Psychological theory and research.* New York, McGraw-Hill, 512-565.

STERN H. (1967) *Foreign Language in primary education.* London, Oxford University Press.

STERN H., SWAIN M., McLEAN L., FREIDMAN R., HARLEY B., LAPKIN S. (1976) *Three approaches to the teaching of French.* Toronto, Ministry of Education, Government of Ontario Press.

STEVENS K., LIBERMAN A., STUDDERT-KENNEDY M., OHMAN S. (1969) *Cross-language study of vowel perception.* Language and Speech 12: 1-23.

STONE J., CHURCH J. (1980) *Childhood and adolescence.* New York. Random House.

STROOP, J. (1935) *Studies of interference in serial verbal reactions.* Journal of Experimental Psychology 18: 643-662.

SWAIN M. (1972) *Bilingualism as a first language.* Doctoral dissertation, University of California, Irvine.

SWAIN M. (1974a) *Child bilingual language learning and linguistic interdependence.* In CAREY S. (ed.) *Bilingualism, biculturalism and education.* Edmonton, University of Alberta Press.

232

SWAIN M. (1974b) *Early and late French immersion programs in Canada: Research findings.* Presented at the Federal-Provincial Conference on Bilingualism in Education, Halifax, Nova Scotia.

SWAIN M., BARIK H. (1976) *Bilingual education for the English Canadian: Recent developments.* In SIMOES A. (ed.) *The bilingual child. Research and analysis of existing educational themes.* New York, Academic Press.

SWAIN M., BURNABY B. (1976) *Personality characteristics and second language learning in young children: A pilot study.* Working Papers on Bilingualism 11: 115-128.

SWAIN M., WESCHE M. (1975) *Linguistic interaction: Case study of a bilingual child.* Language Sciences 37: 17-22.

TAHTA S., WOOD M., LOEWENTHAL K. (1981a) *Age changes in the ability to replicate foreign pronunciation and intonation.* Language and Speech 24: 363-372.

TAHTA S., WOOD M., LOEWENTHAL K. (1981b) *Foreign accents: Factors relating to transfer of accent from the first language to a second language.* Language and Speech 24: 265-272.

TAYLOR M. (1974) *Speculations on bilingualism and the cognitive network.* Working Papers on Bilingualism 2: 68-124.

TITONE R. (1982) *Second language learning: An integrated psycholinguistic model.* In BAIN B. (ed.) *The sociogenesis of language and human conduct.* New York, Plenum.

TOGLIA M., BATTIG W. (1978) *Handbook of semantic word norms.* Hillsdale, N.J., Erlbaum.

TRAVIS L., JOHNSON W., SHOVER J. (1937) *The relation of bilingualism to stuttering.* Journal of Speech Disorders 2: 185:189.

TRIANDIS H., LAMBERT W. (eds.) (1980) *Handbook of cross-cultural psychology. Vol. 1.* Toronto, Allyn and Bacon, Inc.

TRITES R. (1976) *Children with learning difficulties in primary French immersion.* Canadian Modern Language Review 33/2: 193-216.

TRITES R. (1977) *Neuropsychological test manual.* Montreal, Ronalds Federated.

TRITES R. (1981) *Primary French immersion: Disabilities and prediction of success.* The Minister of Education, Ontario, Queen's Park, Toronto.

TRITES R., PRICE M. (1976) *Learning disabilities found in association with French immersion programming.* Toronto, Ontario Ministry of Education.

TRITES R., PRICE M. (1977) *Learning disabilities found in association with French immersion programming: A cross validation.* Toronto, Ontario Ministry of Education.

TRITES R., PRICE M. (1978) *Assessment of readiness for primary French immersion.* Toronto, Ontario Ministry of Education.

TRITES R., PRICE M. (1978-79) *Specific learning disability in primary French immersion.* Interchange 9/4: 73-85.

TRITES R., PRICE M. (1979) *Assessment of readiness for primary French immersion: Kindergarten follow-up assessment.* Toronto, Ontario Ministry of Education.

TRITES R., PRICE M. (1980) *Assessment of readiness for primary French immersion: Grade one follow-up assessment.* Toronto, Ontario Ministry of Education.

TUCKER G. (1975) *The development of reading skills within a bilingual education program.* In SMILEY S., TOWNER J. (eds.) *Language and reading.*

TUCKER, G. (1977) *The linguistic perspective.* In *Bilingual education: Current perspectives,* Vol. 2. Arlington, Virginia, Center for Applied Linguistics.

TWEEDY J., LAPINSKI R., SCHVANEVELDT R. (1977) *Semantic-context effects on word recognition: Influence of varying the proportion of items presented in an appropriate context.* Memory and Cognition 5: 84-89.

URCUIOLI P., KLEIN R., DAY J. (1981) *Hemispheric differences in semantic processing: Category matching is not the same as category membership.* Perception and Psychophysics 28: 343-351.

UZNADZE D. (1966) *The psychology of set.* New York, Consultants.

VAID J. (1981) *Hemisphere differences in bilingual language processing: A task analysis.* Unpublished doctoral dissertation, McGill University.

VAID J. (1983) *Bilingualism and brain lateralization.* In SEGALOWITZ S. (ed.) *Language functions and brain organization.* New York, Academic Press, 315-339.

VAID J., GENESEE F. (1980) *Neuropsychological approaches to bilingualism: A critical review.* Canadian Journal of Psychology 34: 417-445.

VAID J., LAMBERT W. (1979) *Differential cerebral involvement in the cognitive functioning of bilinguals.* Brain and Language 8: 92-110.

VALLENTIN A. (1954) *Le drame d'Albert Einstein.* Paris, Plon.

VAN OVERBEKE M. (1972) *Introduction au problème du bilinguisme.* Bruxelles, Labor.

VIHMAN M., McLAUGHLIN B. (1982) *Bilingualism and second language acquisition in preschool children.* In BRAINERD C., PRESSLEY M. (eds.) *Progress in cognitive development research: Verbal processes in children.* Berlin, Springer.

VILDOMEC V. (1963) *Multilingualism: General linguistics and psychology of speech.* Leyden, Sijthoff.

VOLTERRA V., TAESCHNER T. (1978) *The acquisition and development of language by bilingual children.* In HATCH E. (ed.) *Second language acquisition: A book of readings.* Rowley, Mass., Newbury House.

VYGOTSKY L. (1962) *Thought and language.* Cambridge, Mass., M.I.T. Press.

VYGOTSKY L. (1978) *Mind in society.* Cambridge, Harvard University Press.

WAPER S., WERNER H. (1965) *The body percept.* New York, Random House.

WECHSLER D. (1949) *Manual: Wechsler intelligence scale for children.* New York, Psychological Corporation.

WECHSLER D. (1963) *Wechsler preschool and primary scale of intelligence.* New York, Psychological Corporation.

WEINREICH U. (1953) *Languages in contact.* New York, Columbia University Press.

WEISGERBER L. (1929) *Muttersprache und Geistesbildung.* Göttingen, Vandenhoek und Ruprecht.

WELLS G. (1981) *Learning through interaction: The study of language development.* Cambridge, Cambridge University Press.

WERNER H. (1948) *Comparative psychology of mental development.* Minneapolis, University of Minnesota Press.

WHITE M. (1973) *Does cerebral dominance offer a sufficient explanation for laterality differences in tachistoscopic recognition?* Perceptual and Motor Skills 36: 479-485.

WILLIAMS L. (1979) *The modification of speech perception and production in second-language learning.* Perception and Psychophysics 26: 95-104.

WILLIS B. (1978) *Mentally retarded children - qualitatively different speech.* Unpublished manuscript, Luther College, Decorah, Iowa.

WITKIN H., LEWIS H., HERTZMAN M., MACHOVER K., MEISSNER P., WAPNER S. (1954) *Personality through perception.* New York, Harper.

WITKIN H., PRICE-WILLIAMS D., BERTINI M., CHRISTIANSEN B., OLTMAN P., RAMIREZ M., VAN MEEL J. (1974) *Social conformity and psychological differentiation.* International Journal of Psychology 9: 11-29.

WOBER M. (1969) *Distinguishing centri-cultural from cross-cultural tests and research.* Perceptual and Motor Skills 28: 488.

WRIGHT E., RAMSEY C. (1970) *Students of non-Canadian origin: Age on arrival, academic achievement and ability.* Research Report No. 88, Toronto Board of Education.

YODER D., MILLER J. (1972) *What we may know and what we can do: Input toward a system.* In McLEAN J., YODER D., SCHIEFELBUSH R. (eds.) *Language intervention with the retarded: Developing strategies.* Baltimore, University Park Press, 89-107.

YU A. (1981) *Language, culture, class and cognitive style.* Unpublished Ph.D. thesis, University of Alberta, Canada.

YU A., BAIN B. (1980) *Social class and cultural-educational determinants of first and second language acquisition: Cognitive profiles of Hong Kong and Canadian children.* In *Third Los Angeles Second Language Research Forum.* Los Angeles, University of California Press.

ZAIDEL E. (1978) *Lexical organization in the right hemisphere.* In BUSER, ROUGEUL-BUSER (eds.) *Cerebral correlates of conscious experience.* New York, Elsevier North-Holland Press, 177-197.

ZISK P., BIALER J. (1967) *Speech and language problem in mongolism: A review of the literature.* Journal of Speech and Hearing Disorders 32: 228-241.